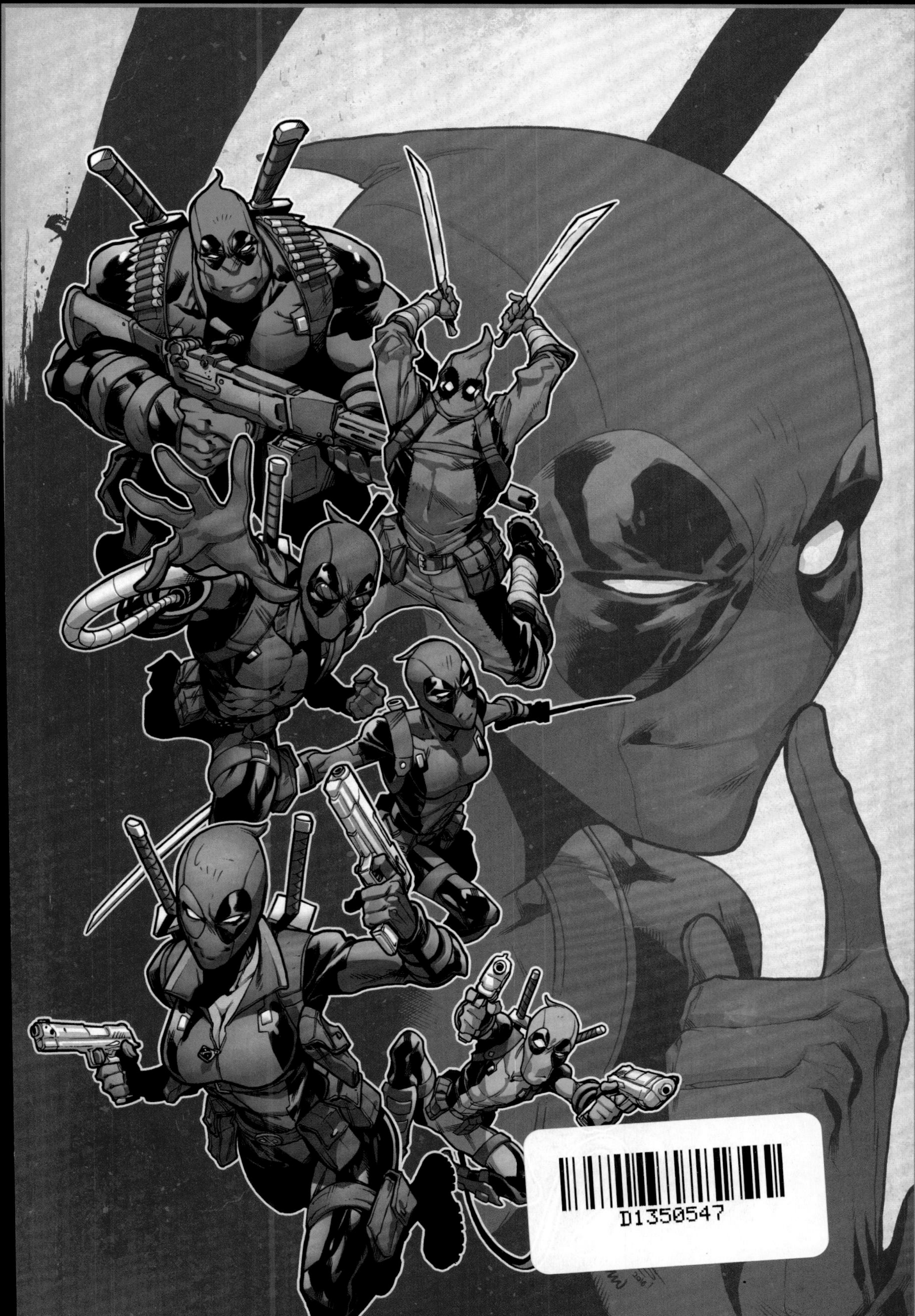

COME ONE, COME ALL... TO THE GREATEST CAVALCADE OF CORRUPTION, THE ULTIMATE VENUE FOR VICE, THE TERRIFIC AND TERRIBLE...

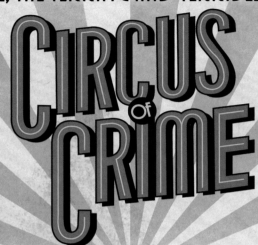

CIRCUS of CRIME

SEE THE FIRE-EATER! THE STRONGMAN! THE CLOWN! PRINCESS PYTHON! THE GAMBINOS! LIVEWIRE! AND THE DIABOLICAL RINGMASTER... VERSUS THE MIGHTY, MESSILY MANAGED...

MERCS for MONEY

YES, INDEED! IT'S GORILLA MAN, HIT-MONKEY, MACHINE MAN, MASACRE AND NEGASONIC TEENAGE WARHEAD—WATCH AS THEY FIGHT THEIR HIGH-FLYING FOES... AND TACKLE AN INTERNAL POWER DISPUTE. THAT'S RIGHT... IT'S THE DEARLY DEPOSED DEADPOOL VERSUS THE DARING, DOMINEERING DOMINO... BATTLING TO BE THE BIG CHEESE... IN THE BIG TOP!!! YOU DON'T WANT TO MISS THIS!

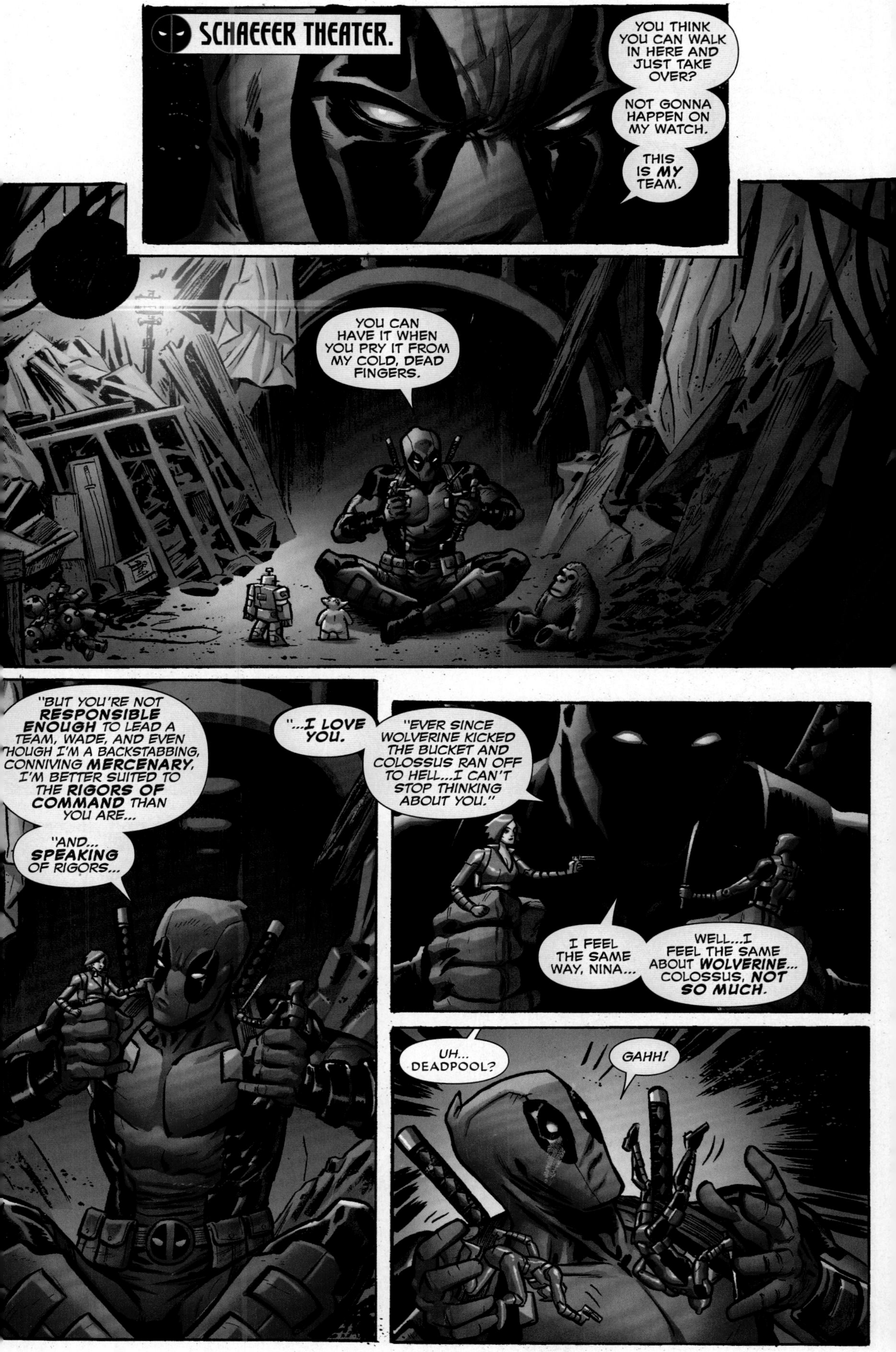
SCHAEFER THEATER.
YOU THINK YOU CAN WALK IN HERE AND JUST TAKE OVER?
NOT GONNA HAPPEN ON MY WATCH.
THIS IS MY TEAM.
YOU CAN HAVE IT WHEN YOU PRY IT FROM MY COLD, DEAD FINGERS.
"BUT YOU'RE NOT RESPONSIBLE ENOUGH TO LEAD A TEAM, WADE, AND EVEN THOUGH I'M A BACKSTABBING, CONNIVING MERCENARY, I'M BETTER SUITED TO THE RIGORS OF COMMAND THAN YOU ARE...
"AND... SPEAKING OF RIGORS...
"...I LOVE YOU.
"EVER SINCE WOLVERINE KICKED THE BUCKET AND COLOSSUS RAN OFF TO HELL...I CAN'T STOP THINKING ABOUT YOU."
I FEEL THE SAME WAY, NINA...
WELL...I FEEL THE SAME ABOUT WOLVERINE... COLOSSUS, NOT SO MUCH.
UH... DEADPOOL?
GAHH!

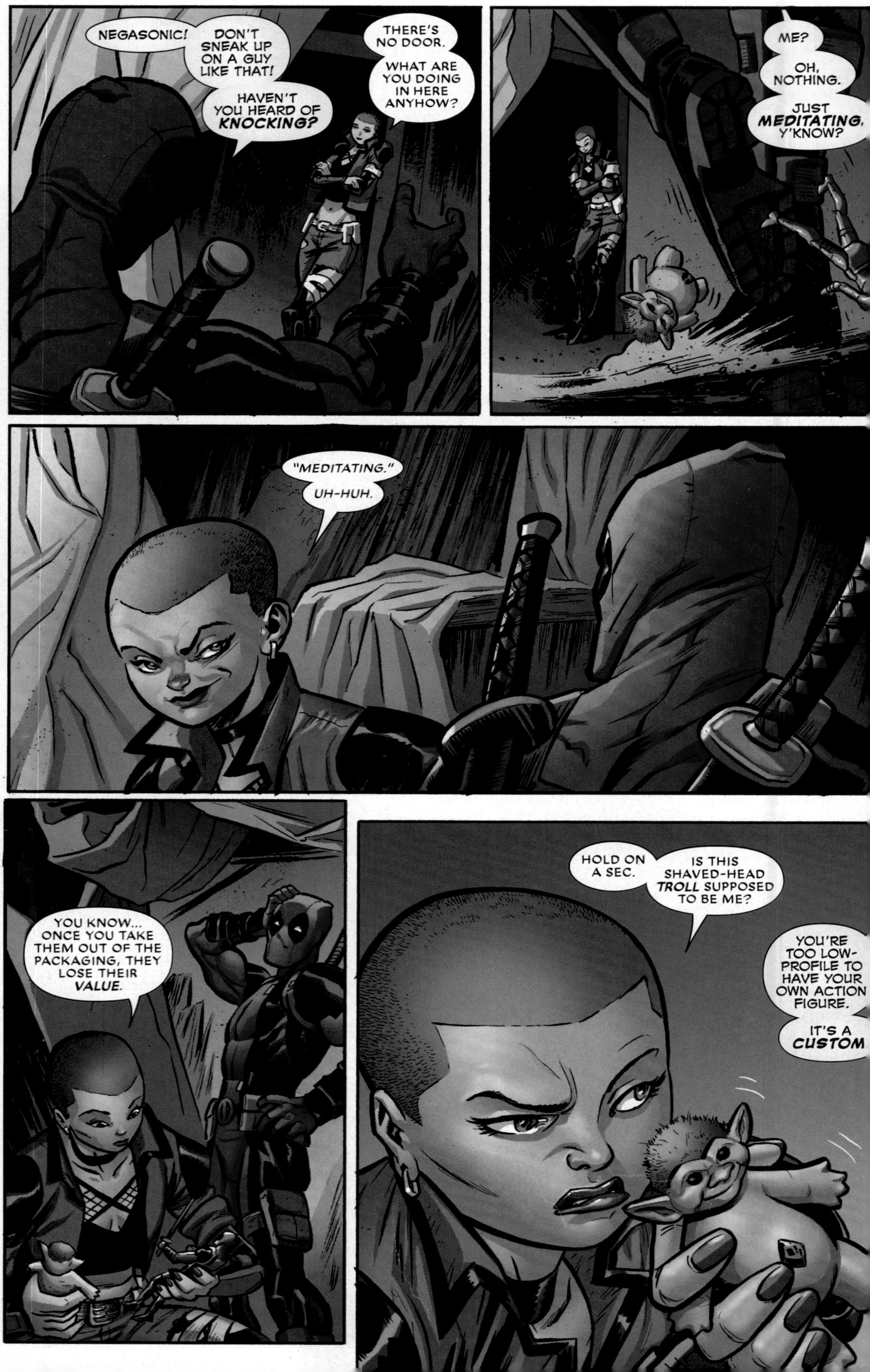
NEGASONIC!
DON'T SNEAK UP ON A GUY LIKE THAT!
HAVEN'T YOU HEARD OF KNOCKING?
THERE'S NO DOOR.
WHAT ARE YOU DOING IN HERE ANYHOW?
ME?
OH, NOTHING.
JUST MEDITATING, Y'KNOW?
"MEDITATING."
UH-HUH.
YOU KNOW... ONCE YOU TAKE THEM OUT OF THE PACKAGING, THEY LOSE THEIR VALUE.
HOLD ON A SEC.
IS THIS SHAVED-HEAD TROLL SUPPOSED TO BE ME?
YOU'RE TOO LOW-PROFILE TO HAVE YOUR OWN ACTION FIGURE.
IT'S A CUSTOM.

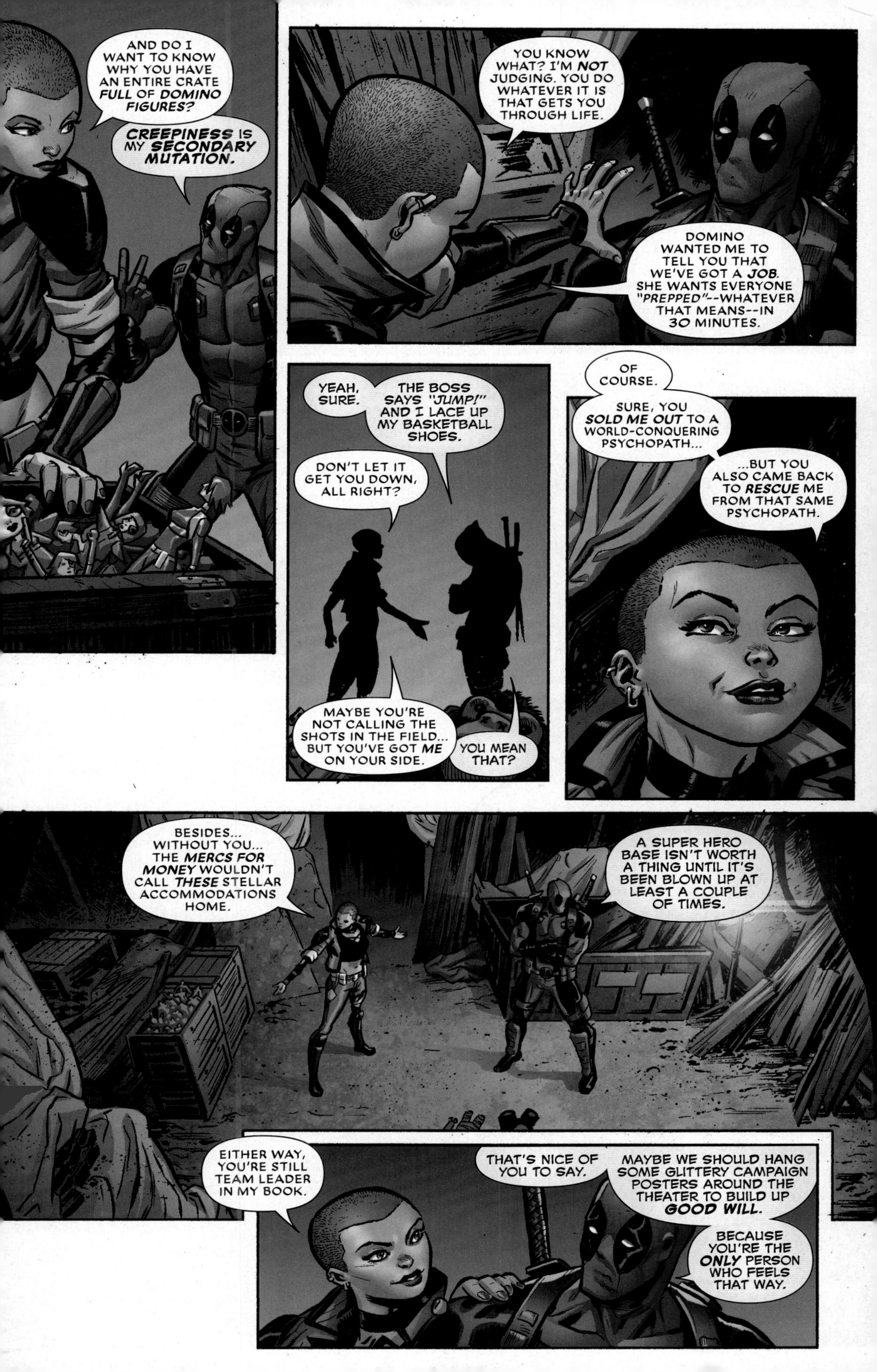
AND DO I WANT TO KNOW WHY YOU HAVE AN ENTIRE CRATE FULL OF DOMINO FIGURES?
CREEPINESS IS MY SECONDARY MUTATION.
YOU KNOW WHAT? I'M NOT JUDGING. YOU DO WHATEVER IT IS THAT GETS YOU THROUGH LIFE.
DOMINO WANTED ME TO TELL YOU THAT WE'VE GOT A JOB. SHE WANTS EVERYONE "PREPPED"--WHATEVER THAT MEANS--IN 30 MINUTES.
YEAH, SURE.
THE BOSS SAYS "JUMP!" AND I LACE UP MY BASKETBALL SHOES.
DON'T LET IT GET YOU DOWN, ALL RIGHT?
MAYBE YOU'RE NOT CALLING THE SHOTS IN THE FIELD... BUT YOU'VE GOT ME ON YOUR SIDE.
YOU MEAN THAT?
OF COURSE.
SURE, YOU SOLD ME OUT TO A WORLD-CONQUERING PSYCHOPATH...
...BUT YOU ALSO CAME BACK TO RESCUE ME FROM THAT SAME PSYCHOPATH.
BESIDES... WITHOUT YOU... THE MERCS FOR MONEY WOULDN'T CALL THESE STELLAR ACCOMMODATIONS HOME.
A SUPER HERO BASE ISN'T WORTH A THING UNTIL IT'S BEEN BLOWN UP AT LEAST A COUPLE OF TIMES.
EITHER WAY, YOU'RE STILL TEAM LEADER IN MY BOOK.
THAT'S NICE OF YOU TO SAY.
MAYBE WE SHOULD HANG SOME GLITTERY CAMPAIGN POSTERS AROUND THE THEATER TO BUILD UP GOOD WILL.
BECAUSE YOU'RE THE ONLY PERSON WHO FEELS THAT WAY.

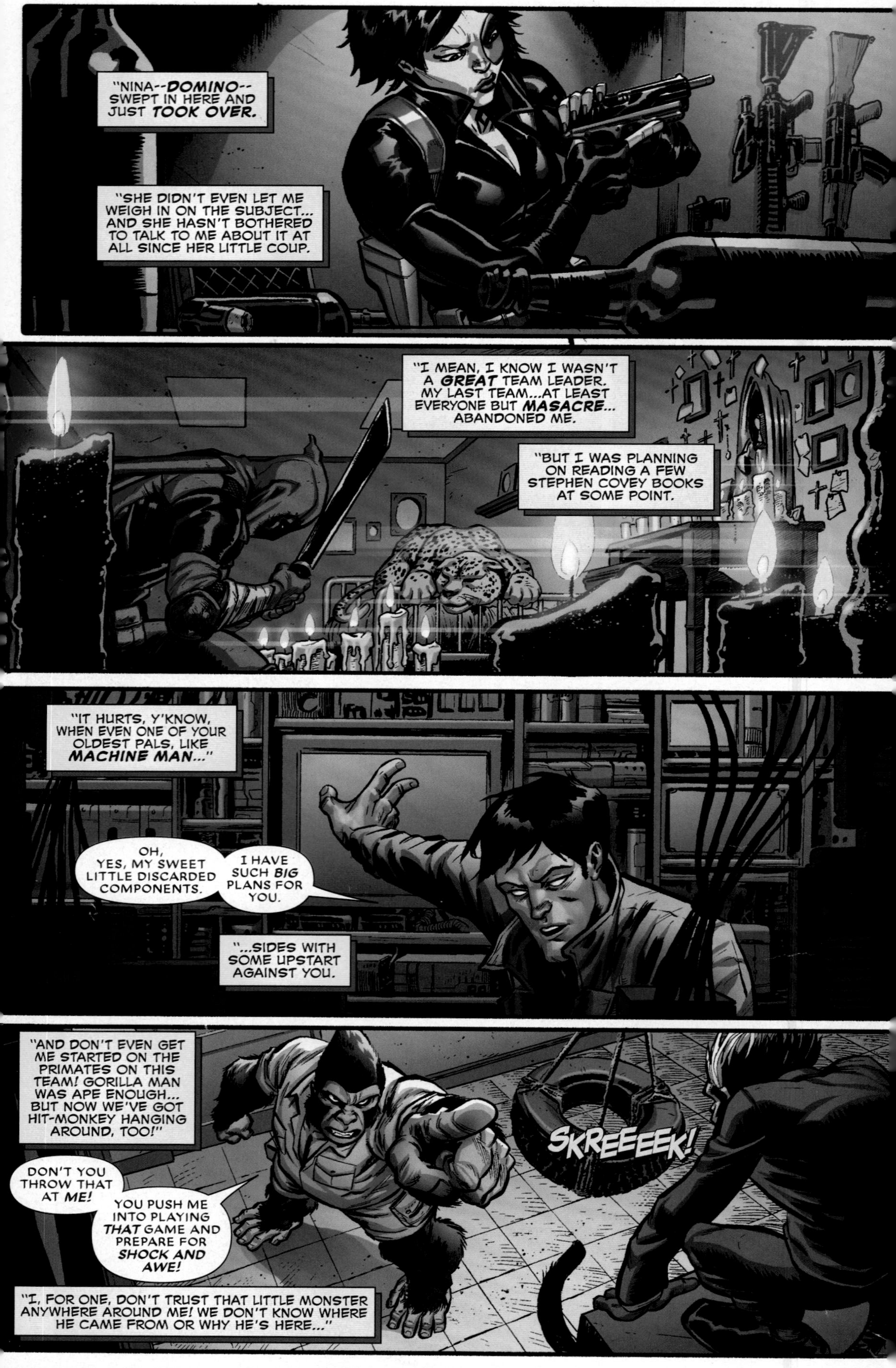
"NINA--DOMINO--SWEPT IN HERE AND JUST TOOK OVER.
"SHE DIDN'T EVEN LET ME WEIGH IN ON THE SUBJECT... AND SHE HASN'T BOTHERED TO TALK TO ME ABOUT IT AT ALL SINCE HER LITTLE COUP.
"I MEAN, I KNOW I WASN'T A GREAT TEAM LEADER. MY LAST TEAM...AT LEAST EVERYONE BUT MASACRE... ABANDONED ME.
"BUT I WAS PLANNING ON READING A FEW STEPHEN COVEY BOOKS AT SOME POINT.
"IT HURTS, Y'KNOW, WHEN EVEN ONE OF YOUR OLDEST PALS, LIKE MACHINE MAN..."
OH, YES, MY SWEET LITTLE DISCARDED COMPONENTS.
I HAVE SUCH BIG PLANS FOR YOU.
"...SIDES WITH SOME UPSTART AGAINST YOU.
"AND DON'T EVEN GET ME STARTED ON THE PRIMATES ON THIS TEAM! GORILLA MAN WAS APE ENOUGH... BUT NOW WE'VE GOT HIT-MONKEY HANGING AROUND, TOO!"
SKREEEEK!
DON'T YOU THROW THAT AT ME!
YOU PUSH ME INTO PLAYING THAT GAME AND PREPARE FOR SHOCK AND AWE!
"I, FOR ONE, DON'T TRUST THAT LITTLE MONSTER ANYWHERE AROUND ME! WE DON'T KNOW WHERE HE CAME FROM OR WHY HE'S HERE..."

...AND HE'S ALREADY **SHOT** ME ONCE SINCE HE ARRIVED!

YEAH. THAT WAS **MESSED UP.**

LOOK, I DON'T WANT YOU TO THINK I'VE GOT **SOUR GRAPES.**

BUT MY **GRAPES** ARE **SOUR!**

SO WHY NOT JUST CUT THE TEAM LOOSE?

TAKE A LOOK AROUND, KID.

I'M UP TO MY NECK IN **REPAIRS** RIGHT NOW.

AND BEING AN AVENGER SLURPS UP **LIQUID ASSETS** LIKE SLUSH-PUPPIES THROUGH A STRAW.

I DON'T NEED TO **QUIT** THE TEAM. THE MERCS BRING IN **CASH.**

I JUST NEED TO BE **IN CHARGE** AGAIN.

ALL RIGHT.

HOW DO YOU MAKE THAT HAPPEN?

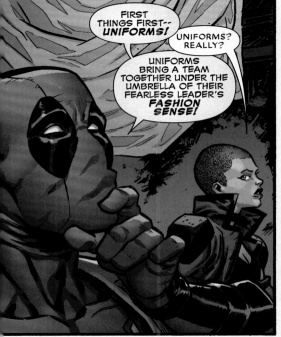

FIRST THINGS FIRST-- **UNIFORMS!**

UNIFORMS? REALLY?

UNIFORMS BRING A TEAM TOGETHER UNDER THE UMBRELLA OF THEIR **FEARLESS LEADER'S FASHION SENSE!**

ALL RIGHT.

YOU WANT **UNIFORMS?**

I CAN HELP MAKE THAT HAPPEN.

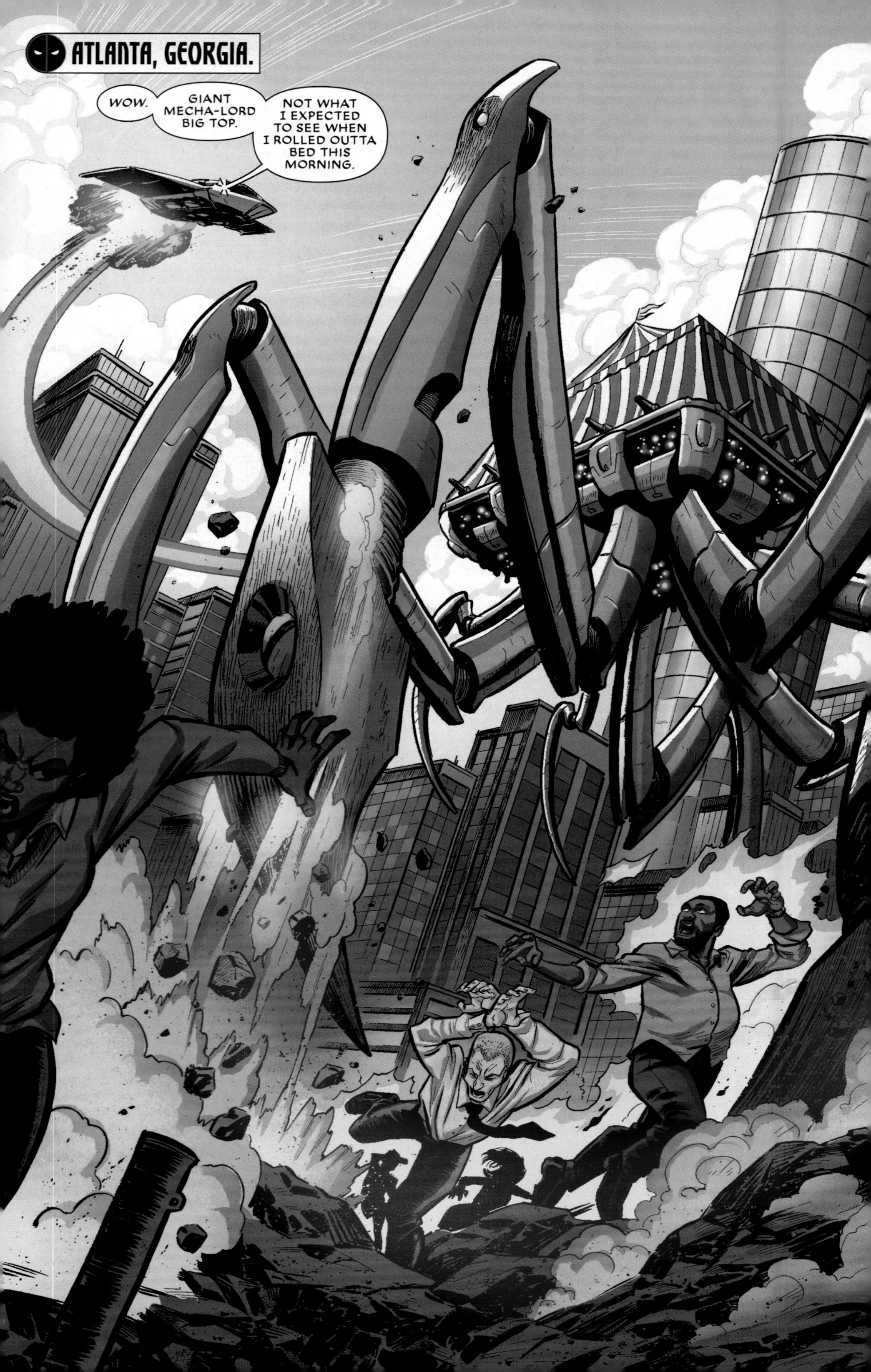
ATLANTA, GEORGIA.
WOW.
GIANT MECHA-LORD BIG TOP.
NOT WHAT I EXPECTED TO SEE WHEN I ROLLED OUTTA BED THIS MORNING.

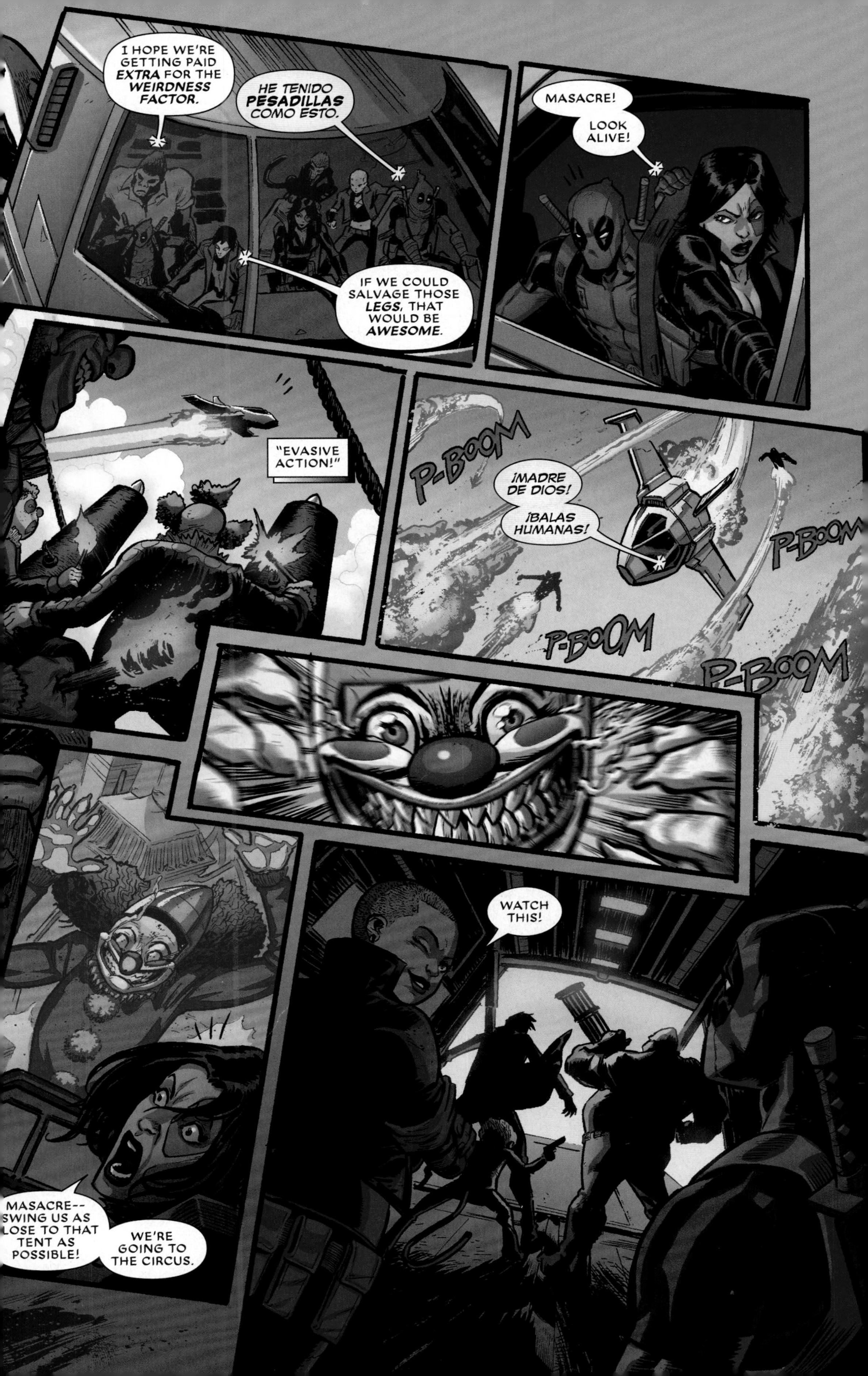
I HOPE WE'RE GETTING PAID EXTRA FOR THE WEIRDNESS FACTOR.
HE TENIDO PESADILLAS COMO ESTO.
IF WE COULD SALVAGE THOSE LEGS, THAT WOULD BE AWESOME.
MASACRE!
LOOK ALIVE!
"EVASIVE ACTION!"
P-BOOM
¡MADRE DE DIOS!
¡BALAS HUMANAS!
P-BOOM
P-BOOM
P-BOOM
MASACRE-- SWING US AS LOSE TO THAT TENT AS POSSIBLE!
WE'RE GOING TO THE CIRCUS.
WATCH THIS!

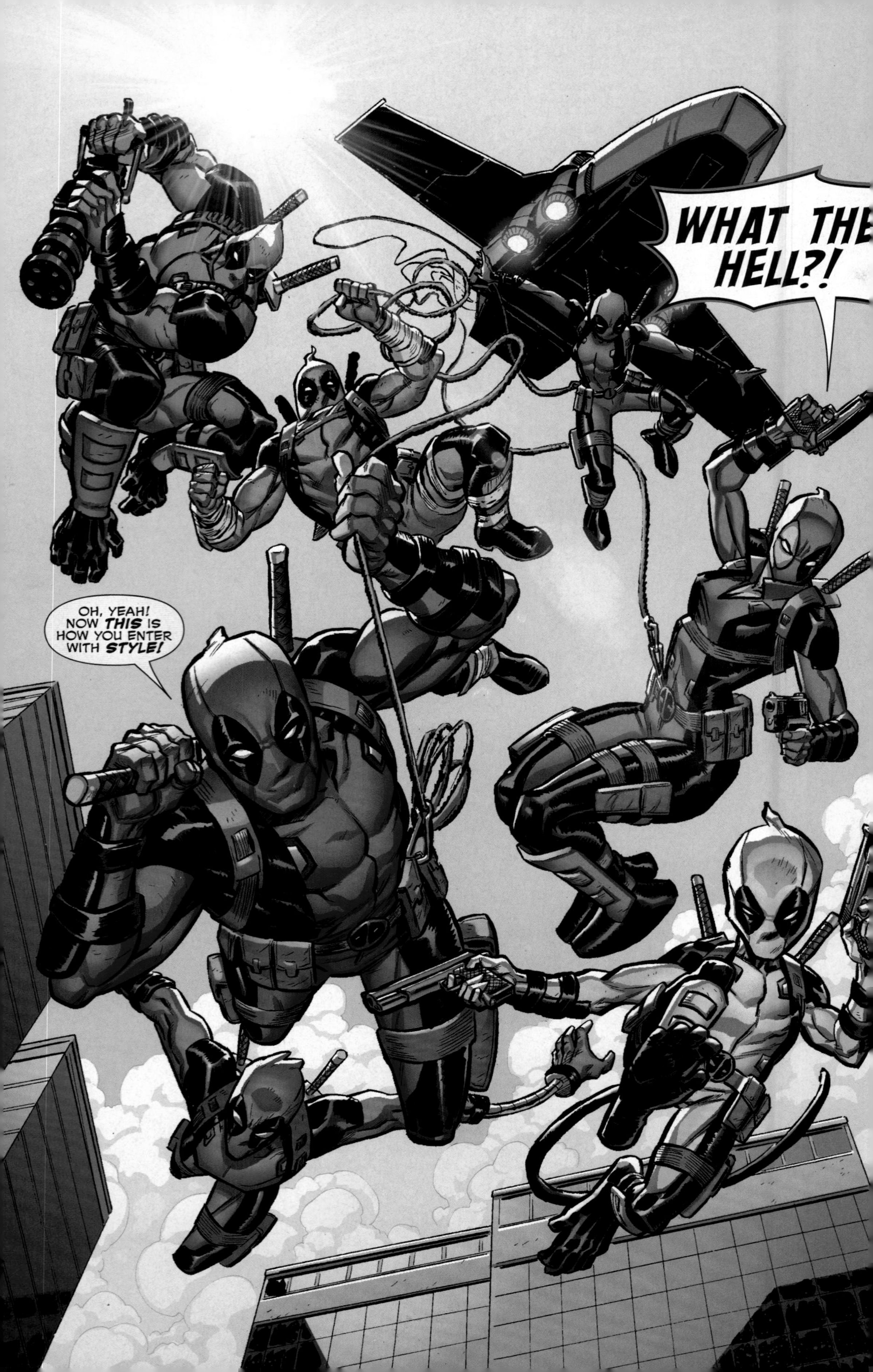
WHAT THE HELL?!
OH, YEAH! NOW THIS IS HOW YOU ENTER WITH STYLE!

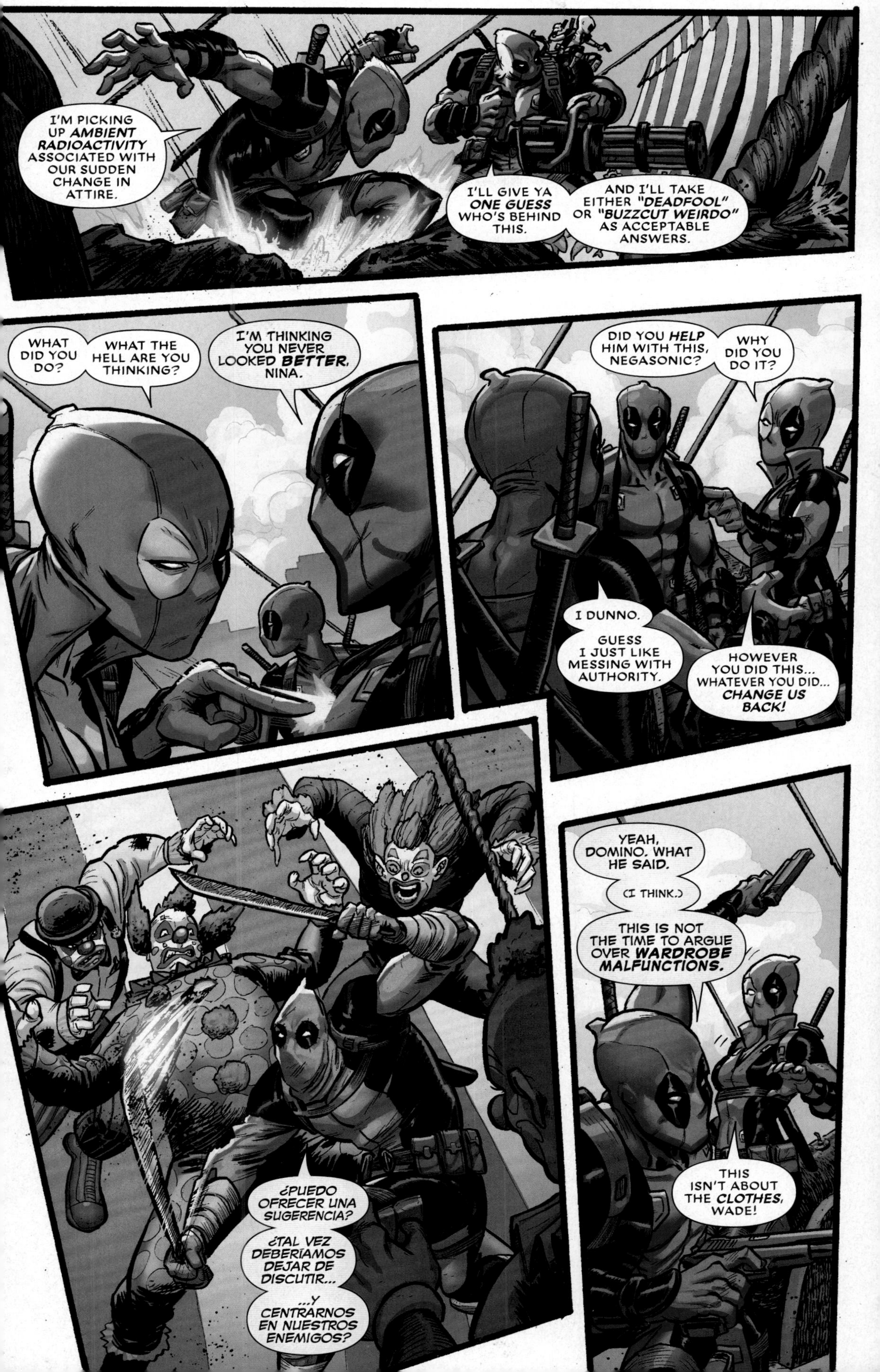

I'M PICKING UP AMBIENT RADIOACTIVITY ASSOCIATED WITH OUR SUDDEN CHANGE IN ATTIRE.
I'LL GIVE YA ONE GUESS WHO'S BEHIND THIS.
AND I'LL TAKE EITHER "DEADFOOL" OR "BUZZCUT WEIRDO" AS ACCEPTABLE ANSWERS.
WHAT DID YOU DO?
WHAT THE HELL ARE YOU THINKING?
I'M THINKING YOU NEVER LOOKED BETTER, NINA.
DID YOU HELP HIM WITH THIS, NEGASONIC?
WHY DID YOU DO IT?
I DUNNO.
GUESS I JUST LIKE MESSING WITH AUTHORITY.
HOWEVER YOU DID THIS... WHATEVER YOU DID... CHANGE US BACK!
¿PUEDO OFRECER UNA SUGERENCIA?
¿TAL VEZ DEBERÍAMOS DEJAR DE DISCUTIR...
...Y CENTRARNOS EN NUESTROS ENEMIGOS?
YEAH, DOMINO. WHAT HE SAID.
(I THINK.)
THIS IS NOT THE TIME TO ARGUE OVER WARDROBE MALFUNCTIONS.
THIS ISN'T ABOUT THE CLOTHES, WADE!

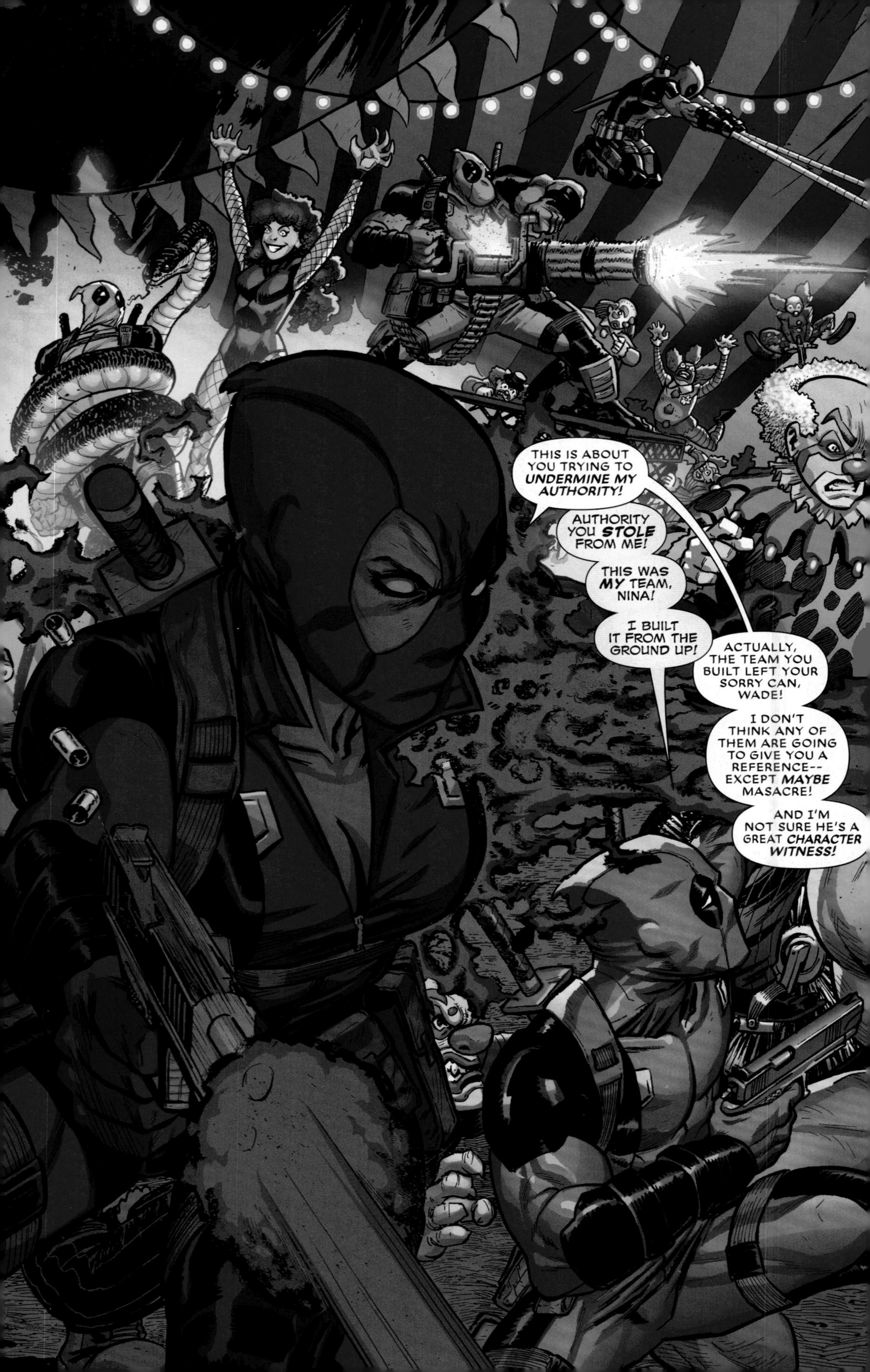

THIS IS ABOUT YOU TRYING TO UNDERMINE MY AUTHORITY!
AUTHORITY YOU STOLE FROM ME!
THIS WAS MY TEAM, NINA!
I BUILT IT FROM THE GROUND UP!
ACTUALLY, THE TEAM YOU BUILT LEFT YOUR SORRY CAN, WADE!
I DON'T THINK ANY OF THEM ARE GOING TO GIVE YOU A REFERENCE-- EXCEPT MAYBE MASACRE!
AND I'M NOT SURE HE'S A GREAT CHARACTER WITNESS!

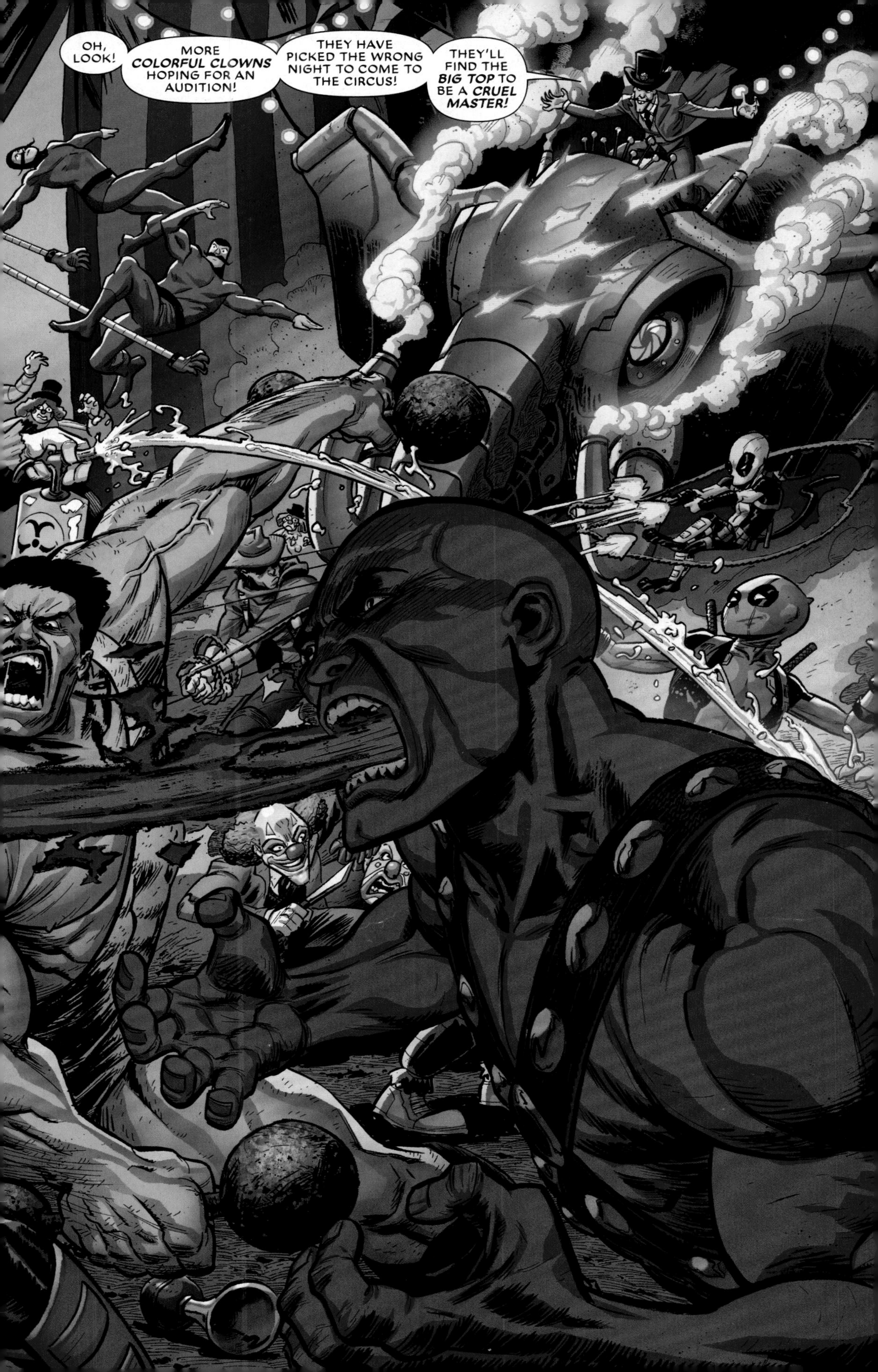
OH, LOOK!
MORE COLORFUL CLOWNS HOPING FOR AN AUDITION!
THEY HAVE PICKED THE WRONG NIGHT TO COME TO THE CIRCUS!
THEY'LL FIND THE BIG TOP TO BE A CRUEL MASTER!

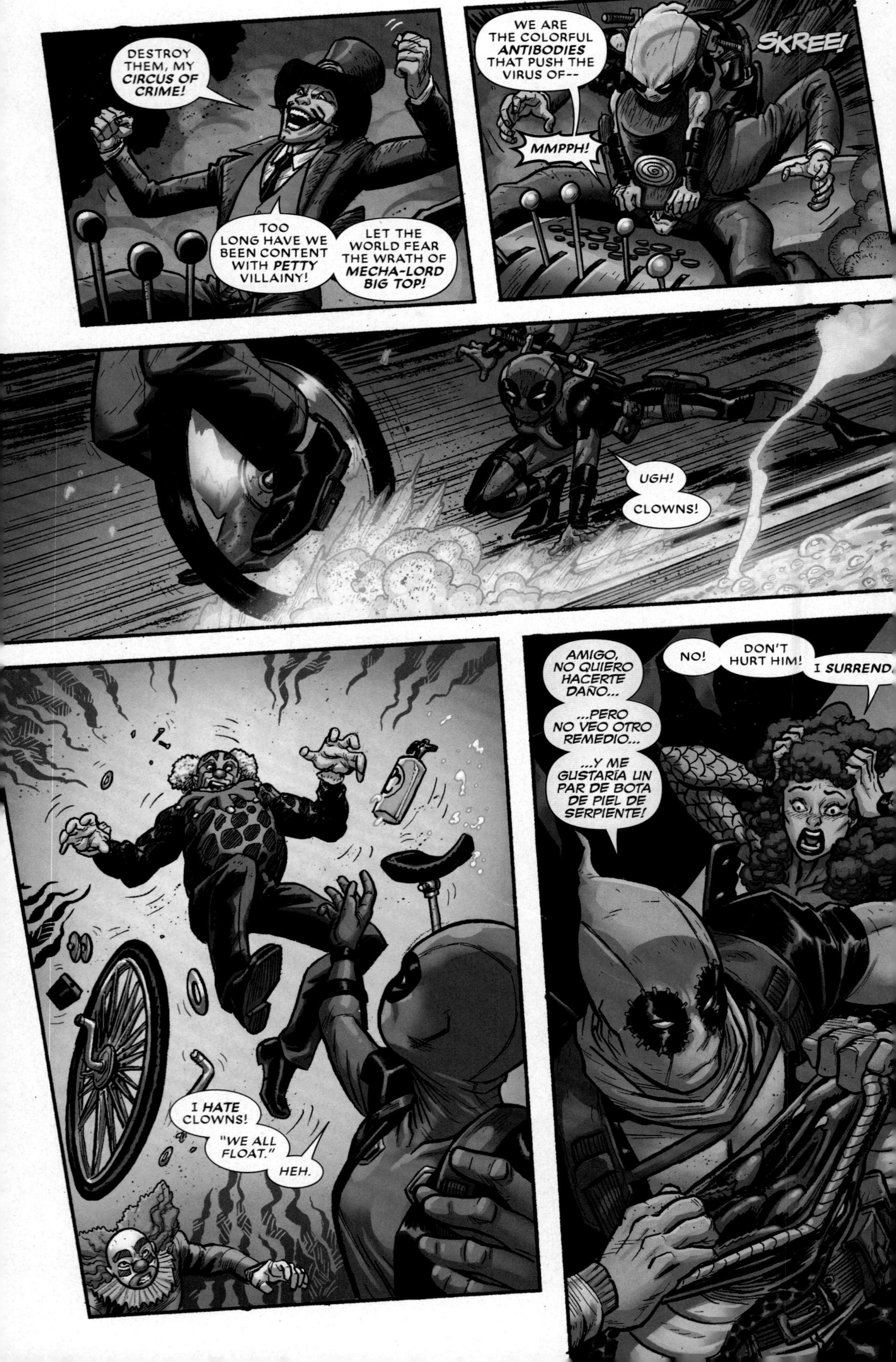
DESTROY THEM, MY CIRCUS OF CRIME!
TOO LONG HAVE WE BEEN CONTENT WITH PETTY VILLAINY!
LET THE WORLD FEAR THE WRATH OF MECHA-LORD BIG TOP!
WE ARE THE COLORFUL ANTIBODIES THAT PUSH THE VIRUS OF--
MMPPH!
SKREE!
UGH!
CLOWNS!
I HATE CLOWNS!
"WE ALL FLOAT."
HEH.
AMIGO, NO QUIERO HACERTE DAÑO...
...PERO NO VEO OTRO REMEDIO...
...Y ME GUSTARÍA UN PAR DE BOTA DE PIEL DE SERPIENTE!
NO!
DON'T HURT HIM!
I SURREND

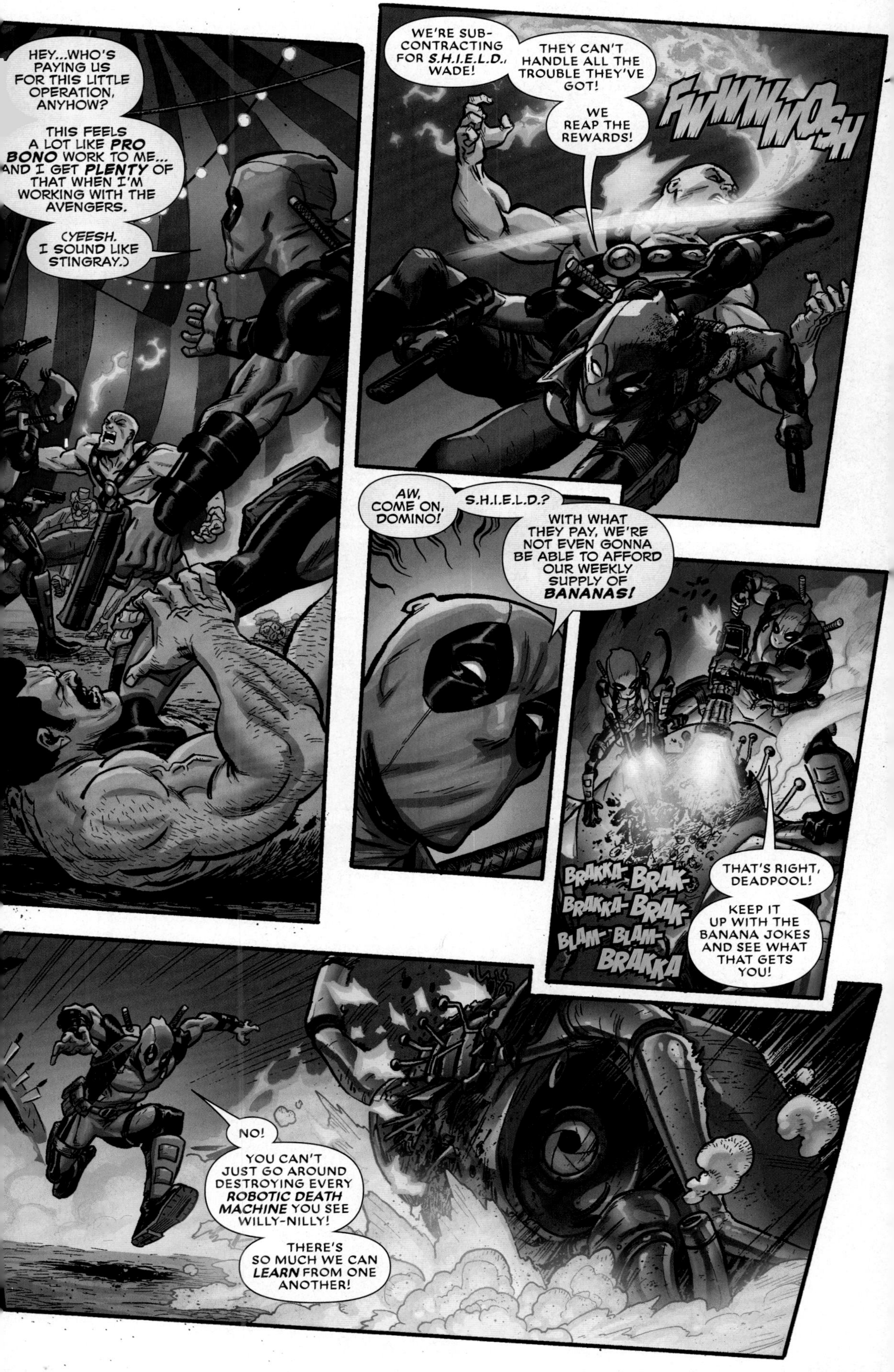
HEY...WHO'S PAYING US FOR THIS LITTLE OPERATION, ANYHOW?
THIS FEELS A LOT LIKE PRO BONO WORK TO ME... AND I GET PLENTY OF THAT WHEN I'M WORKING WITH THE AVENGERS.
(YEESH. I SOUND LIKE STINGRAY.)
WE'RE SUB-CONTRACTING FOR S.H.I.E.L.D., WADE!
THEY CAN'T HANDLE ALL THE TROUBLE THEY'VE GOT!
WE REAP THE REWARDS!
FWWWWOOSH
AW, COME ON, DOMINO!
S.H.I.E.L.D.?
WITH WHAT THEY PAY, WE'RE NOT EVEN GONNA BE ABLE TO AFFORD OUR WEEKLY SUPPLY OF BANANAS!
BRAKKA-BRAK-BRAKKA-BRAK-BLAM-BLAM-BRAKKA
THAT'S RIGHT, DEADPOOL!
KEEP IT UP WITH THE BANANA JOKES AND SEE WHAT THAT GETS YOU!
NO!
YOU CAN'T JUST GO AROUND DESTROYING EVERY ROBOTIC DEATH MACHINE YOU SEE WILLY-NILLY!
THERE'S SO MUCH WE CAN LEARN FROM ONE ANOTHER!

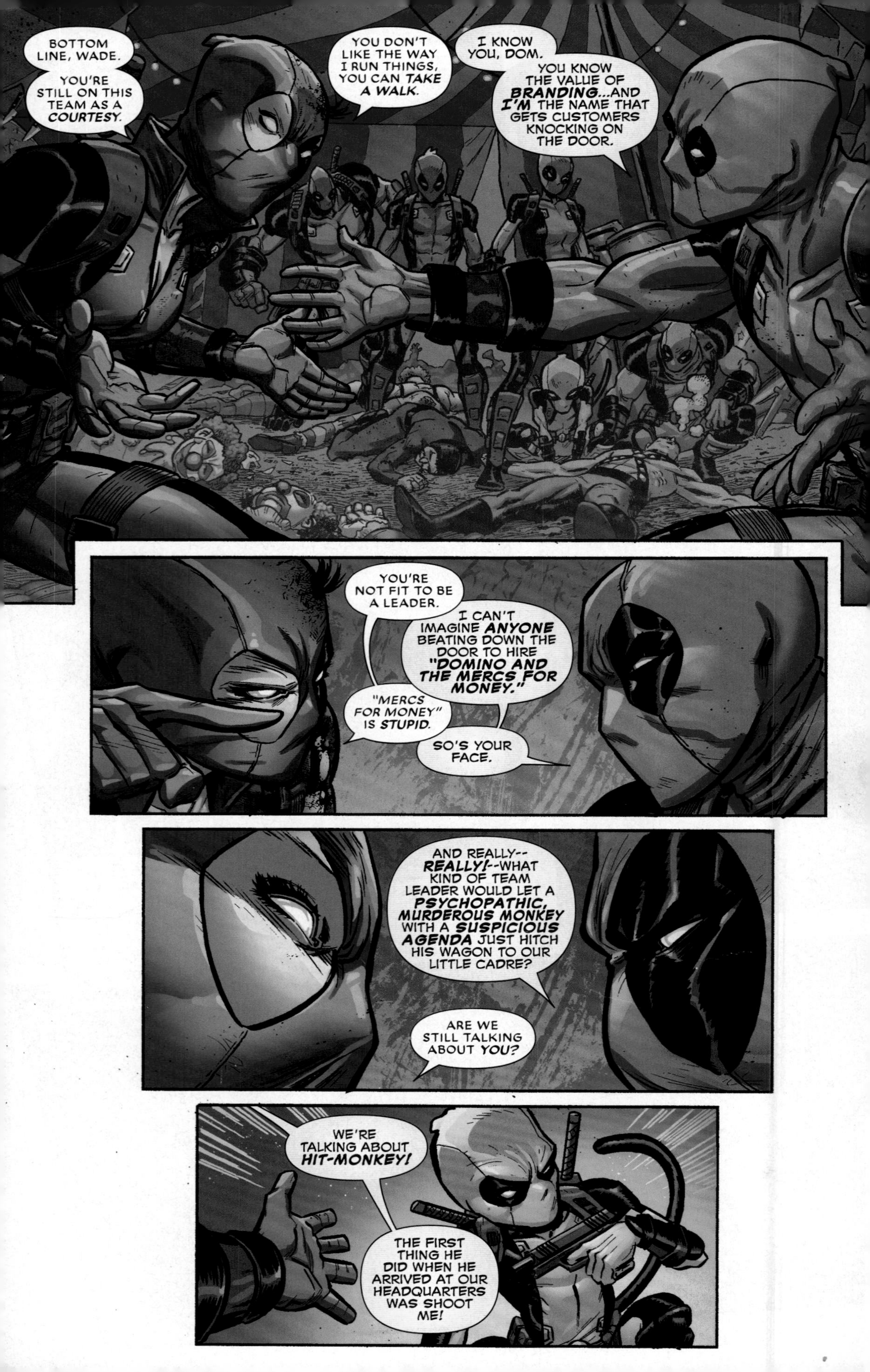
BOTTOM LINE, WADE.
YOU'RE STILL ON THIS TEAM AS A COURTESY.
YOU DON'T LIKE THE WAY I RUN THINGS, YOU CAN TAKE A WALK.
I KNOW YOU, DOM.
YOU KNOW THE VALUE OF BRANDING...AND I'M THE NAME THAT GETS CUSTOMERS KNOCKING ON THE DOOR.
YOU'RE NOT FIT TO BE A LEADER.
I CAN'T IMAGINE ANYONE BEATING DOWN THE DOOR TO HIRE "DOMINO AND THE MERCS FOR MONEY."
"MERCS FOR MONEY" IS STUPID.
SO'S YOUR FACE.
AND REALLY-- REALLY!--WHAT KIND OF TEAM LEADER WOULD LET A PSYCHOPATHIC, MURDEROUS MONKEY WITH A SUSPICIOUS AGENDA JUST HITCH HIS WAGON TO OUR LITTLE CADRE?
ARE WE STILL TALKING ABOUT YOU?
WE'RE TALKING ABOUT HIT-MONKEY!
THE FIRST THING HE DID WHEN HE ARRIVED AT OUR HEADQUARTERS WAS SHOOT ME!

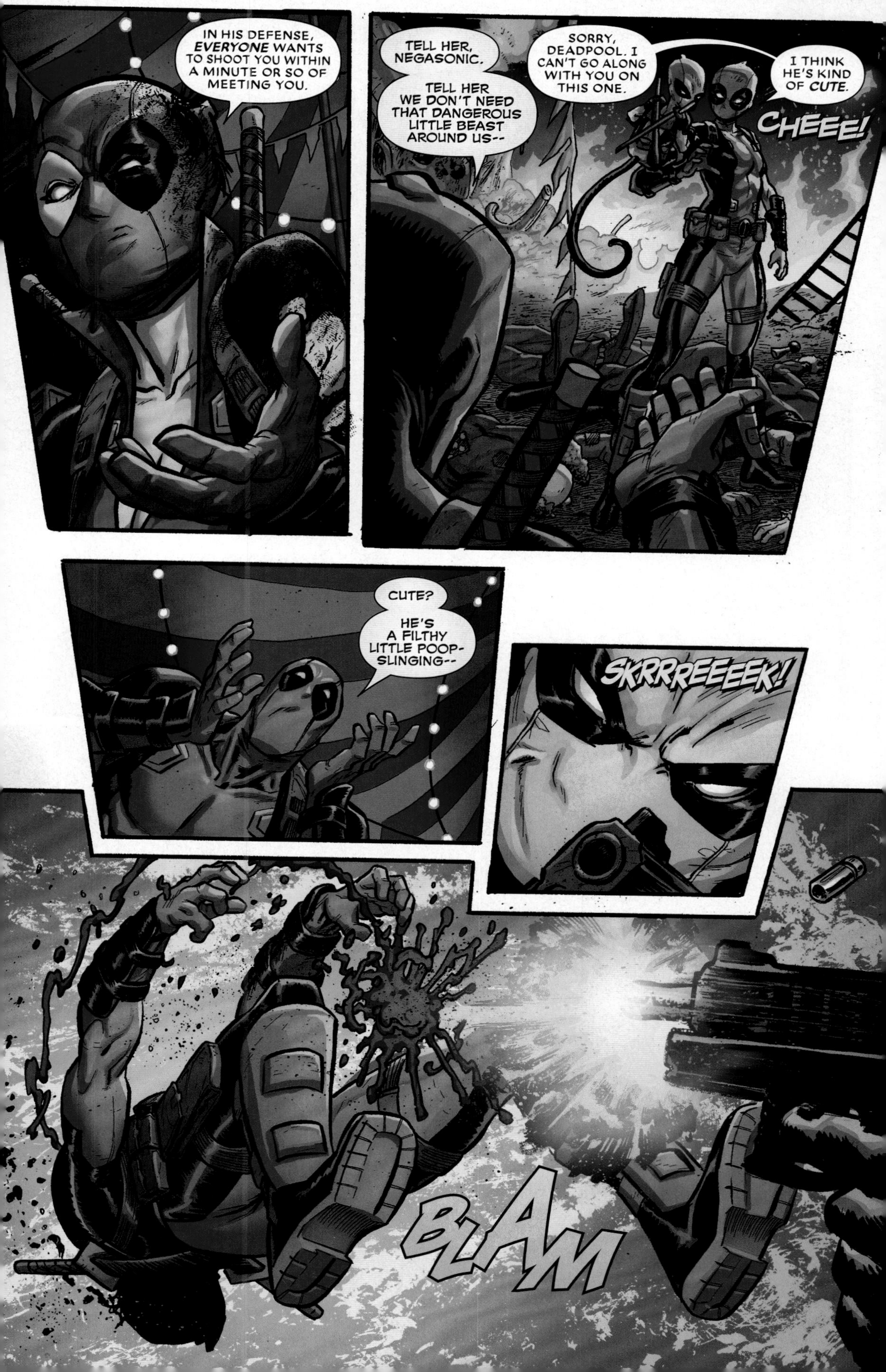
IN HIS DEFENSE, EVERYONE WANTS TO SHOOT YOU WITHIN A MINUTE OR SO OF MEETING YOU.
TELL HER, NEGASONIC.
TELL HER WE DON'T NEED THAT DANGEROUS LITTLE BEAST AROUND US--
SORRY, DEADPOOL. I CAN'T GO ALONG WITH YOU ON THIS ONE.
I THINK HE'S KIND OF CUTE.
CHEEE!
CUTE?
HE'S A FILTHY LITTLE POOP-SLINGING--
SKRRREEEEK!
BLAM

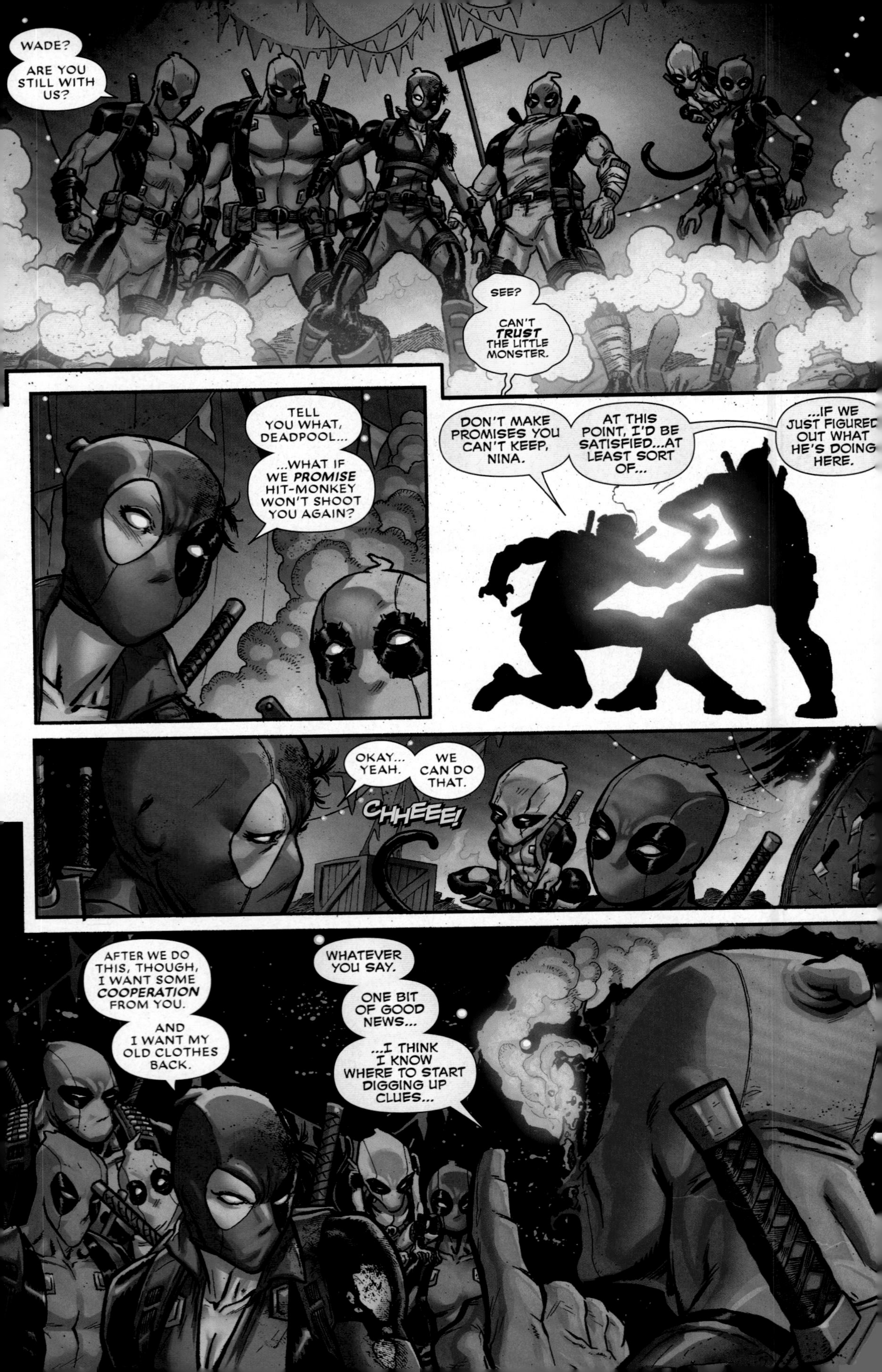
WADE?
ARE YOU STILL WITH US?
SEE?
CAN'T TRUST THE LITTLE MONSTER.
TELL YOU WHAT, DEADPOOL...
...WHAT IF WE PROMISE HIT-MONKEY WON'T SHOOT YOU AGAIN?
DON'T MAKE PROMISES YOU CAN'T KEEP, NINA.
AT THIS POINT, I'D BE SATISFIED...AT LEAST SORT OF...
...IF WE JUST FIGURED OUT WHAT HE'S DOING HERE.
OKAY... YEAH.
WE CAN DO THAT.
CHHEEE!
AFTER WE DO THIS, THOUGH, I WANT SOME COOPERATION FROM YOU.
AND I WANT MY OLD CLOTHES BACK.
WHATEVER YOU SAY.
ONE BIT OF GOOD NEWS...
...I THINK I KNOW WHERE TO START DIGGING UP CLUES...

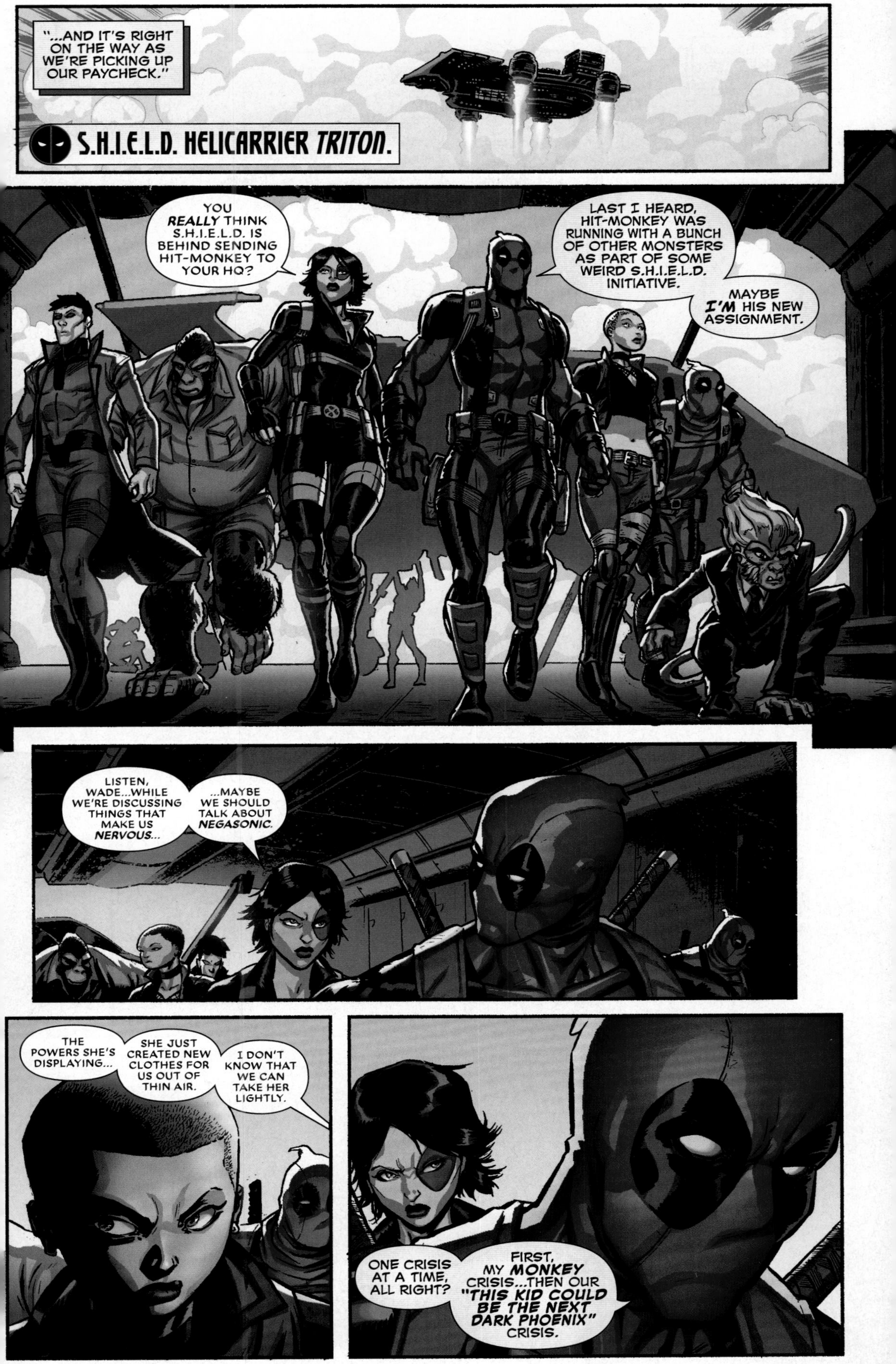
"...AND IT'S RIGHT ON THE WAY AS WE'RE PICKING UP OUR PAYCHECK."
S.H.I.E.L.D. HELICARRIER TRITON.
YOU REALLY THINK S.H.I.E.L.D. IS BEHIND SENDING HIT-MONKEY TO YOUR HQ?
LAST I HEARD, HIT-MONKEY WAS RUNNING WITH A BUNCH OF OTHER MONSTERS AS PART OF SOME WEIRD S.H.I.E.L.D. INITIATIVE.
MAYBE I'M HIS NEW ASSIGNMENT.
LISTEN, WADE...WHILE WE'RE DISCUSSING THINGS THAT MAKE US NERVOUS...
...MAYBE WE SHOULD TALK ABOUT NEGASONIC.
THE POWERS SHE'S DISPLAYING...
SHE JUST CREATED NEW CLOTHES FOR US OUT OF THIN AIR.
I DON'T KNOW THAT WE CAN TAKE HER LIGHTLY.
ONE CRISIS AT A TIME, ALL RIGHT?
FIRST, MY MONKEY CRISIS...THEN OUR "THIS KID COULD BE THE NEXT DARK PHOENIX" CRISIS.

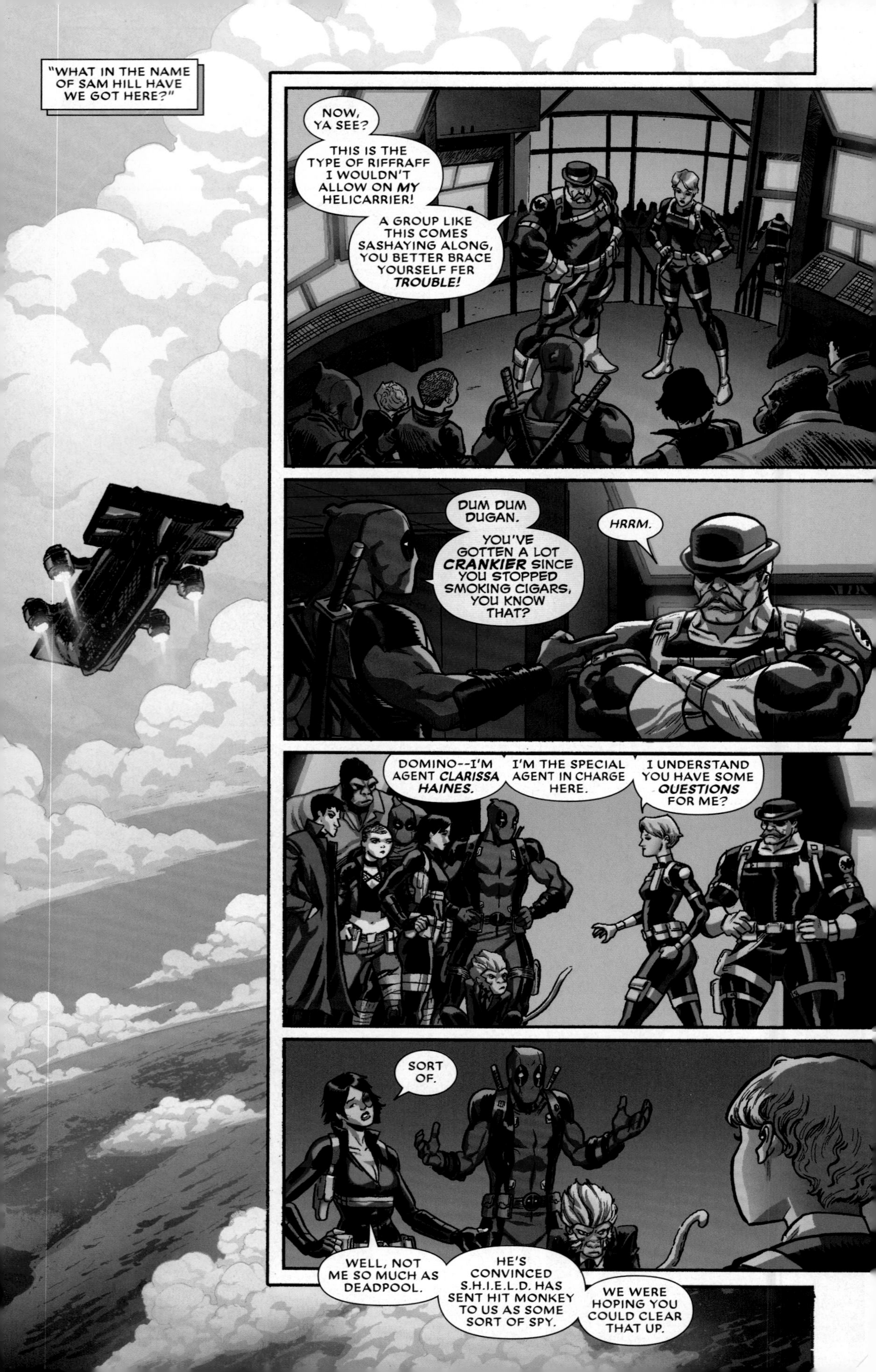
"WHAT IN THE NAME OF SAM HILL HAVE WE GOT HERE?"
NOW, YA SEE?
THIS IS THE TYPE OF RIFFRAFF I WOULDN'T ALLOW ON MY HELICARRIER!
A GROUP LIKE THIS COMES SASHAYING ALONG, YOU BETTER BRACE YOURSELF FER TROUBLE!
DUM DUM DUGAN.
YOU'VE GOTTEN A LOT CRANKIER SINCE YOU STOPPED SMOKING CIGARS, YOU KNOW THAT?
HRRM.
DOMINO--I'M AGENT CLARISSA HAINES.
I'M THE SPECIAL AGENT IN CHARGE HERE.
I UNDERSTAND YOU HAVE SOME QUESTIONS FOR ME?
SORT OF.
WELL, NOT ME SO MUCH AS DEADPOOL.
HE'S CONVINCED S.H.I.E.L.D. HAS SENT HIT MONKEY TO US AS SOME SORT OF SPY.
WE WERE HOPING YOU COULD CLEAR THAT UP.

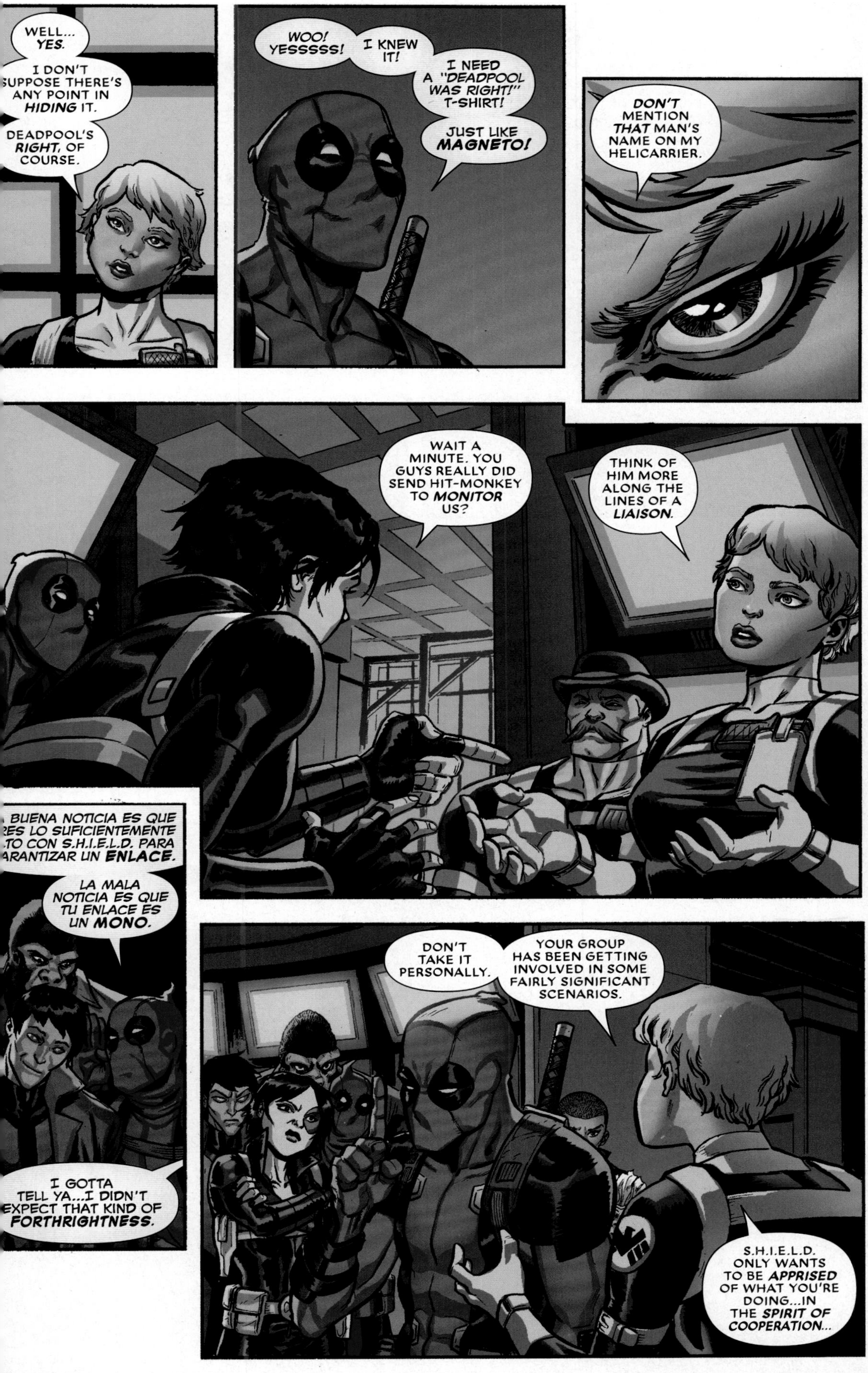
WELL... YES.
I DON'T SUPPOSE THERE'S ANY POINT IN HIDING IT.
DEADPOOL'S RIGHT, OF COURSE.
WOO! YESSSSS!
I KNEW IT!
I NEED A "DEADPOOL WAS RIGHT!" T-SHIRT!
JUST LIKE MAGNETO!
DON'T MENTION THAT MAN'S NAME ON MY HELICARRIER.
WAIT A MINUTE. YOU GUYS REALLY DID SEND HIT-MONKEY TO MONITOR US?
THINK OF HIM MORE ALONG THE LINES OF A LIAISON.
BUENA NOTICIA ES QUE RES LO SUFICIENTEMENTE TO CON S.H.I.E.L.D. PARA ARANTIZAR UN ENLACE.
LA MALA NOTICIA ES QUE TU ENLACE ES UN MONO.
I GOTTA TELL YA...I DIDN'T EXPECT THAT KIND OF FORTHRIGHTNESS.
DON'T TAKE IT PERSONALLY.
YOUR GROUP HAS BEEN GETTING INVOLVED IN SOME FAIRLY SIGNIFICANT SCENARIOS.
S.H.I.E.L.D. ONLY WANTS TO BE APPRISED OF WHAT YOU'RE DOING...IN THE SPIRIT OF COOPERATION...

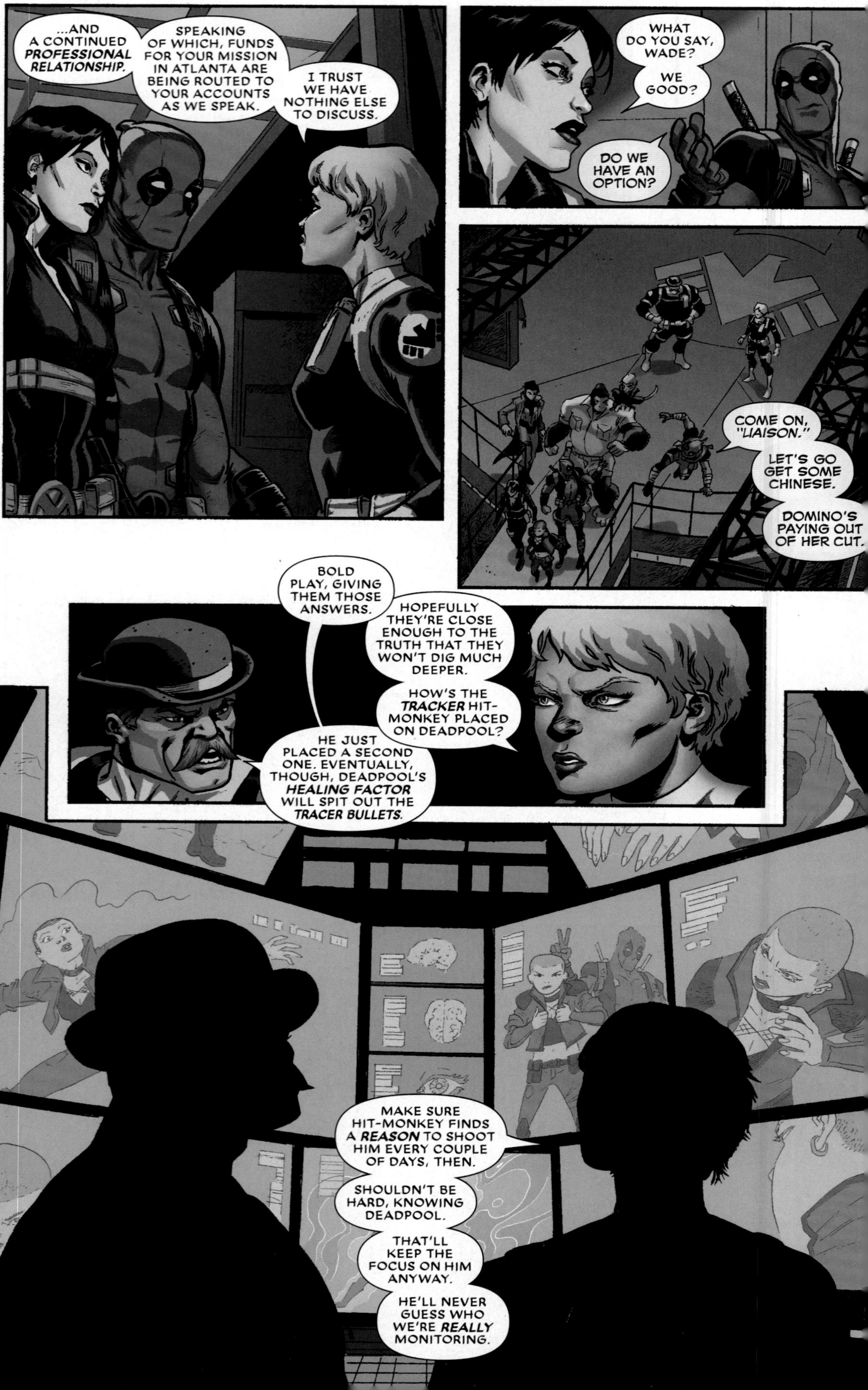
...AND A CONTINUED PROFESSIONAL RELATIONSHIP.
SPEAKING OF WHICH, FUNDS FOR YOUR MISSION IN ATLANTA ARE BEING ROUTED TO YOUR ACCOUNTS AS WE SPEAK.
I TRUST WE HAVE NOTHING ELSE TO DISCUSS.
WHAT DO YOU SAY, WADE?
WE GOOD?
DO WE HAVE AN OPTION?
COME ON, "LIAISON."
LET'S GO GET SOME CHINESE.
DOMINO'S PAYING OUT OF HER CUT.
BOLD PLAY, GIVING THEM THOSE ANSWERS.
HOPEFULLY THEY'RE CLOSE ENOUGH TO THE TRUTH THAT THEY WON'T DIG MUCH DEEPER.
HOW'S THE TRACKER HIT-MONKEY PLACED ON DEADPOOL?
HE JUST PLACED A SECOND ONE. EVENTUALLY, THOUGH, DEADPOOL'S HEALING FACTOR WILL SPIT OUT THE TRACER BULLETS.
MAKE SURE HIT-MONKEY FINDS A REASON TO SHOOT HIM EVERY COUPLE OF DAYS, THEN.
SHOULDN'T BE HARD, KNOWING DEADPOOL.
THAT'LL KEEP THE FOCUS ON HIM ANYWAY.
HE'LL NEVER GUESS WHO WE'RE REALLY MONITORING.

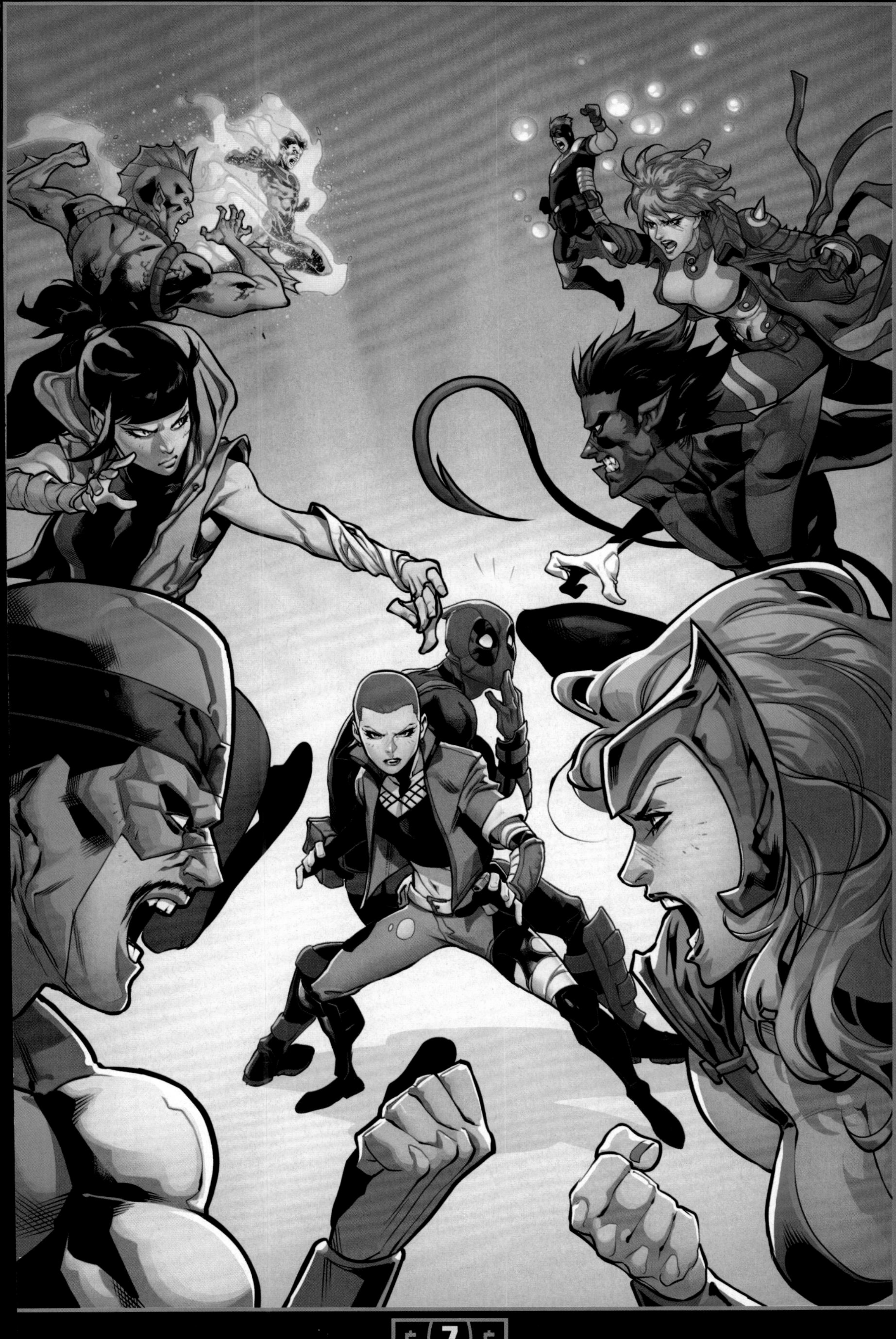

INHUMANS VS X-MEN

DEADPOOL & THE MERCS FOR MONEY

When the Terrigen mists — the catalyst that grants Inhumans their powers — were discovered to be poisonous to mutants, veteran X-Men Cyclops and Emma Frost rallied their mutant brothers and sisters to destroy the Terrigen Clouds circling the Earth. The mutants succeeded in eradicating half of the Terrigen but both sides suffered extreme loss. The time for truce has come to an end.

Now it is 5 years from the initial release of the mists and the Mercs for Money roam the streets of New York for their cause in protecting those who cannot protect themselves from the mists. Meanwhile, Negasonic Teenage Warhead has gone missing, and it's up to Domino, Deadpool, Gorilla-Man, Hit-Monkey, Machine Man, and new team member Ren Kimura to find her...

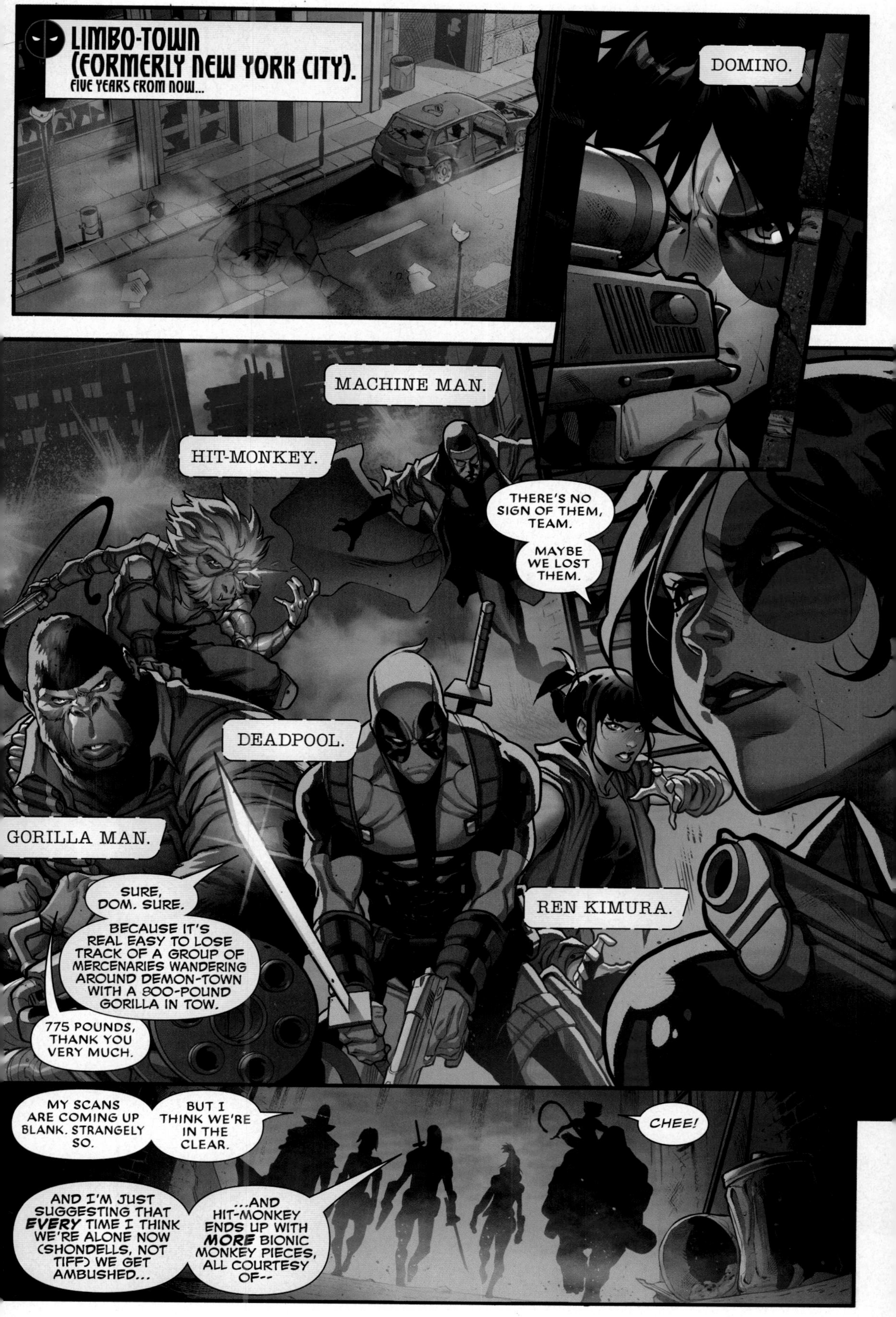

LIMBO-TOWN (FORMERLY NEW YORK CITY).
FIVE YEARS FROM NOW...
DOMINO.
MACHINE MAN.
HIT-MONKEY.
THERE'S NO SIGN OF THEM, TEAM.
MAYBE WE LOST THEM.
DEADPOOL.
GORILLA MAN.
REN KIMURA.
SURE, DOM. SURE.
BECAUSE IT'S REAL EASY TO LOSE TRACK OF A GROUP OF MERCENARIES WANDERING AROUND DEMON-TOWN WITH A 800-POUND GORILLA IN TOW.
775 POUNDS, THANK YOU VERY MUCH.
MY SCANS ARE COMING UP BLANK. STRANGELY SO.
BUT I THINK WE'RE IN THE CLEAR.
CHEE!
AND I'M JUST SUGGESTING THAT EVERY TIME I THINK WE'RE ALONE NOW (SHONDELLS, NOT TIFF) WE GET AMBUSHED...
...AND HIT-MONKEY ENDS UP WITH MORE BIONIC MONKEY PIECES, ALL COURTESY OF--

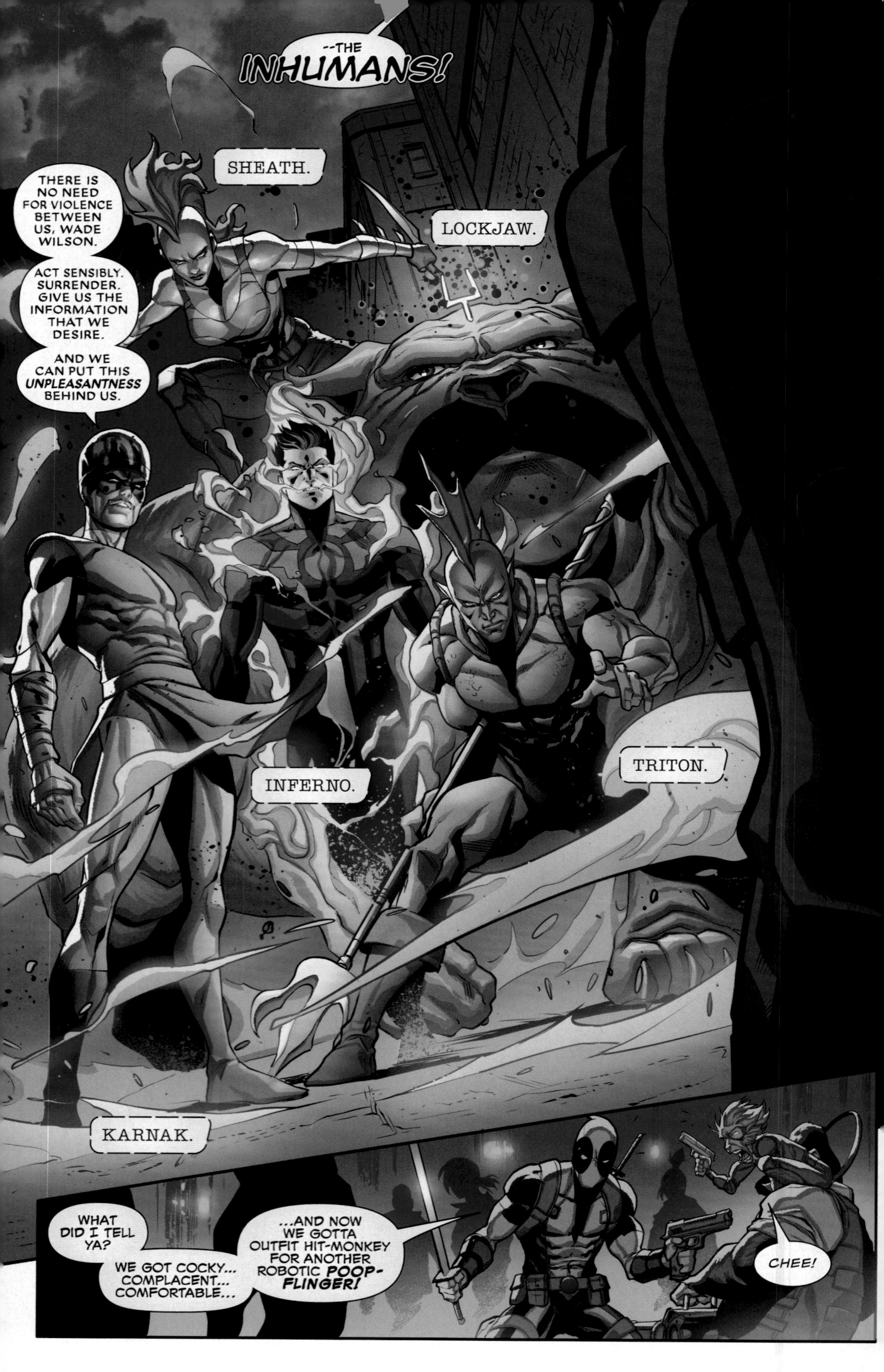
--THE INHUMANS!
THERE IS NO NEED FOR VIOLENCE BETWEEN US, WADE WILSON.
ACT SENSIBLY. SURRENDER. GIVE US THE INFORMATION THAT WE DESIRE.
AND WE CAN PUT THIS UNPLEASANTNESS BEHIND US.
SHEATH.
LOCKJAW.
INFERNO.
TRITON.
KARNAK.
WHAT DID I TELL YA?
WE GOT COCKY... COMPLACENT... COMFORTABLE...
...AND NOW WE GOTTA OUTFIT HIT-MONKEY FOR ANOTHER ROBOTIC POOP-FLINGER!
CHEE!

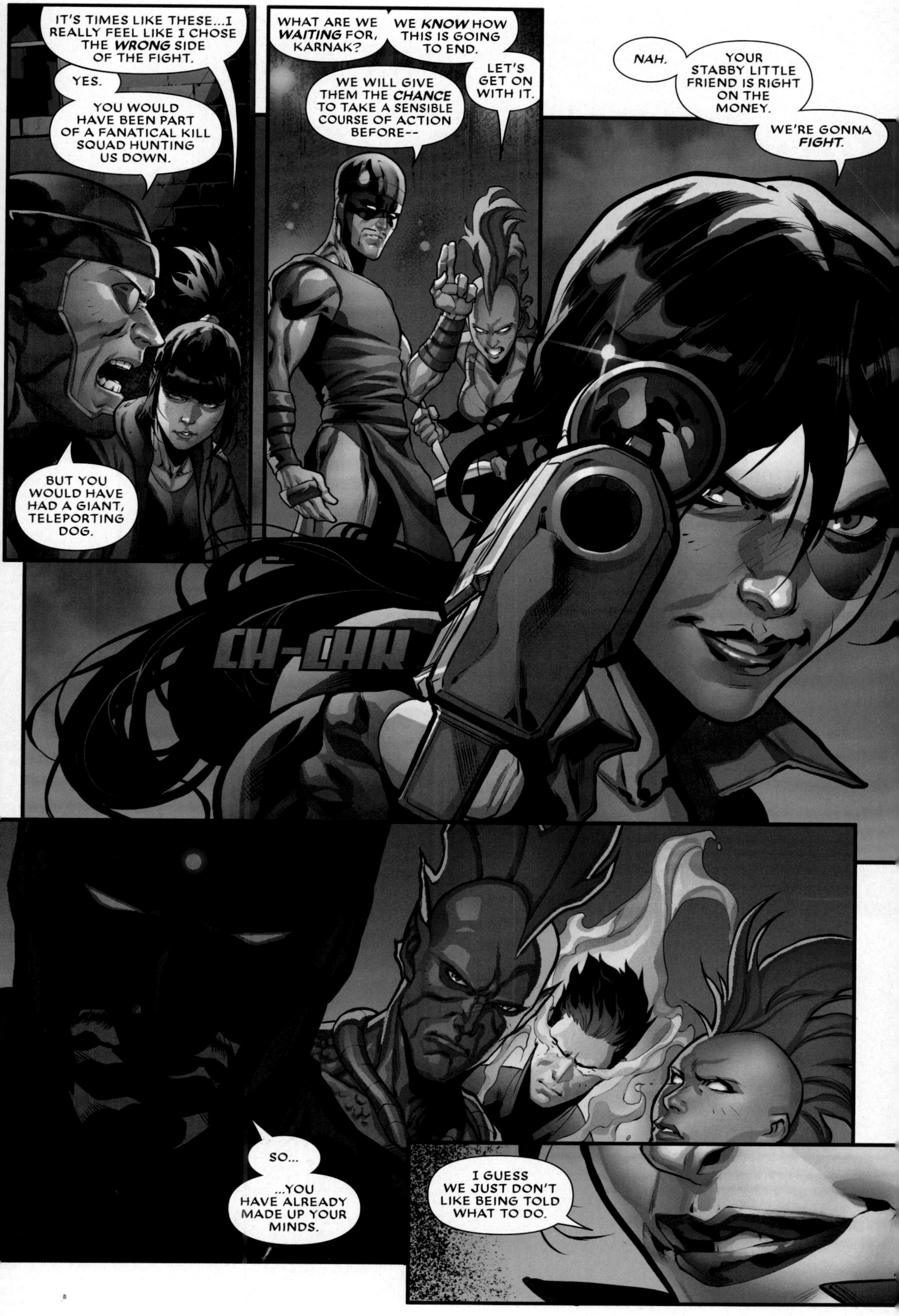

IT'S TIMES LIKE THESE...I REALLY FEEL LIKE I CHOSE THE *WRONG* SIDE OF THE FIGHT.
YES.
YOU WOULD HAVE BEEN PART OF A FANATICAL KILL SQUAD HUNTING US DOWN.
BUT YOU WOULD HAVE HAD A GIANT, TELEPORTING DOG.
WHAT ARE WE *WAITING* FOR, KARNAK?
WE *KNOW* HOW THIS IS GOING TO END.
LET'S GET ON WITH IT.
WE WILL GIVE THEM THE *CHANCE* TO TAKE A SENSIBLE COURSE OF ACTION BEFORE--
NAH.
YOUR STABBY LITTLE FRIEND IS RIGHT ON THE MONEY.
WE'RE GONNA *FIGHT.*
CH-CHK
SO...
...YOU HAVE ALREADY MADE UP YOUR MINDS.
I GUESS WE JUST DON'T LIKE BEING TOLD WHAT TO DO.

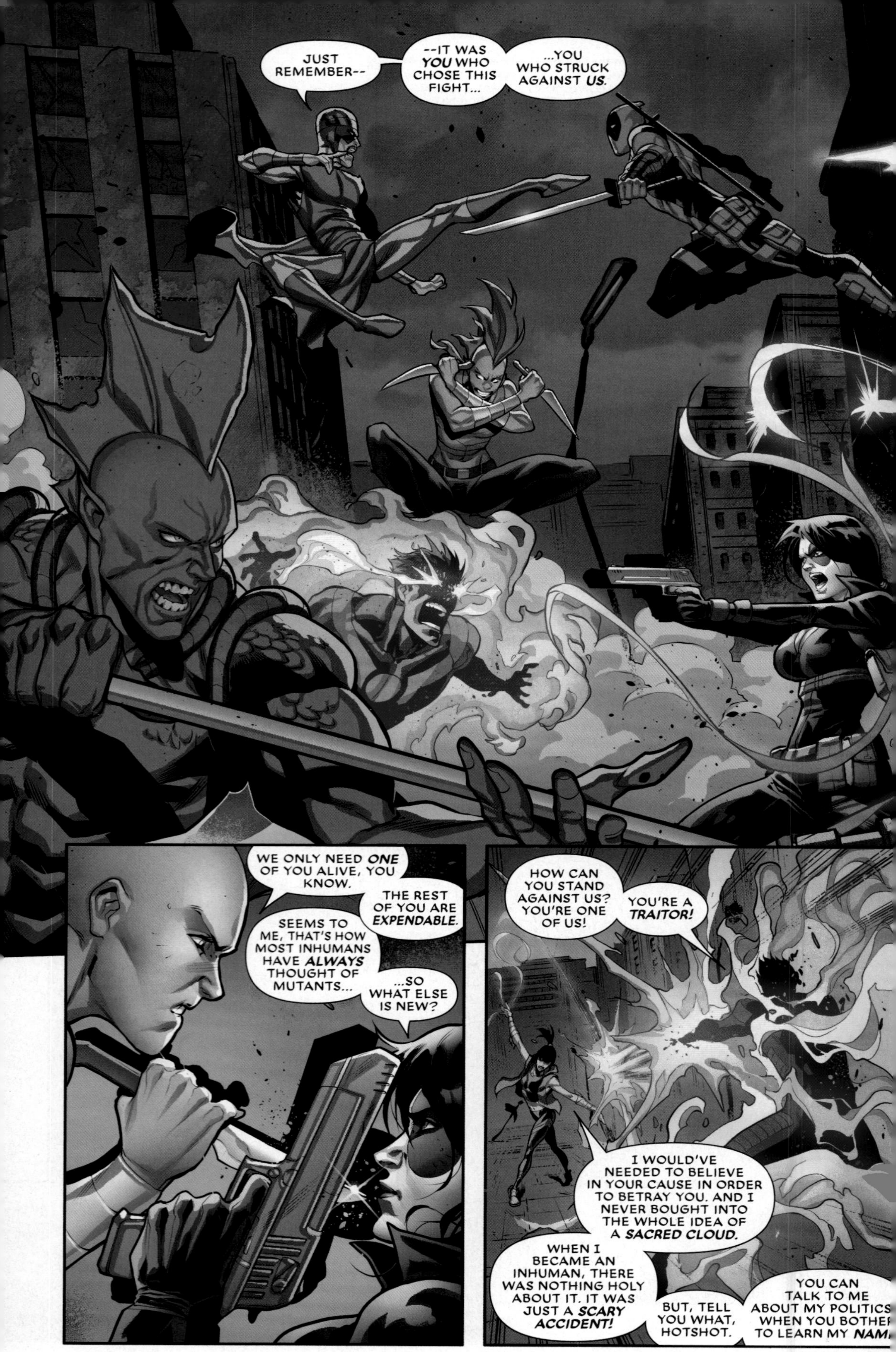
JUST REMEMBER--
--IT WAS YOU WHO CHOSE THIS FIGHT...
...YOU WHO STRUCK AGAINST US.
WE ONLY NEED ONE OF YOU ALIVE, YOU KNOW.
THE REST OF YOU ARE EXPENDABLE.
SEEMS TO ME, THAT'S HOW MOST INHUMANS HAVE ALWAYS THOUGHT OF MUTANTS...
...SO WHAT ELSE IS NEW?
HOW CAN YOU STAND AGAINST US? YOU'RE ONE OF US!
YOU'RE A TRAITOR!
I WOULD'VE NEEDED TO BELIEVE IN YOUR CAUSE IN ORDER TO BETRAY YOU. AND I NEVER BOUGHT INTO THE WHOLE IDEA OF A SACRED CLOUD.
WHEN I BECAME AN INHUMAN, THERE WAS NOTHING HOLY ABOUT IT. IT WAS JUST A SCARY ACCIDENT!
BUT, TELL YOU WHAT, HOTSHOT.
YOU CAN TALK TO ME ABOUT MY POLITICS WHEN YOU BOTHER TO LEARN MY NAM

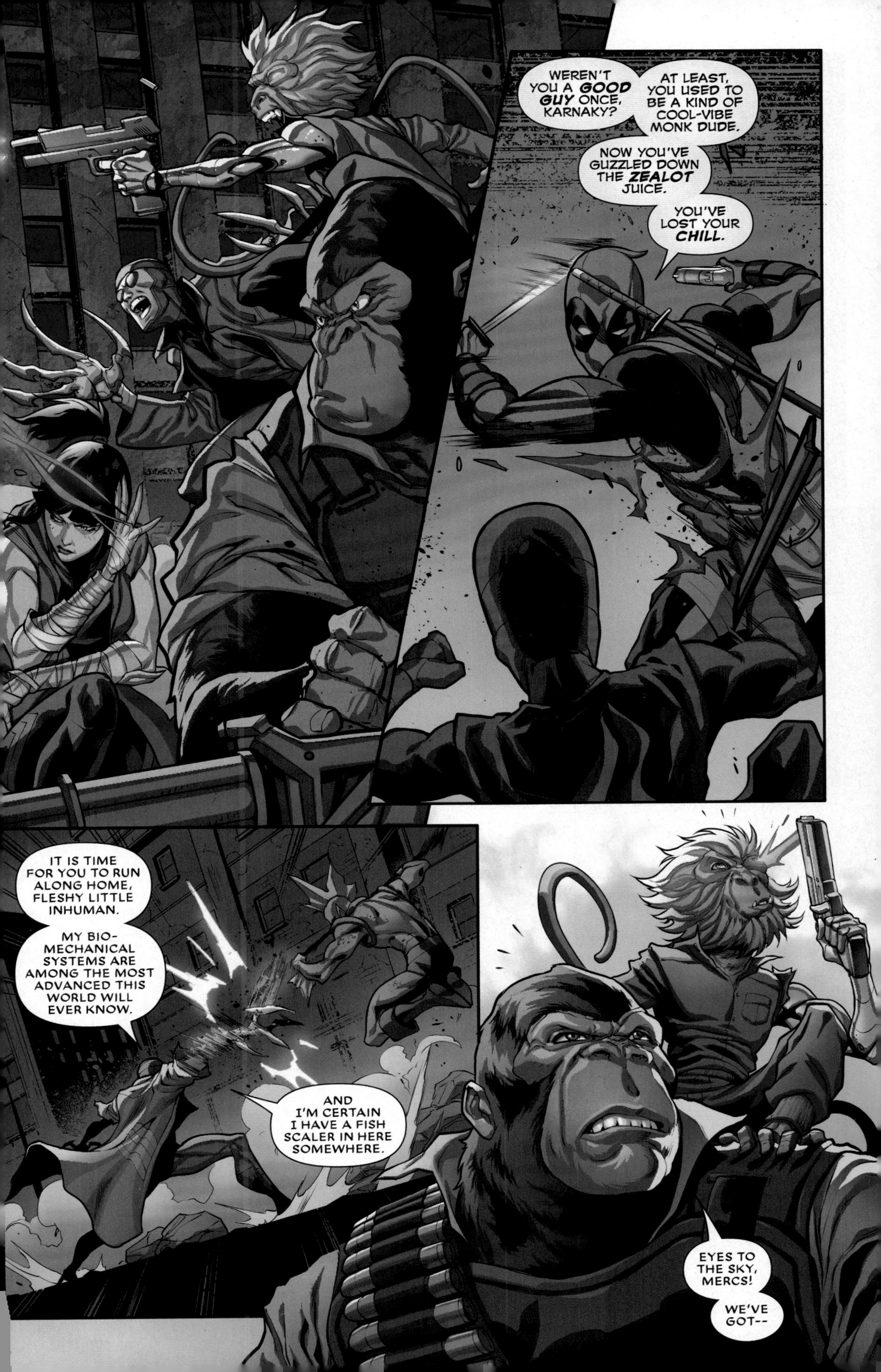
WEREN'T YOU A GOOD GUY ONCE, KARNAKY?
AT LEAST, YOU USED TO BE A KIND OF COOL-VIBE MONK DUDE.
NOW YOU'VE GUZZLED DOWN THE ZEALOT JUICE.
YOU'VE LOST YOUR CHILL.
IT IS TIME FOR YOU TO RUN ALONG HOME, FLESHY LITTLE INHUMAN.
MY BIO-MECHANICAL SYSTEMS ARE AMONG THE MOST ADVANCED THIS WORLD WILL EVER KNOW.
AND I'M CERTAIN I HAVE A FISH SCALER IN HERE SOMEWHERE.
EYES TO THE SKY, MERCS!
WE'VE GOT--

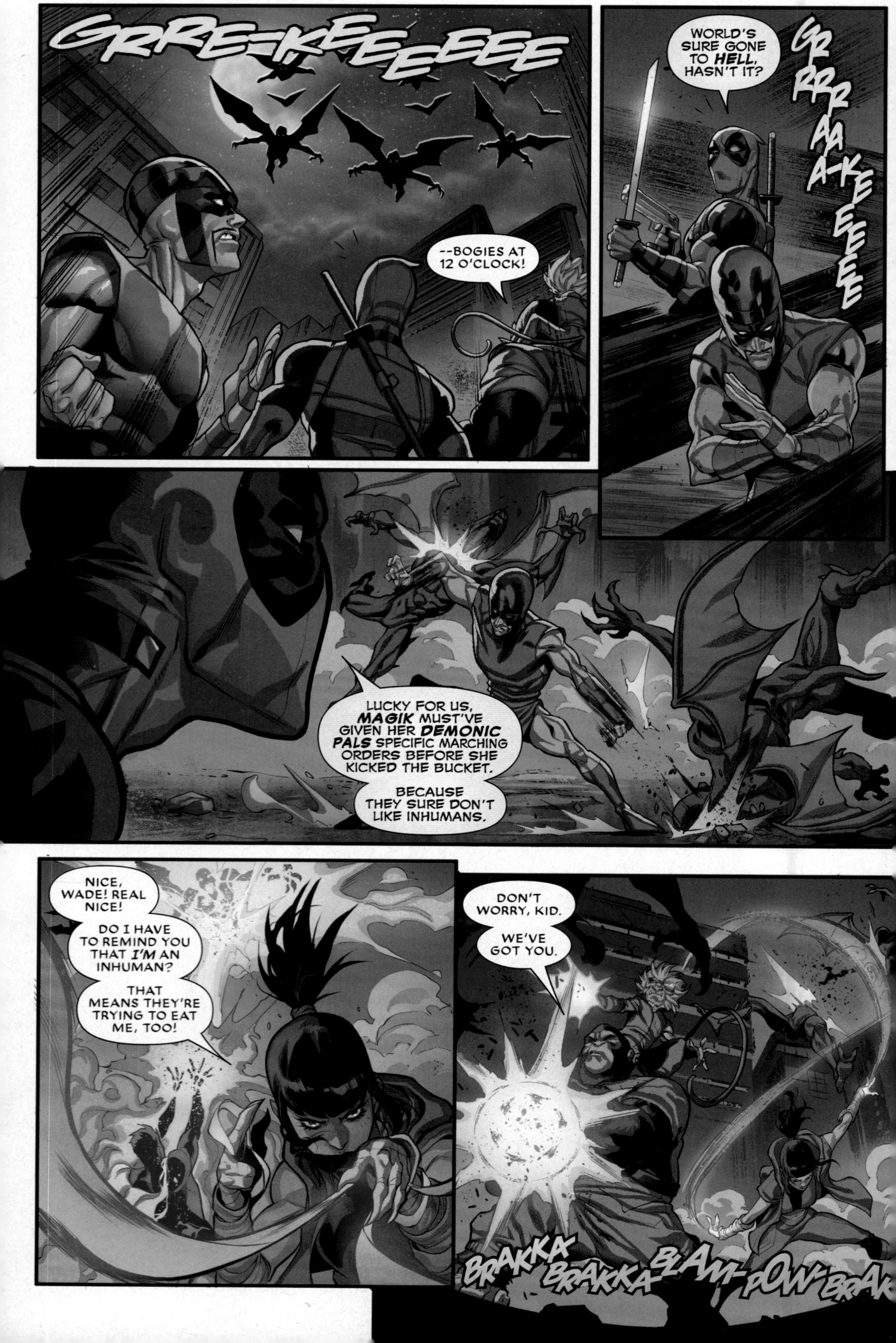
GRRE-KEEEEEEE
--BOGIES AT 12 O'CLOCK!
WORLD'S SURE GONE TO HELL, HASN'T IT?
GRRRAAA-KEEEEEE
LUCKY FOR US, MAGIK MUST'VE GIVEN HER DEMONIC PALS SPECIFIC MARCHING ORDERS BEFORE SHE KICKED THE BUCKET.
BECAUSE THEY SURE DON'T LIKE INHUMANS.
NICE, WADE! REAL NICE!
DO I HAVE TO REMIND YOU THAT I'M AN INHUMAN?
THAT MEANS THEY'RE TRYING TO EAT ME, TOO!
DON'T WORRY, KID.
WE'VE GOT YOU.
BRAKKA BRAKKA BLAM POW

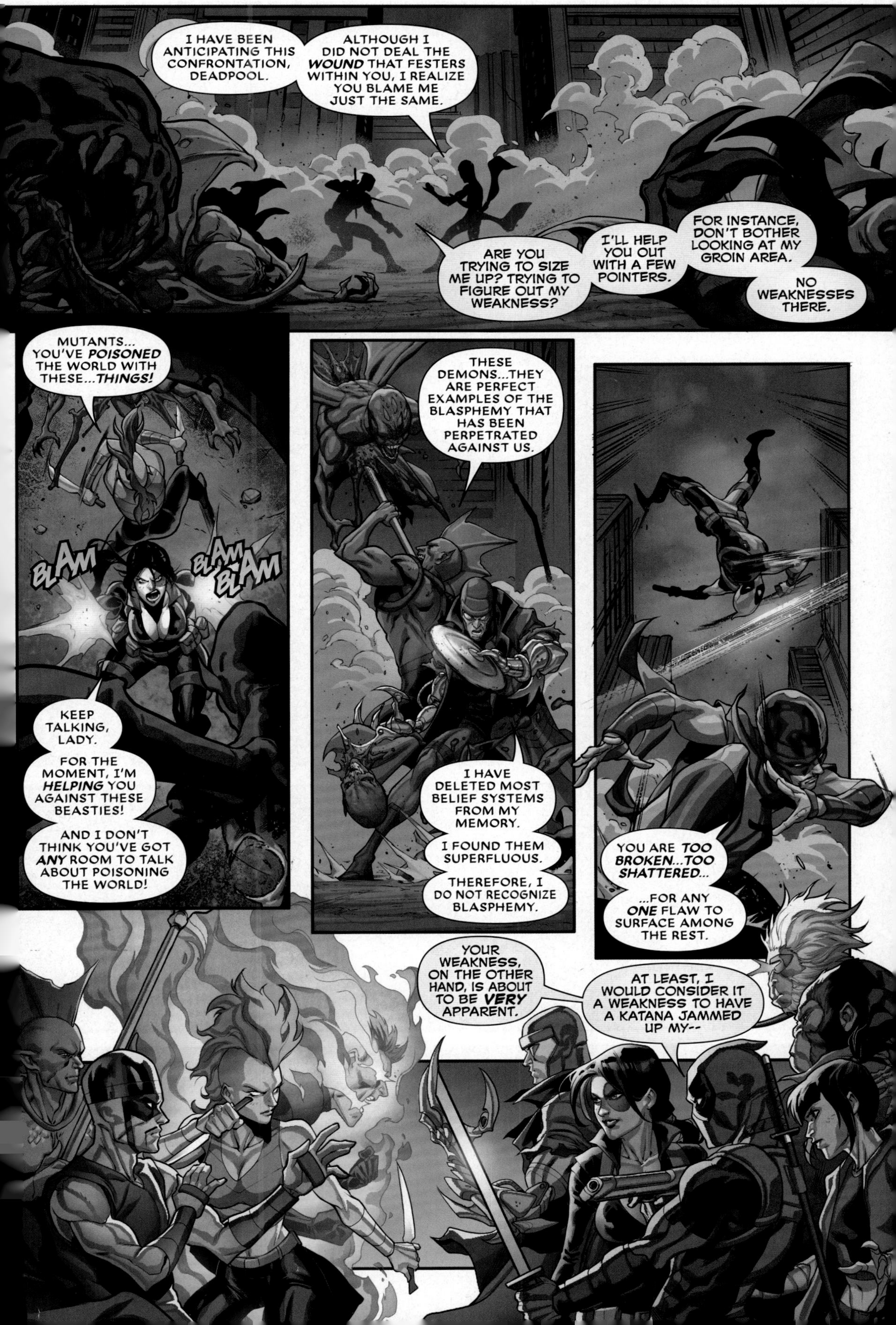
I HAVE BEEN ANTICIPATING THIS CONFRONTATION, DEADPOOL.
ALTHOUGH I DID NOT DEAL THE WOUND THAT FESTERS WITHIN YOU, I REALIZE YOU BLAME ME JUST THE SAME.
ARE YOU TRYING TO SIZE ME UP? TRYING TO FIGURE OUT MY WEAKNESS?
I'LL HELP YOU OUT WITH A FEW POINTERS.
FOR INSTANCE, DON'T BOTHER LOOKING AT MY GROIN AREA.
NO WEAKNESSES THERE.
MUTANTS... YOU'VE POISONED THE WORLD WITH THESE... THINGS!
BLAM
BLAM BLAM
KEEP TALKING, LADY.
FOR THE MOMENT, I'M HELPING YOU AGAINST THESE BEASTIES!
AND I DON'T THINK YOU'VE GOT ANY ROOM TO TALK ABOUT POISONING THE WORLD!
THESE DEMONS...THEY ARE PERFECT EXAMPLES OF THE BLASPHEMY THAT HAS BEEN PERPETRATED AGAINST US.
I HAVE DELETED MOST BELIEF SYSTEMS FROM MY MEMORY.
I FOUND THEM SUPERFLUOUS.
THEREFORE, I DO NOT RECOGNIZE BLASPHEMY.
YOU ARE TOO BROKEN...TOO SHATTERED...
...FOR ANY ONE FLAW TO SURFACE AMONG THE REST.
YOUR WEAKNESS, ON THE OTHER HAND, IS ABOUT TO BE VERY APPARENT.
AT LEAST, I WOULD CONSIDER IT A WEAKNESS TO HAVE A KATANA JAMMED UP MY--

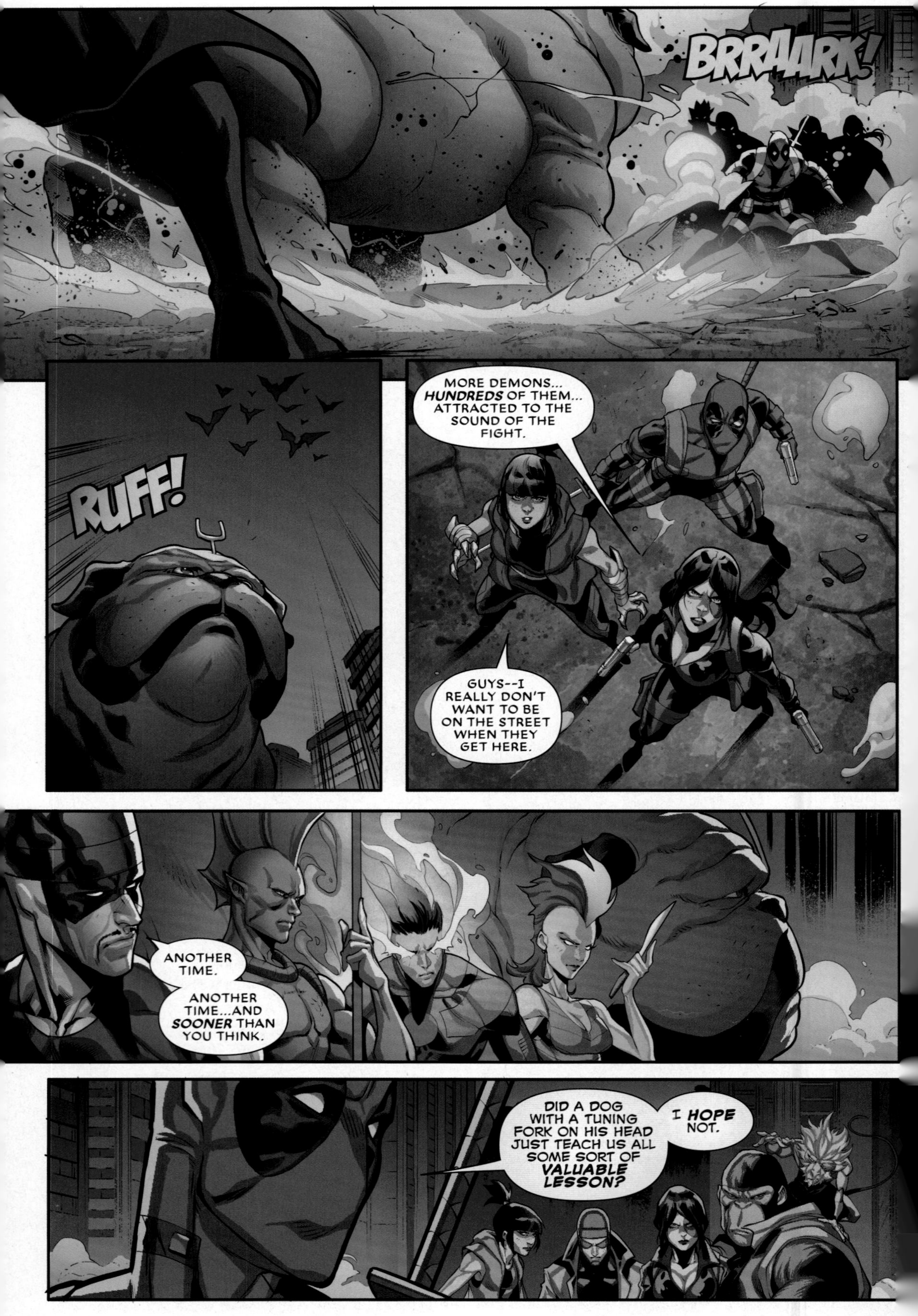
BRRAARK!
RUFF!
MORE DEMONS... HUNDREDS OF THEM... ATTRACTED TO THE SOUND OF THE FIGHT.
GUYS--I REALLY DON'T WANT TO BE ON THE STREET WHEN THEY GET HERE.
ANOTHER TIME.
ANOTHER TIME...AND SOONER THAN YOU THINK.
DID A DOG WITH A TUNING FORK ON HIS HEAD JUST TEACH US ALL SOME SORT OF VALUABLE LESSON?
I HOPE NOT.

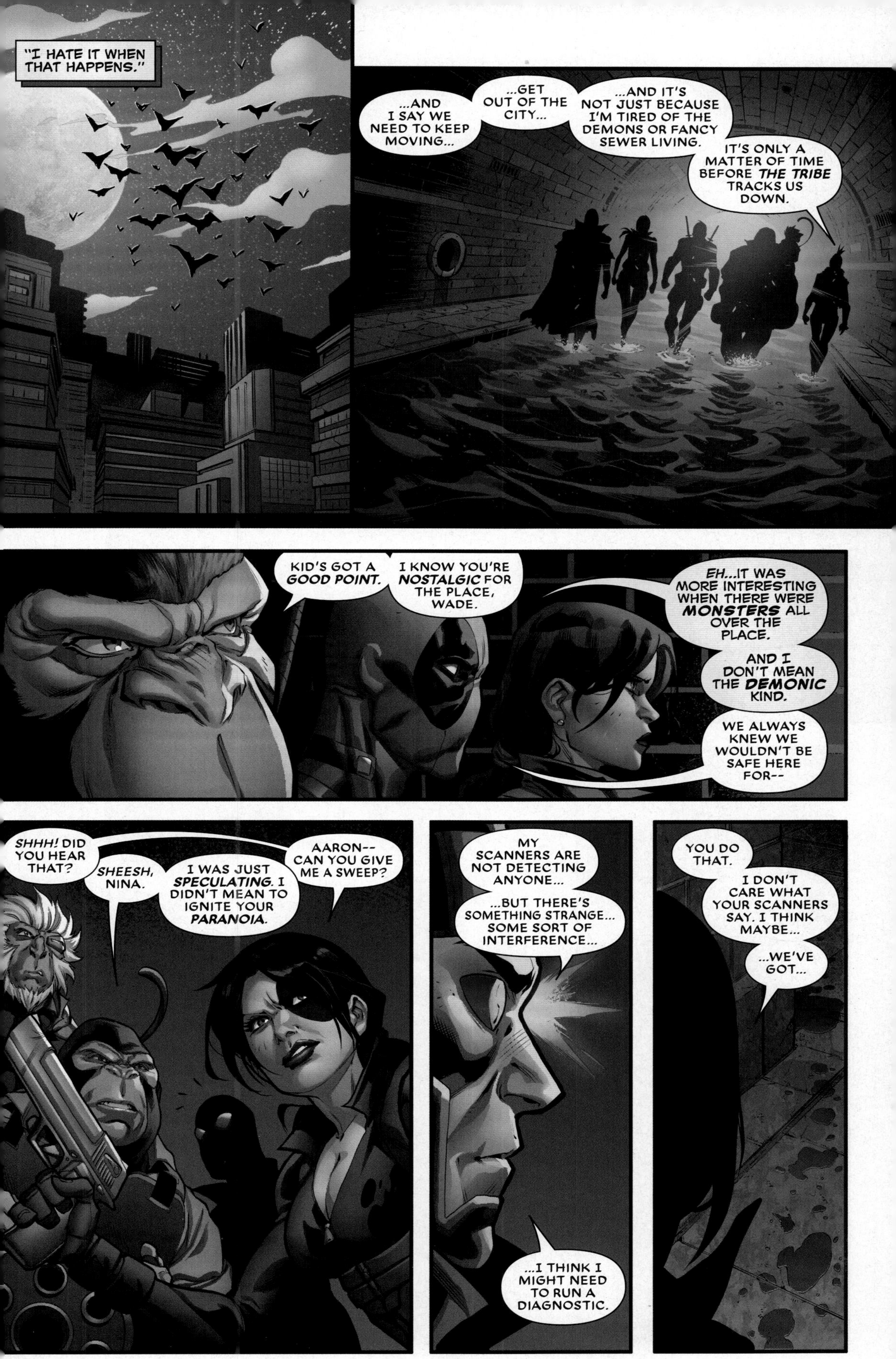
"I HATE IT WHEN THAT HAPPENS."
...AND I SAY WE NEED TO KEEP MOVING...
...GET OUT OF THE CITY...
...AND IT'S NOT JUST BECAUSE I'M TIRED OF THE DEMONS OR FANCY SEWER LIVING.
IT'S ONLY A MATTER OF TIME BEFORE THE TRIBE TRACKS US DOWN.
KID'S GOT A GOOD POINT.
I KNOW YOU'RE NOSTALGIC FOR THE PLACE, WADE.
EH...IT WAS MORE INTERESTING WHEN THERE WERE MONSTERS ALL OVER THE PLACE.
AND I DON'T MEAN THE DEMONIC KIND.
WE ALWAYS KNEW WE WOULDN'T BE SAFE HERE FOR--
SHHH! DID YOU HEAR THAT?
SHEESH, NINA.
I WAS JUST SPECULATING. I DIDN'T MEAN TO IGNITE YOUR PARANOIA.
AARON-- CAN YOU GIVE ME A SWEEP?
MY SCANNERS ARE NOT DETECTING ANYONE...
...BUT THERE'S SOMETHING STRANGE... SOME SORT OF INTERFERENCE...
...I THINK I MIGHT NEED TO RUN A DIAGNOSTIC.
YOU DO THAT.
I DON'T CARE WHAT YOUR SCANNERS SAY. I THINK MAYBE...
...WE'VE GOT...

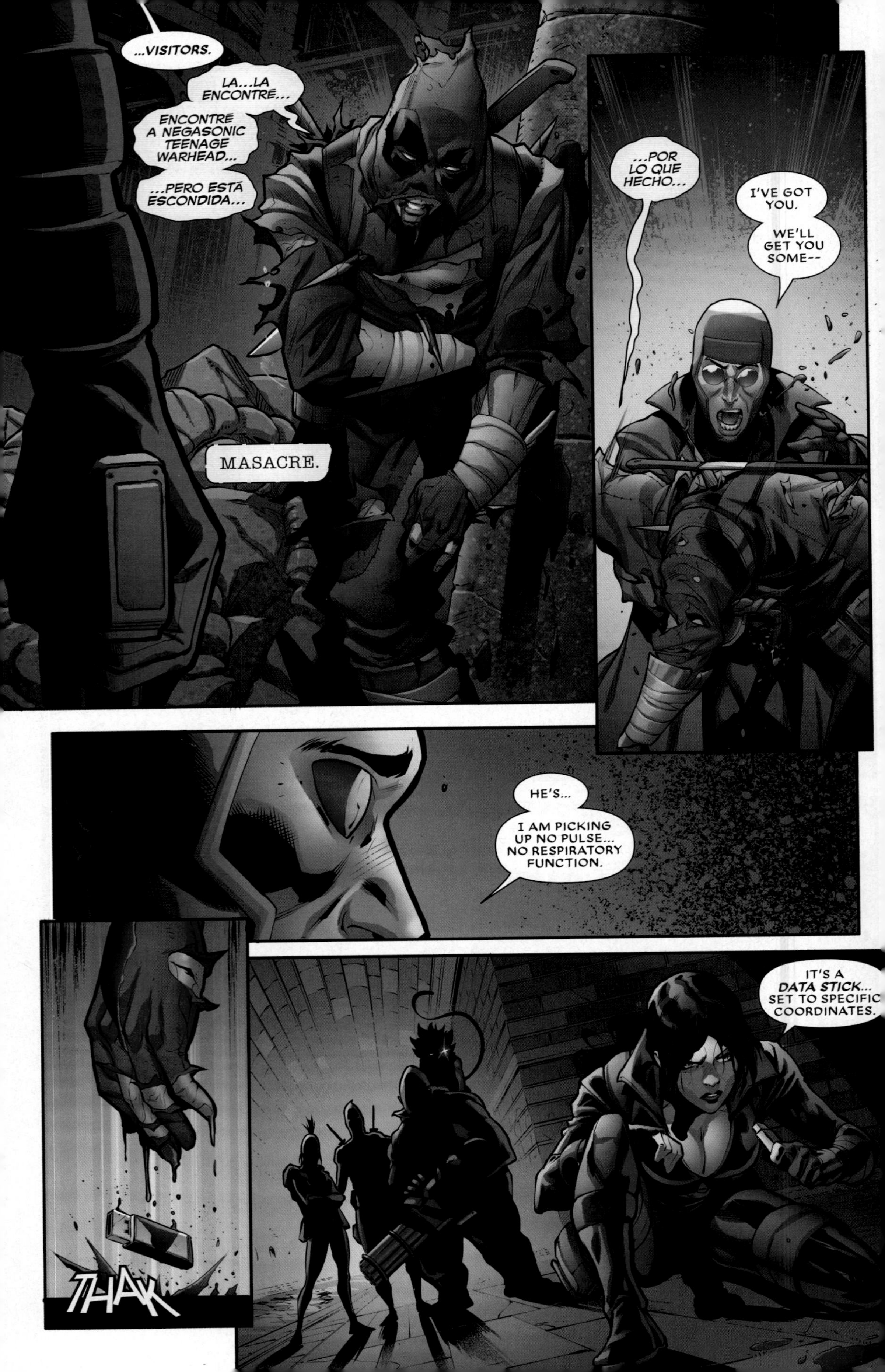
...VISITORS.
LA...LA ENCONTRÉ...
ENCONTRÉ A NEGASONIC TEENAGE WARHEAD...
...PERO ESTÁ ESCONDIDA...
MASACRE.
...POR LO QUE HECHO...
I'VE GOT YOU.
WE'LL GET YOU SOME--
HE'S...
I AM PICKING UP NO PULSE... NO RESPIRATORY FUNCTION.
THAK
IT'S A DATA STICK... SET TO SPECIFIC COORDINATES.

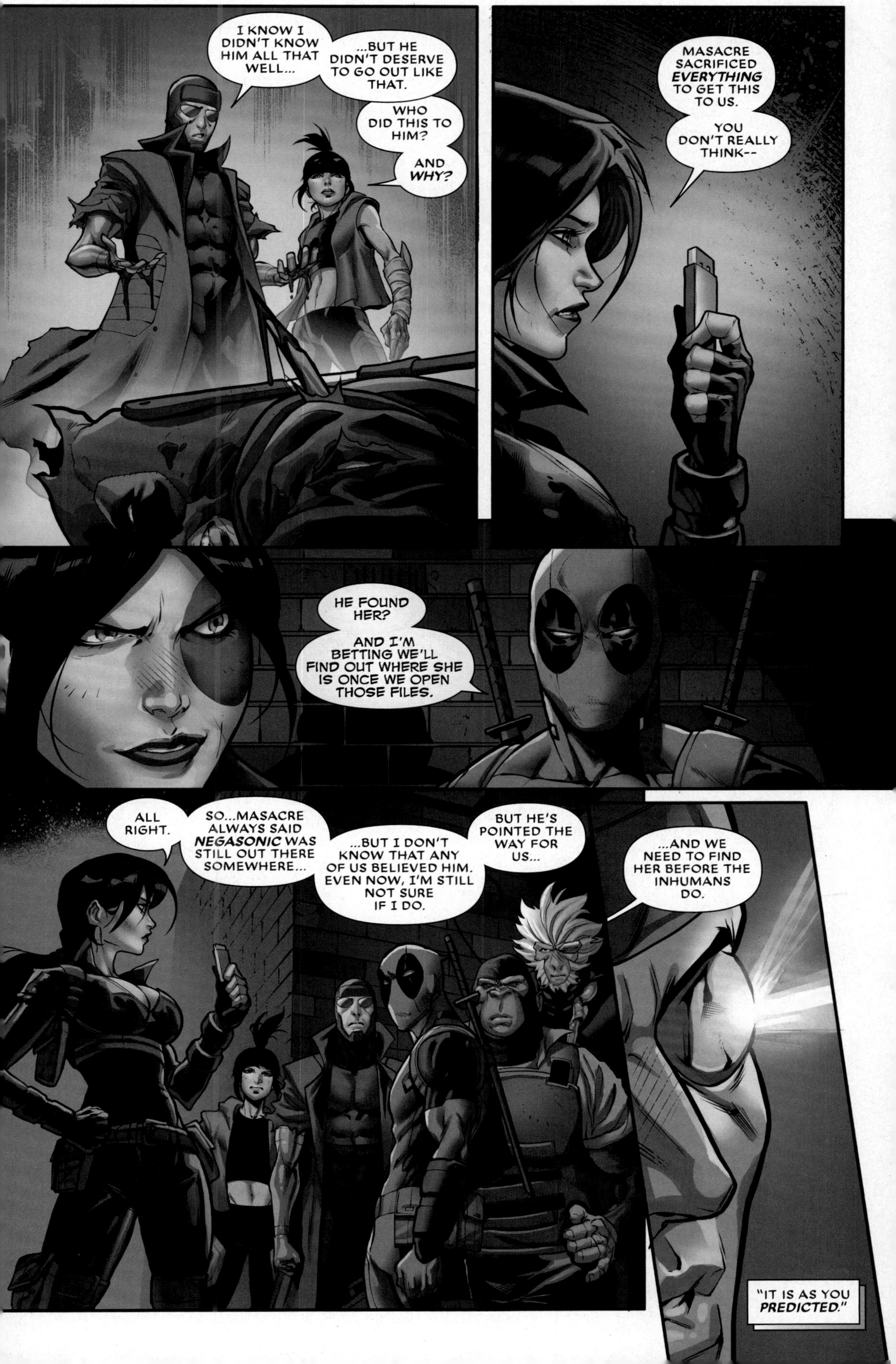
I KNOW I DIDN'T KNOW HIM ALL THAT WELL...
...BUT HE DIDN'T DESERVE TO GO OUT LIKE THAT.
WHO DID THIS TO HIM?
AND *WHY?*
MASACRE SACRIFICED *EVERYTHING* TO GET THIS TO US.
YOU DON'T REALLY THINK--
HE FOUND HER?
AND I'M BETTING WE'LL FIND OUT WHERE SHE IS ONCE WE OPEN THOSE FILES.
ALL RIGHT.
SO...MASACRE ALWAYS SAID *NEGASONIC* WAS STILL OUT THERE SOMEWHERE...
...BUT I DON'T KNOW THAT ANY OF US BELIEVED HIM. EVEN NOW, I'M STILL NOT SURE IF I DO.
BUT HE'S POINTED THE WAY FOR US...
...AND WE NEED TO FIND HER BEFORE THE INHUMANS DO.
"IT IS AS YOU *PREDICTED.*"

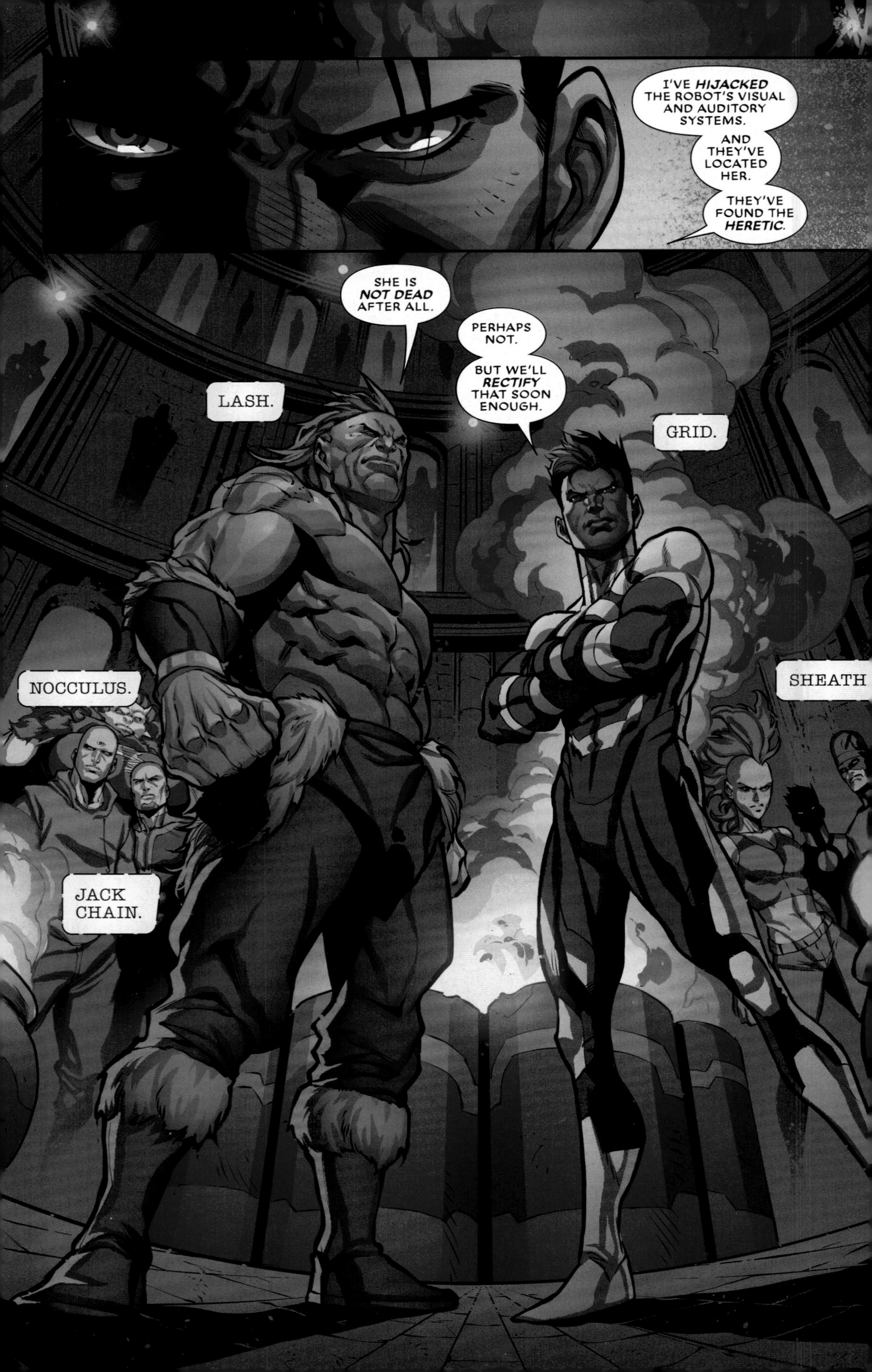

I'VE HIJACKED THE ROBOT'S VISUAL AND AUDITORY SYSTEMS.
AND THEY'VE LOCATED HER.
THEY'VE FOUND THE HERETIC.
SHE IS NOT DEAD AFTER ALL.
PERHAPS NOT.
BUT WE'LL RECTIFY THAT SOON ENOUGH.
LASH.
GRID.
NOCCULUS.
SHEATH
JACK CHAIN.

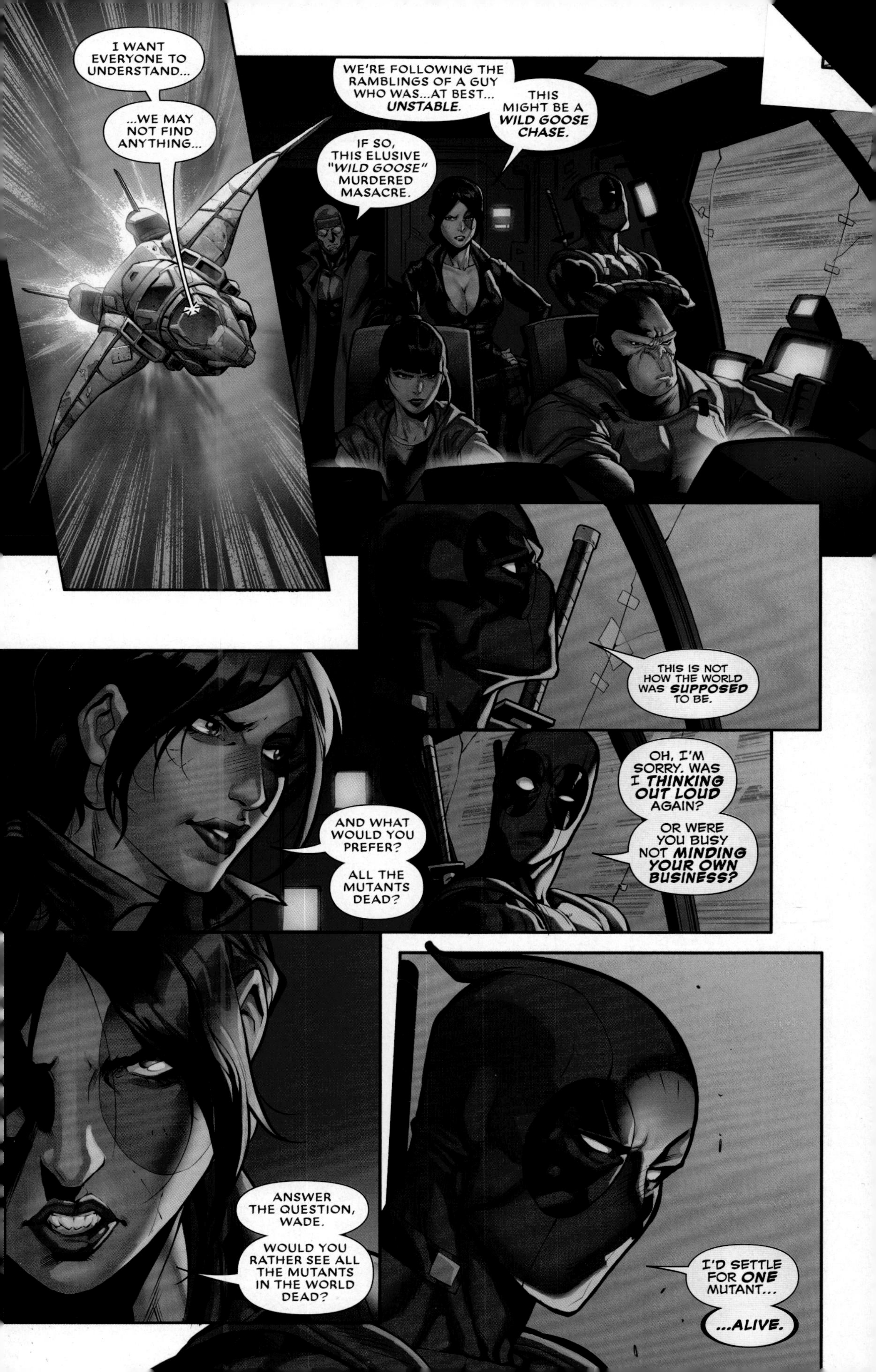

I WANT EVERYONE TO UNDERSTAND...
...WE MAY NOT FIND ANYTHING...
WE'RE FOLLOWING THE RAMBLINGS OF A GUY WHO WAS...AT BEST... UNSTABLE.
THIS MIGHT BE A WILD GOOSE CHASE.
IF SO, THIS ELUSIVE "WILD GOOSE" MURDERED MASACRE.
THIS IS NOT HOW THE WORLD WAS SUPPOSED TO BE.
AND WHAT WOULD YOU PREFER?
ALL THE MUTANTS DEAD?
OH, I'M SORRY. WAS I THINKING OUT LOUD AGAIN?
OR WERE YOU BUSY NOT MINDING YOUR OWN BUSINESS?
ANSWER THE QUESTION, WADE.
WOULD YOU RATHER SEE ALL THE MUTANTS IN THE WORLD DEAD?
I'D SETTLE FOR ONE MUTANT...
...ALIVE.

SO...WHAT'S IT GONNA BE?

THIS AIN'T OUR FIGHT.

WE'RE *MERCENARIES*... AND IT DOESN'T SOUND LIKE THERE'S ANY *MONEY* TO BE MADE HERE.

THIS ISN'T *ABOUT* MONEY, KEN.

SOMETIMES YOU STRAP ON YOUR GUNS FOR *CASH*.

SOMETIMES, YOU DO IT BECAUSE IT'S WHAT'S *RIGHT*.

YUP. I KNOW.

JUST WANTED TO HEAR *YOU* SAY IT.

IT'S PRETTY CLEAR TO ME WHICH TEAM WE'RE PLAYING FOR.

WE'VE GOT TWO MUTANTS AMONG US...

...AND ONE PERSON--ME--WITH A *VESTED INTEREST* IN MUTANT SURVIVAL.

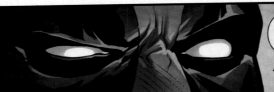

THE TERRIGEN CLOUD IS *TOXIC*.

IT'S GOING TO KILL EVERY MUTANT ON THE PLANET IN A MATTER OF *WEEKS*.

THE X-MEN-- AND I'M TALKING ALL TWO BAZILLION OF THEM--ARE TAKING A SHOT AT THE CLOUD.

THE INHUMAN WON'T L[I] THAT.

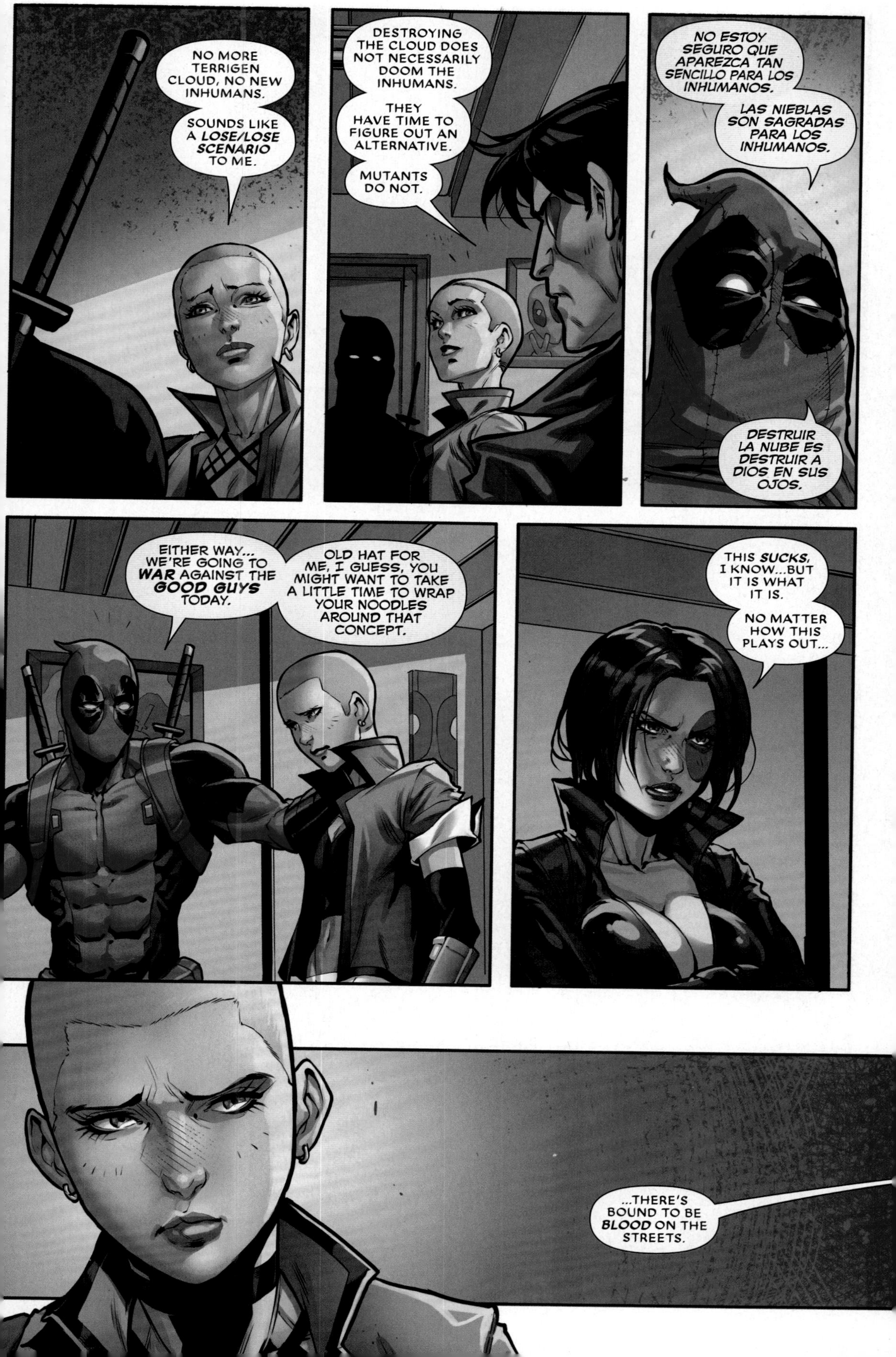
NO MORE TERRIGEN CLOUD, NO NEW INHUMANS.
SOUNDS LIKE A *LOSE/LOSE SCENARIO* TO ME.
DESTROYING THE CLOUD DOES NOT NECESSARILY DOOM THE INHUMANS.
THEY HAVE TIME TO FIGURE OUT AN ALTERNATIVE.
MUTANTS DO NOT.
NO ESTOY SEGURO QUE APAREZCA TAN SENCILLO PARA LOS INHUMANOS.
LAS NIEBLAS SON SAGRADAS PARA LOS INHUMANOS.
DESTRUIR LA NUBE ES DESTRUIR A DIOS EN SUS OJOS.
EITHER WAY... WE'RE GOING TO **WAR** AGAINST THE ***GOOD GUYS*** TODAY.
OLD HAT FOR ME, I GUESS, YOU MIGHT WANT TO TAKE A LITTLE TIME TO WRAP YOUR NOODLES AROUND THAT CONCEPT.
THIS *SUCKS*, I KNOW...BUT IT IS WHAT IT IS.
NO MATTER HOW THIS PLAYS OUT...
...THERE'S BOUND TO BE ***BLOOD*** ON THE STREETS.

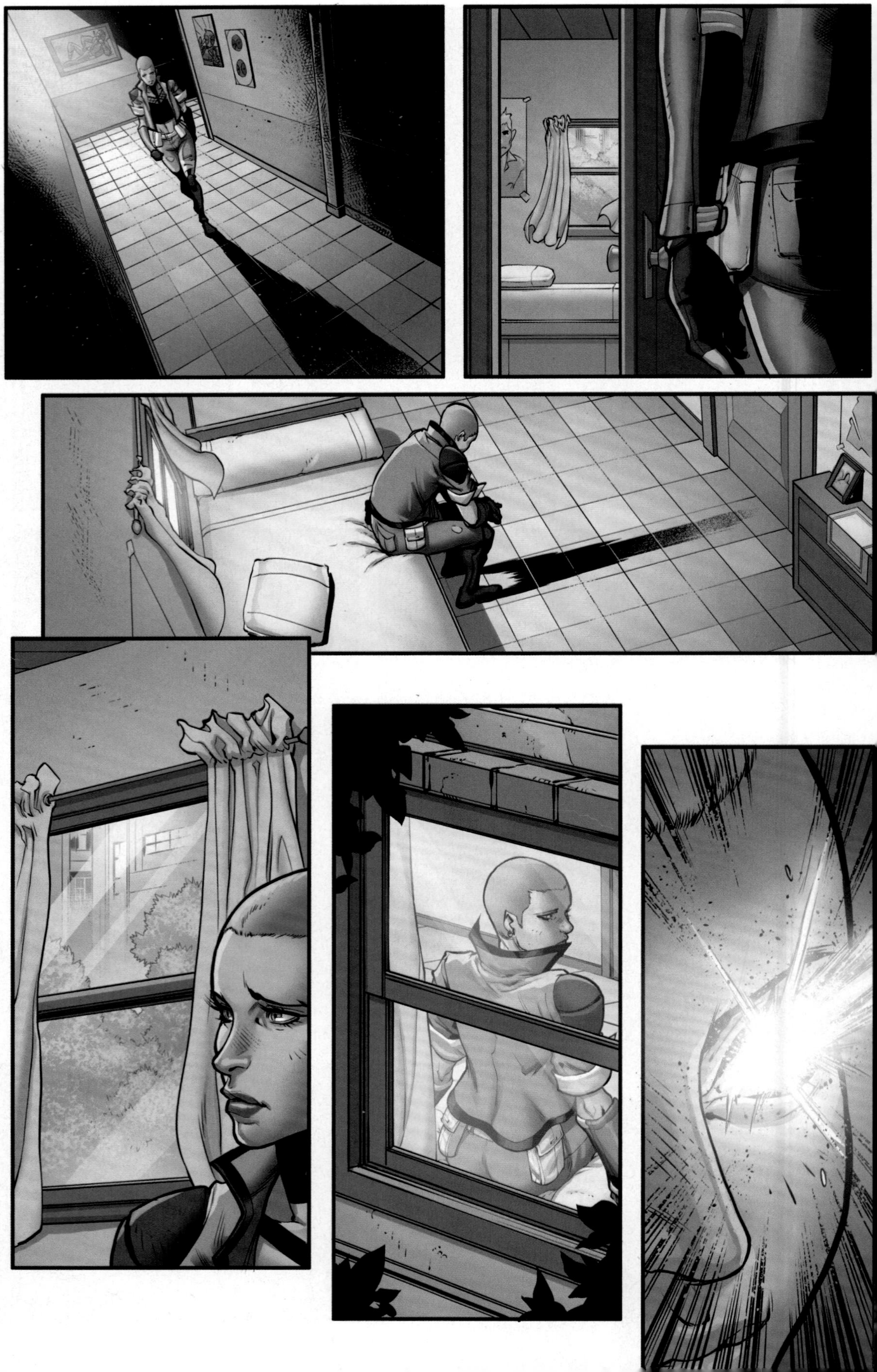

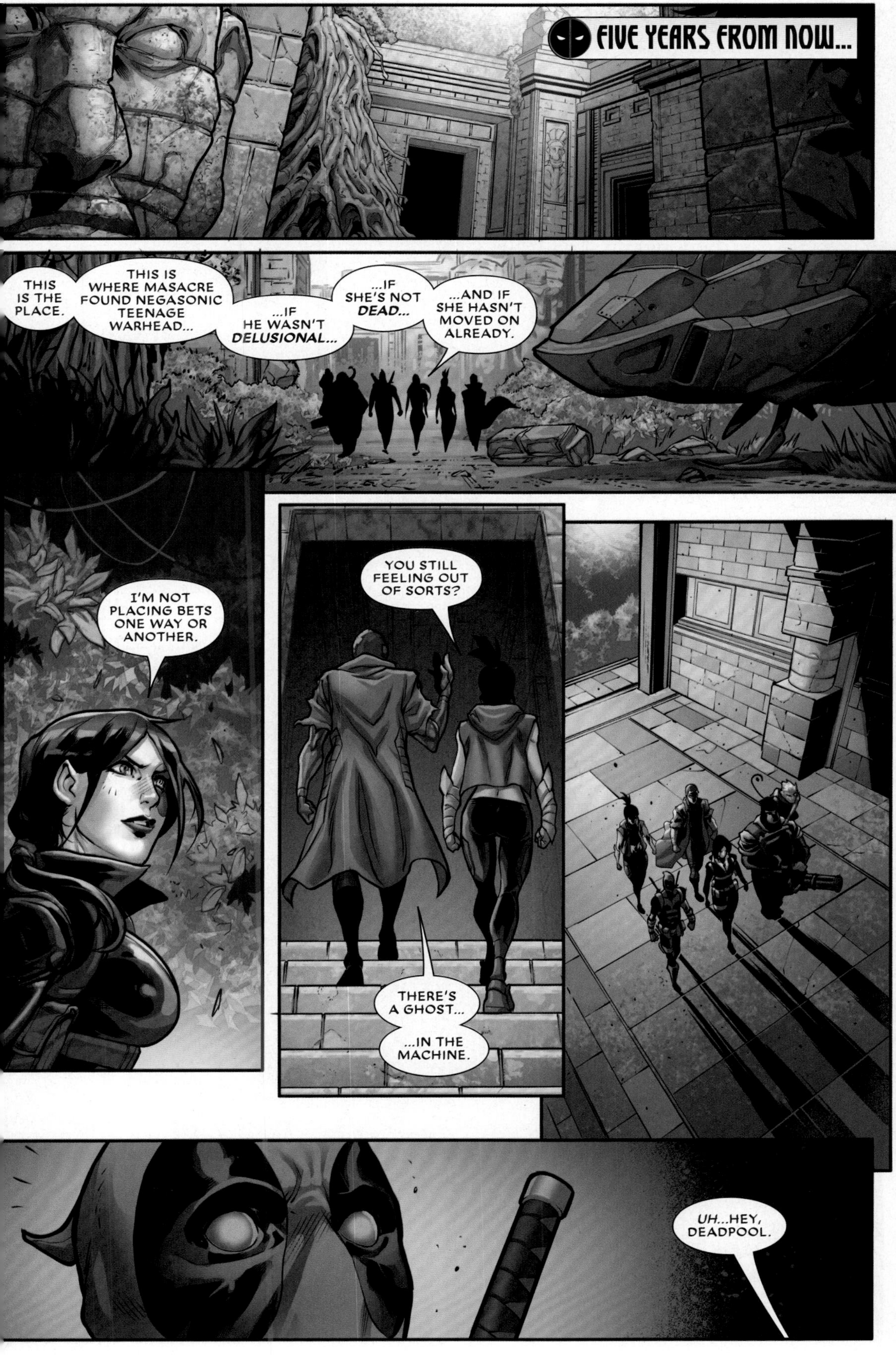
FIVE YEARS FROM NOW...
THIS IS THE PLACE.
THIS IS WHERE MASACRE FOUND NEGASONIC TEENAGE WARHEAD...
...IF HE WASN'T *DELUSIONAL...*
...IF SHE'S NOT *DEAD...*
...AND IF SHE HASN'T MOVED ON ALREADY.
I'M NOT PLACING BETS ONE WAY OR ANOTHER.
YOU STILL FEELING OUT OF SORTS?
THERE'S A GHOST...
...IN THE MACHINE.
*UH...*HEY, DEADPOOL.

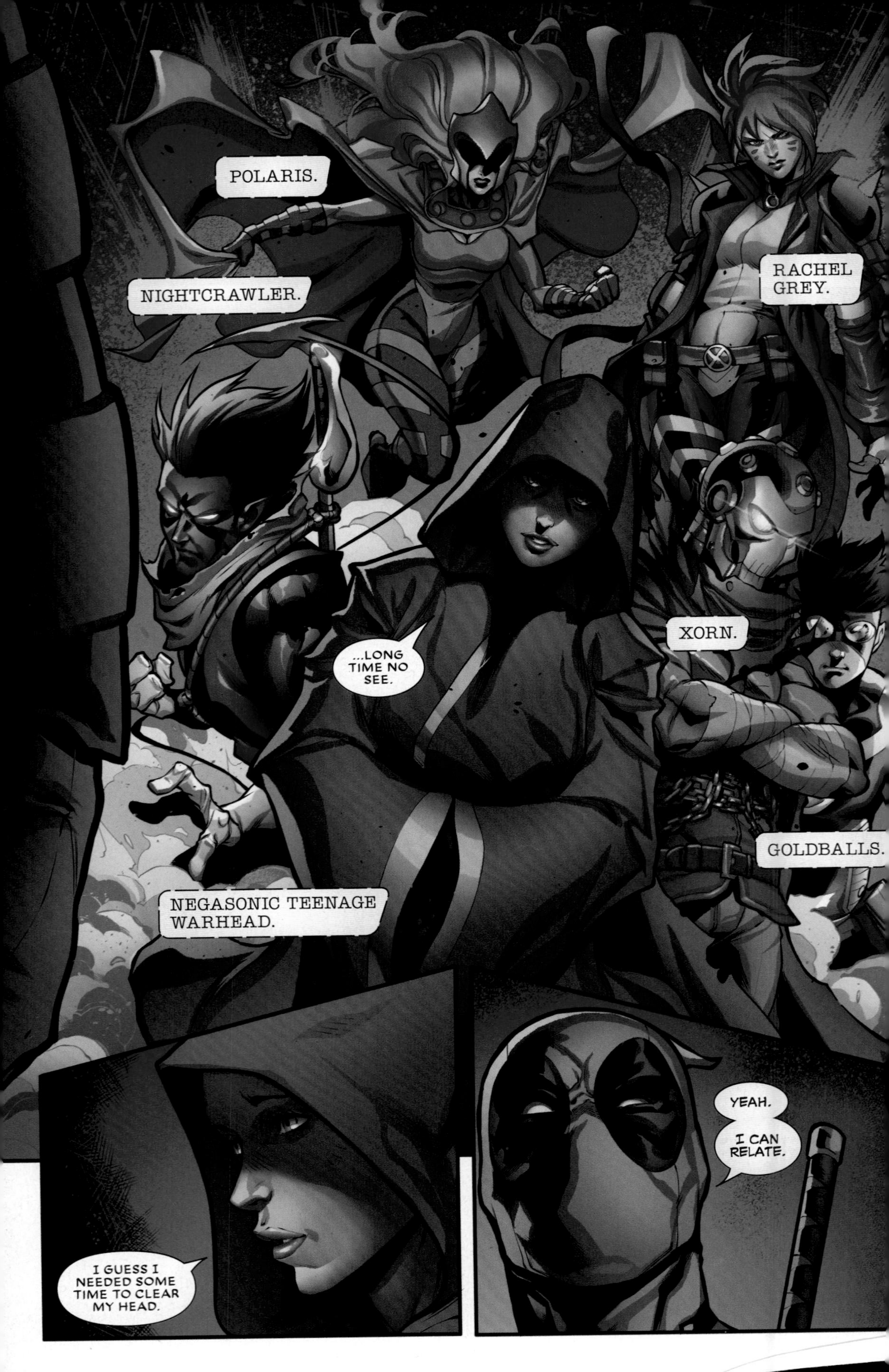
POLARIS.
NIGHTCRAWLER.
RACHEL GREY.
XORN.
...LONG TIME NO SEE.
GOLDBALLS.
NEGASONIC TEENAGE WARHEAD.
I GUESS I NEEDED SOME TIME TO CLEAR MY HEAD.
YEAH.
I CAN RELATE.

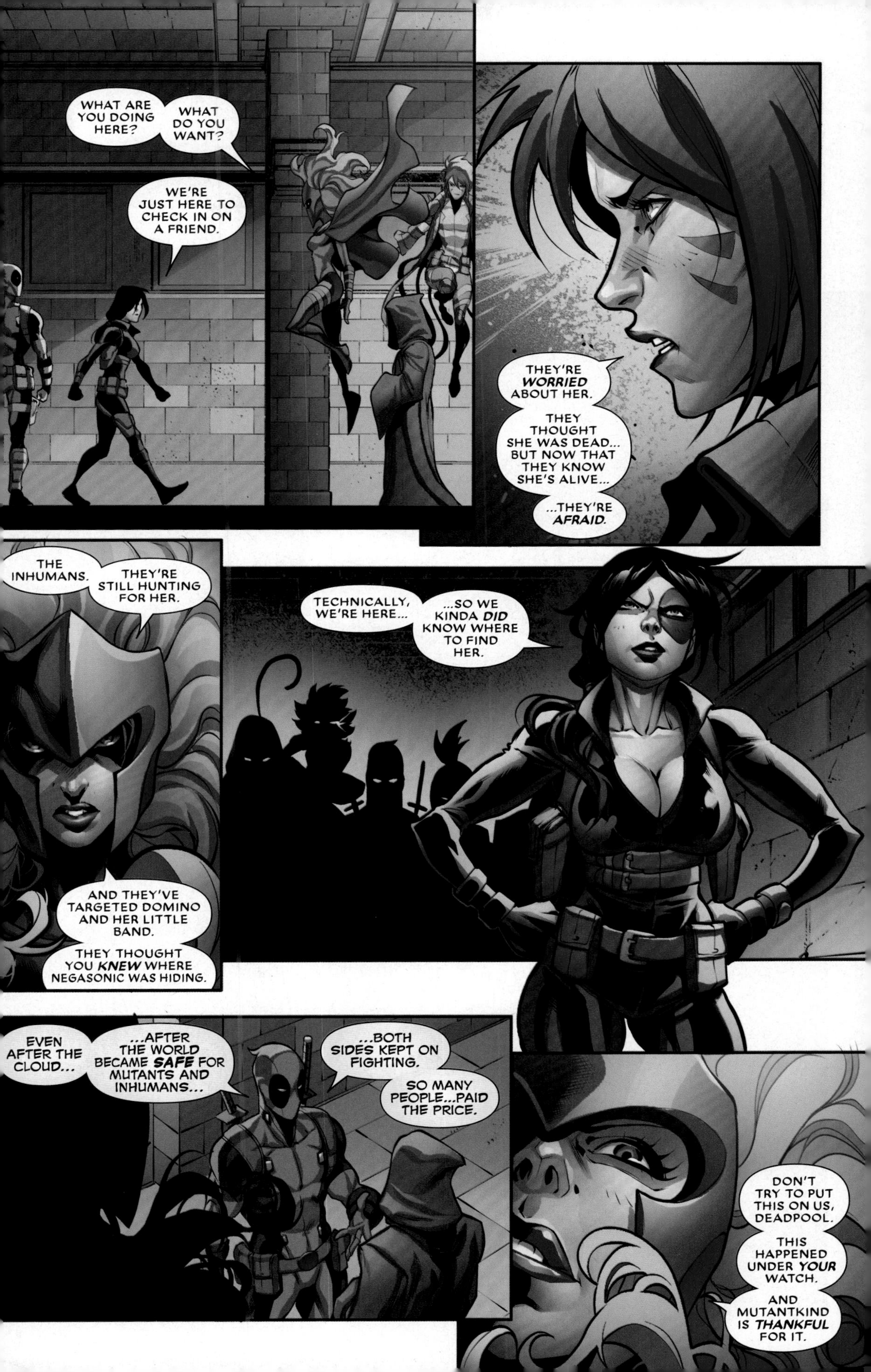

WHAT ARE YOU DOING HERE?
WHAT DO YOU WANT?
WE'RE JUST HERE TO CHECK IN ON A FRIEND.
THEY'RE WORRIED ABOUT HER.
THEY THOUGHT SHE WAS DEAD... BUT NOW THAT THEY KNOW SHE'S ALIVE...
...THEY'RE AFRAID.
THE INHUMANS.
THEY'RE STILL HUNTING FOR HER.
AND THEY'VE TARGETED DOMINO AND HER LITTLE BAND.
THEY THOUGHT YOU KNEW WHERE NEGASONIC WAS HIDING.
TECHNICALLY, WE'RE HERE...
...SO WE KINDA DID KNOW WHERE TO FIND HER.
EVEN AFTER THE CLOUD...
...AFTER THE WORLD BECAME SAFE FOR MUTANTS AND INHUMANS...
...BOTH SIDES KEPT ON FIGHTING.
SO MANY PEOPLE...PAID THE PRICE.
DON'T TRY TO PUT THIS ON US, DEADPOOL.
THIS HAPPENED UNDER YOUR WATCH.
AND MUTANTKIND IS THANKFUL FOR IT.

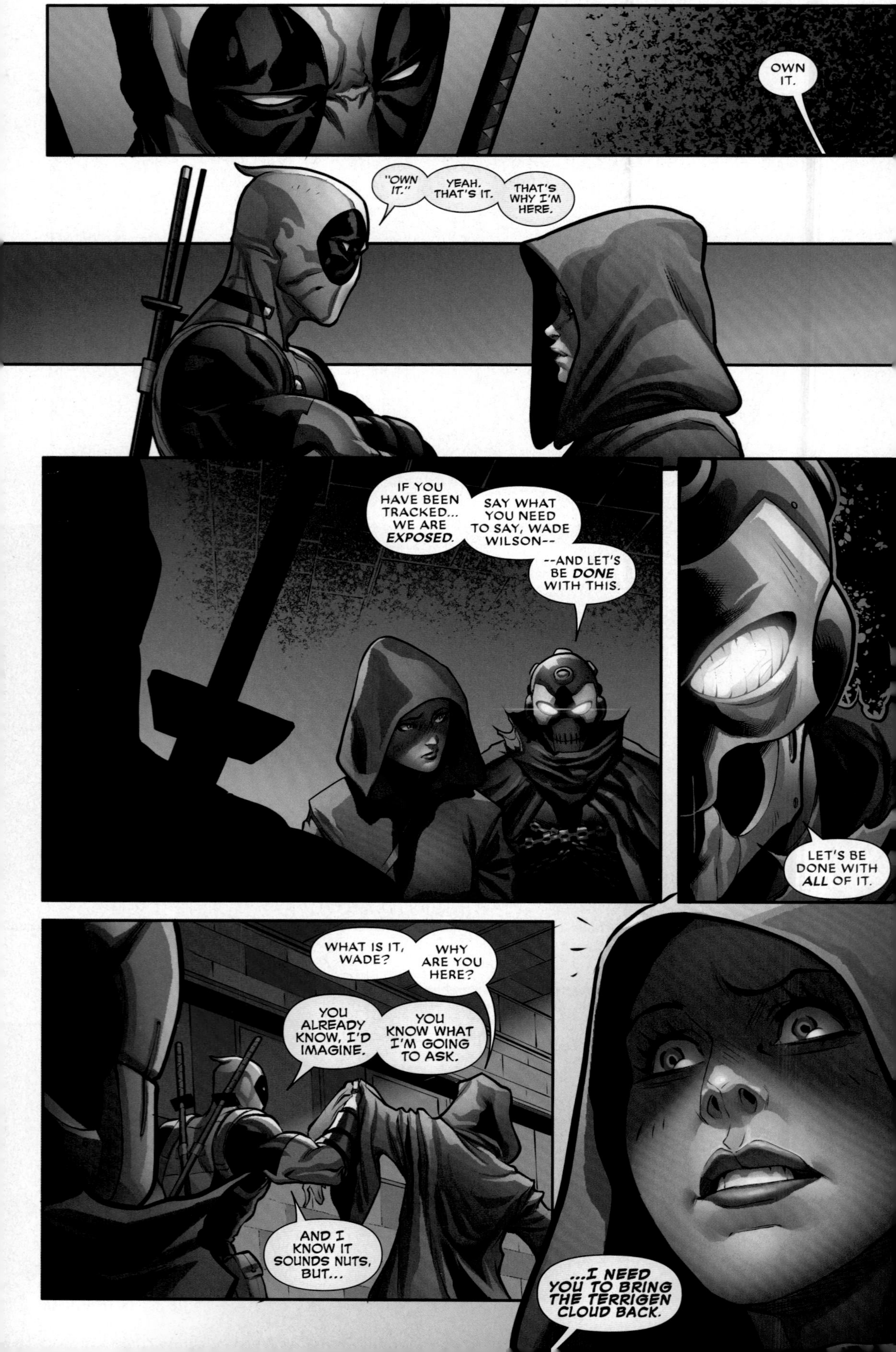
OWN IT.
"OWN IT."
YEAH. THAT'S IT.
THAT'S WHY I'M HERE.
IF YOU HAVE BEEN TRACKED... WE ARE EXPOSED.
SAY WHAT YOU NEED TO SAY, WADE WILSON--
--AND LET'S BE DONE WITH THIS.
LET'S BE DONE WITH ALL OF IT.
WHAT IS IT, WADE?
WHY ARE YOU HERE?
YOU ALREADY KNOW, I'D IMAGINE.
YOU KNOW WHAT I'M GOING TO ASK.
AND I KNOW IT SOUNDS NUTS, BUT...
...I NEED YOU TO BRING THE TERRIGEN CLOUD BACK.

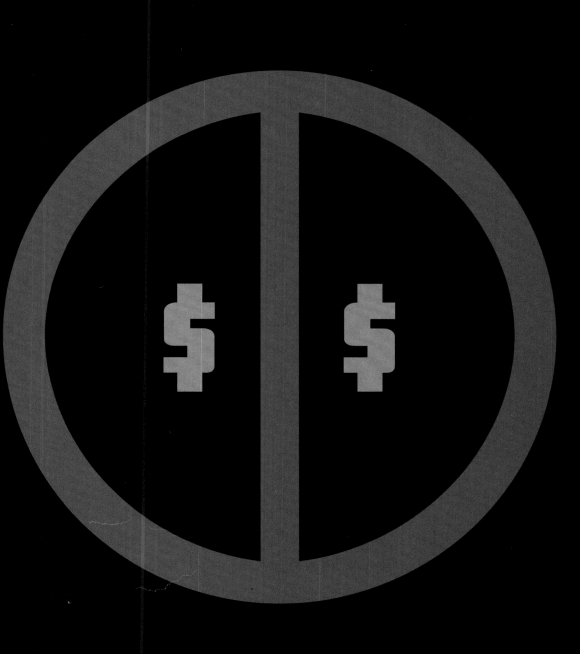

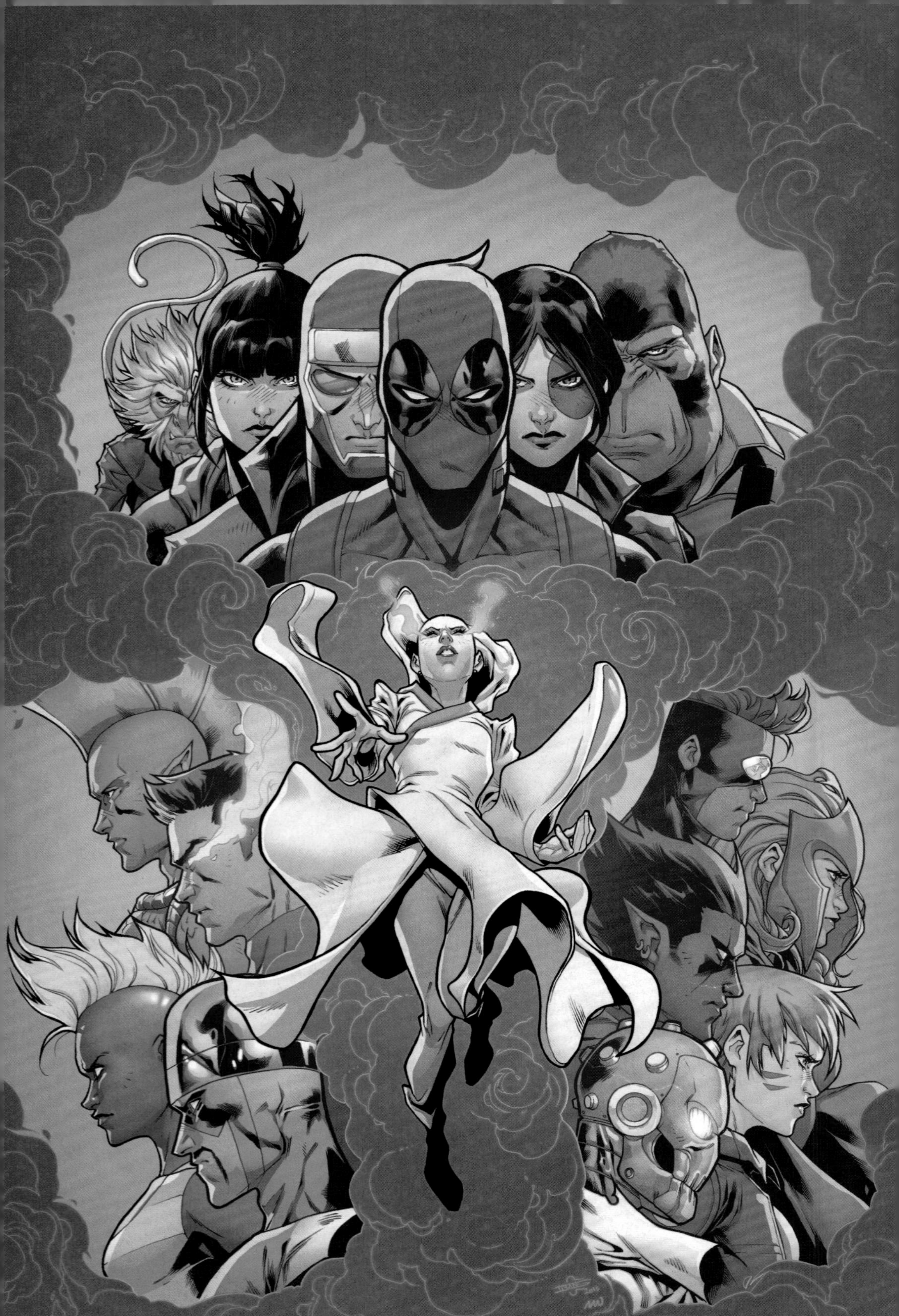

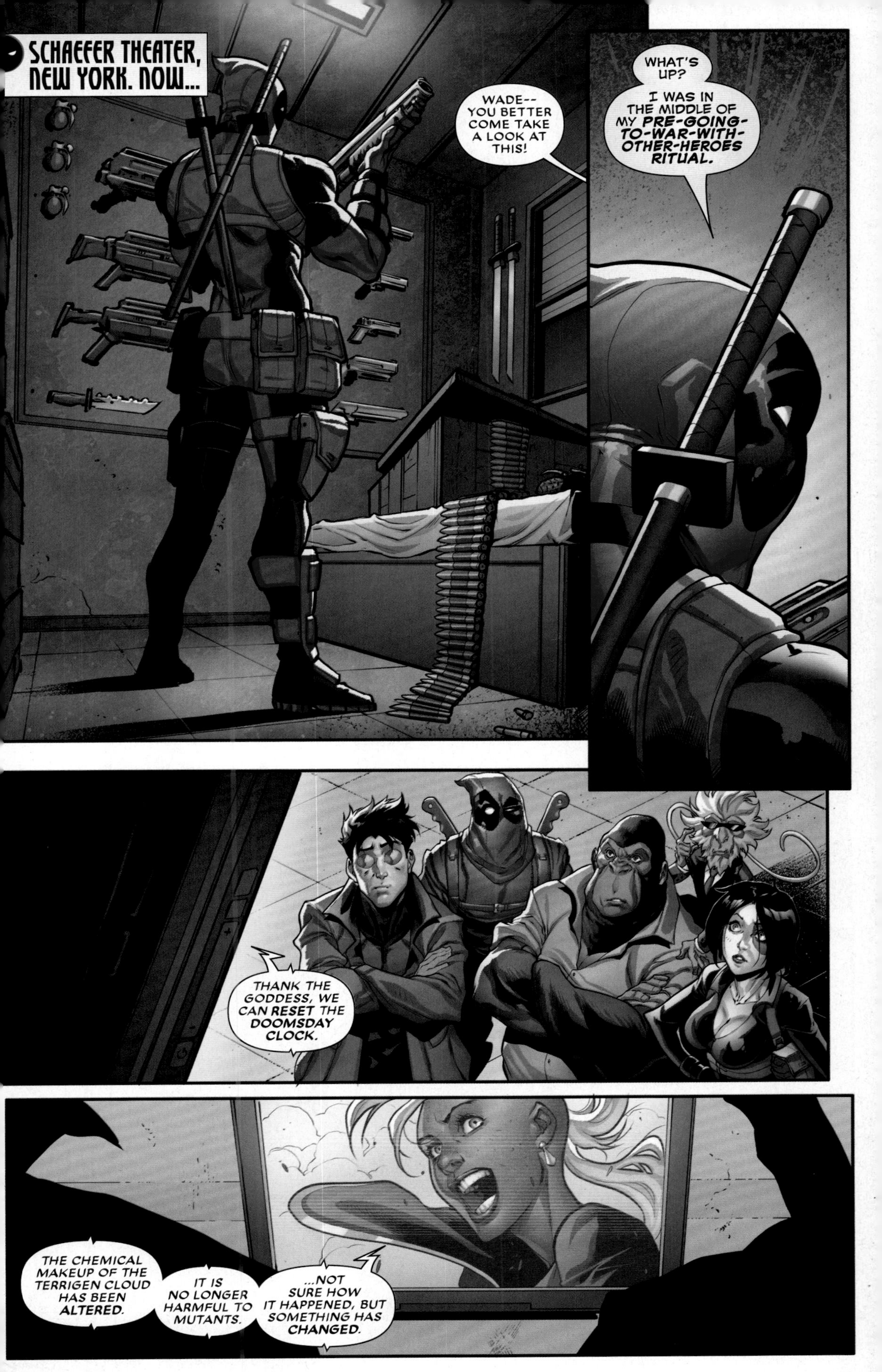
SCHAEFER THEATER, NEW YORK. NOW...
WADE-- YOU BETTER COME TAKE A LOOK AT THIS!
WHAT'S UP?
I WAS IN THE MIDDLE OF MY PRE-GOING-TO-WAR-WITH-OTHER-HEROES RITUAL.
THANK THE GODDESS, WE CAN RESET THE DOOMSDAY CLOCK.
THE CHEMICAL MAKEUP OF THE TERRIGEN CLOUD HAS BEEN ALTERED.
IT IS NO LONGER HARMFUL TO MUTANTS.
...NOT SURE HOW IT HAPPENED, BUT SOMETHING HAS CHANGED.

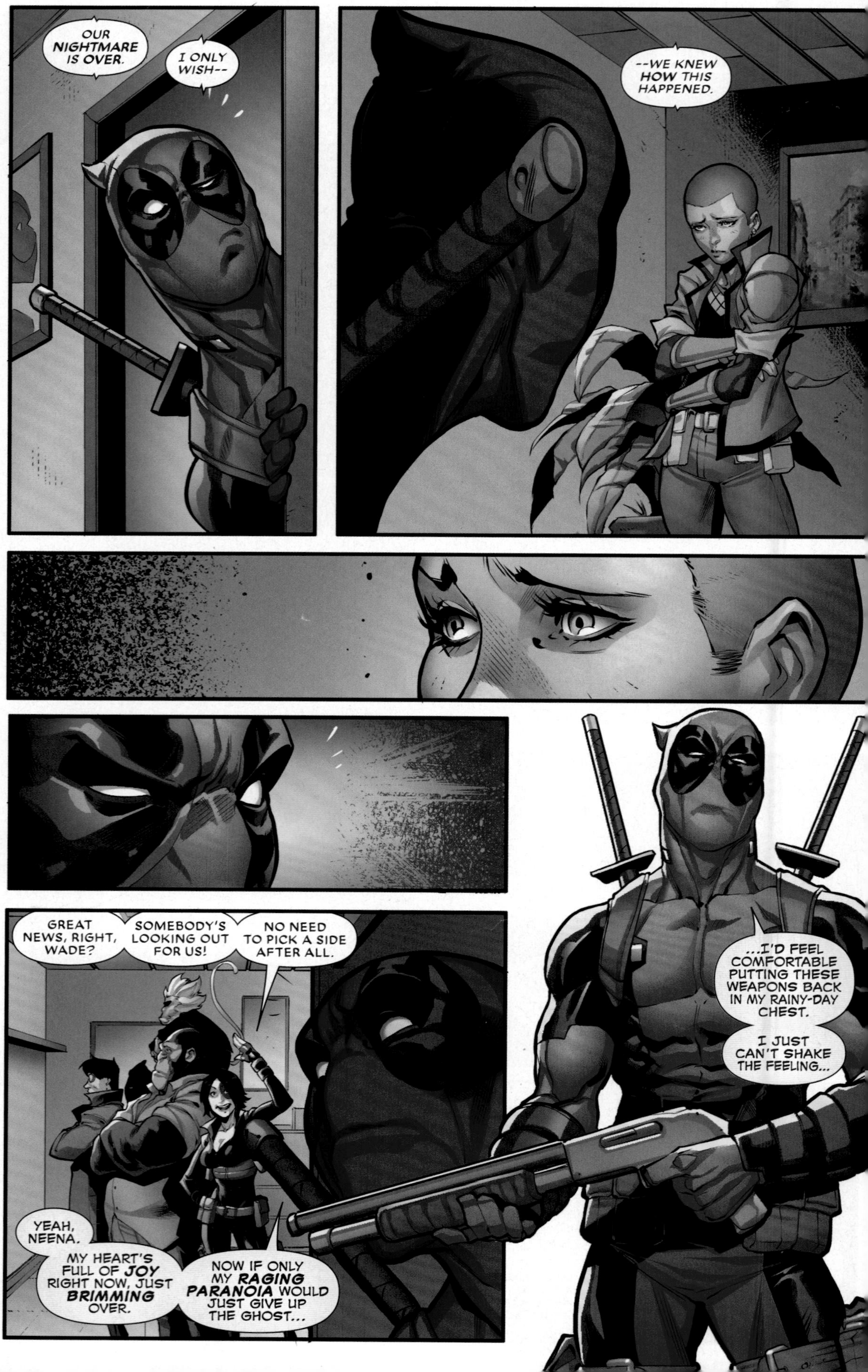
OUR NIGHTMARE IS OVER.
I ONLY WISH--
--WE KNEW HOW THIS HAPPENED.
GREAT NEWS, RIGHT, WADE?
SOMEBODY'S LOOKING OUT FOR US!
NO NEED TO PICK A SIDE AFTER ALL.
YEAH, NEENA.
MY HEART'S FULL OF JOY RIGHT NOW, JUST BRIMMING OVER.
NOW IF ONLY MY RAGING PARANOIA WOULD JUST GIVE UP THE GHOST...
...I'D FEEL COMFORTABLE PUTTING THESE WEAPONS BACK IN MY RAINY-DAY CHEST.
I JUST CAN'T SHAKE THE FEELING...

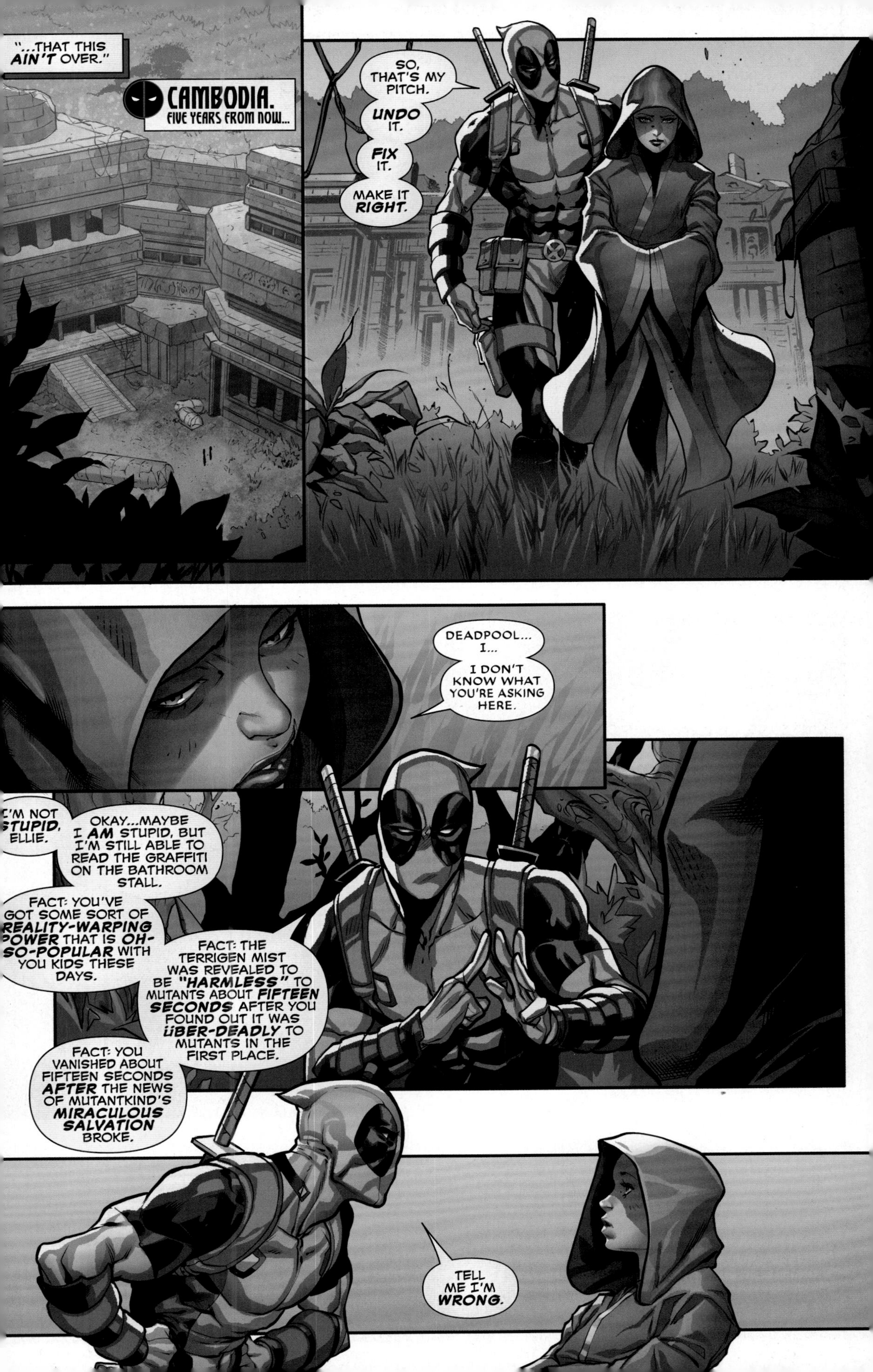
"...THAT THIS AIN'T OVER."
CAMBODIA. FIVE YEARS FROM NOW...
SO, THAT'S MY PITCH.
UNDO IT.
FIX IT.
MAKE IT RIGHT.
DEADPOOL... I...
I DON'T KNOW WHAT YOU'RE ASKING HERE.
I'M NOT STUPID, ELLIE.
OKAY...MAYBE I AM STUPID, BUT I'M STILL ABLE TO READ THE GRAFFITI ON THE BATHROOM STALL.
FACT: YOU'VE GOT SOME SORT OF REALITY-WARPING POWER THAT IS OH-SO-POPULAR WITH YOU KIDS THESE DAYS.
FACT: THE TERRIGEN MIST WAS REVEALED TO BE "HARMLESS" TO MUTANTS ABOUT FIFTEEN SECONDS AFTER YOU FOUND OUT IT WAS ÜBER-DEADLY TO MUTANTS IN THE FIRST PLACE.
FACT: YOU VANISHED ABOUT FIFTEEN SECONDS AFTER THE NEWS OF MUTANTKIND'S MIRACULOUS SALVATION BROKE.
TELL ME I'M WRONG.

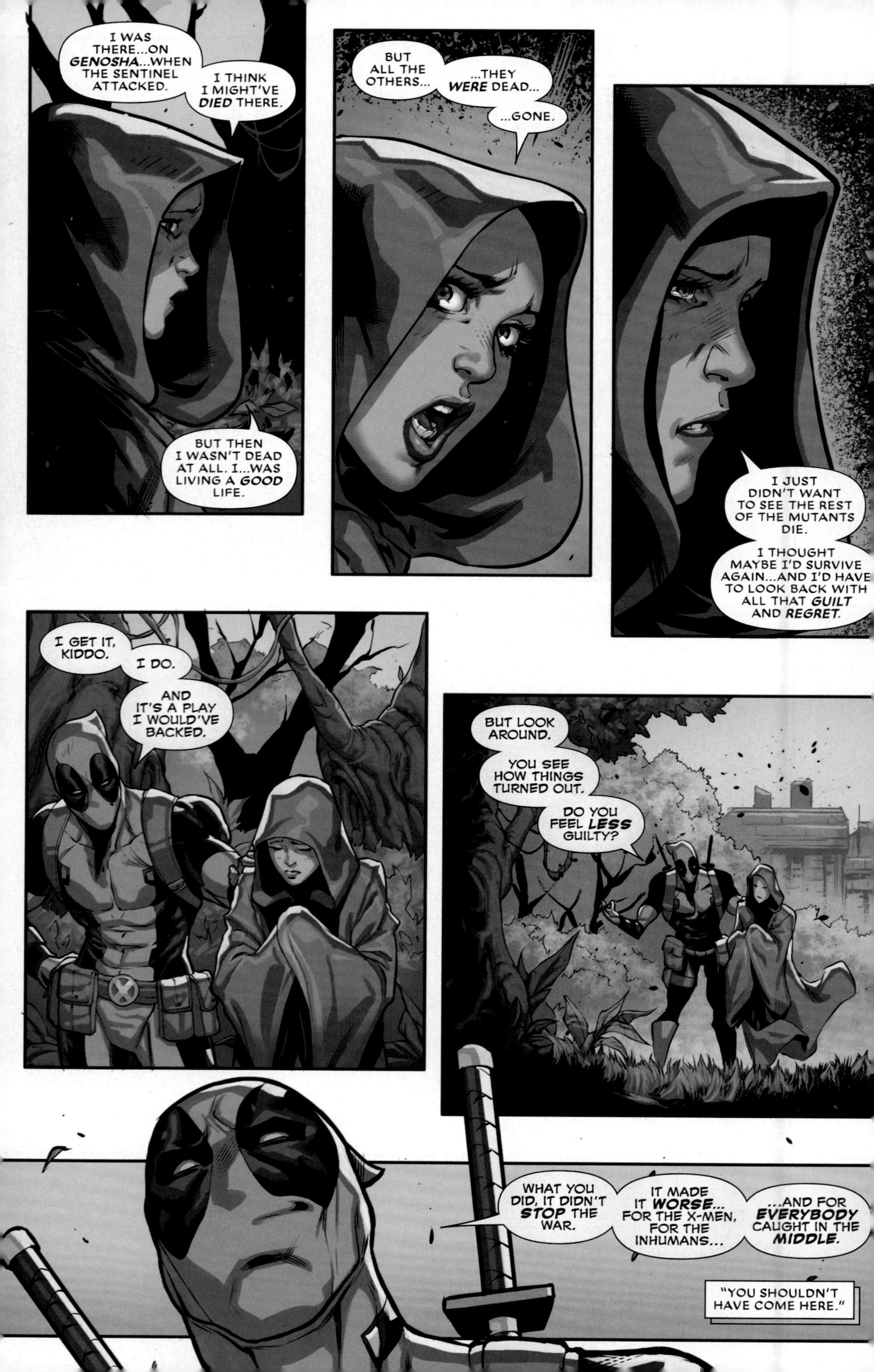
I WAS THERE...ON GENOSHA...WHEN THE SENTINEL ATTACKED.
I THINK I MIGHT'VE DIED THERE.
BUT THEN I WASN'T DEAD AT ALL. I...WAS LIVING A GOOD LIFE.
BUT ALL THE OTHERS...
...THEY WERE DEAD...
...GONE.
I JUST DIDN'T WANT TO SEE THE REST OF THE MUTANTS DIE.
I THOUGHT MAYBE I'D SURVIVE AGAIN...AND I'D HAVE TO LOOK BACK WITH ALL THAT GUILT AND REGRET.
I GET IT, KIDDO.
I DO.
AND IT'S A PLAY I WOULD'VE BACKED.
BUT LOOK AROUND.
YOU SEE HOW THINGS TURNED OUT.
DO YOU FEEL LESS GUILTY?
WHAT YOU DID, IT DIDN'T STOP THE WAR.
IT MADE IT WORSE... FOR THE X-MEN, FOR THE INHUMANS...
...AND FOR EVERYBODY CAUGHT IN THE MIDDLE.
"YOU SHOULDN'T HAVE COME HERE."

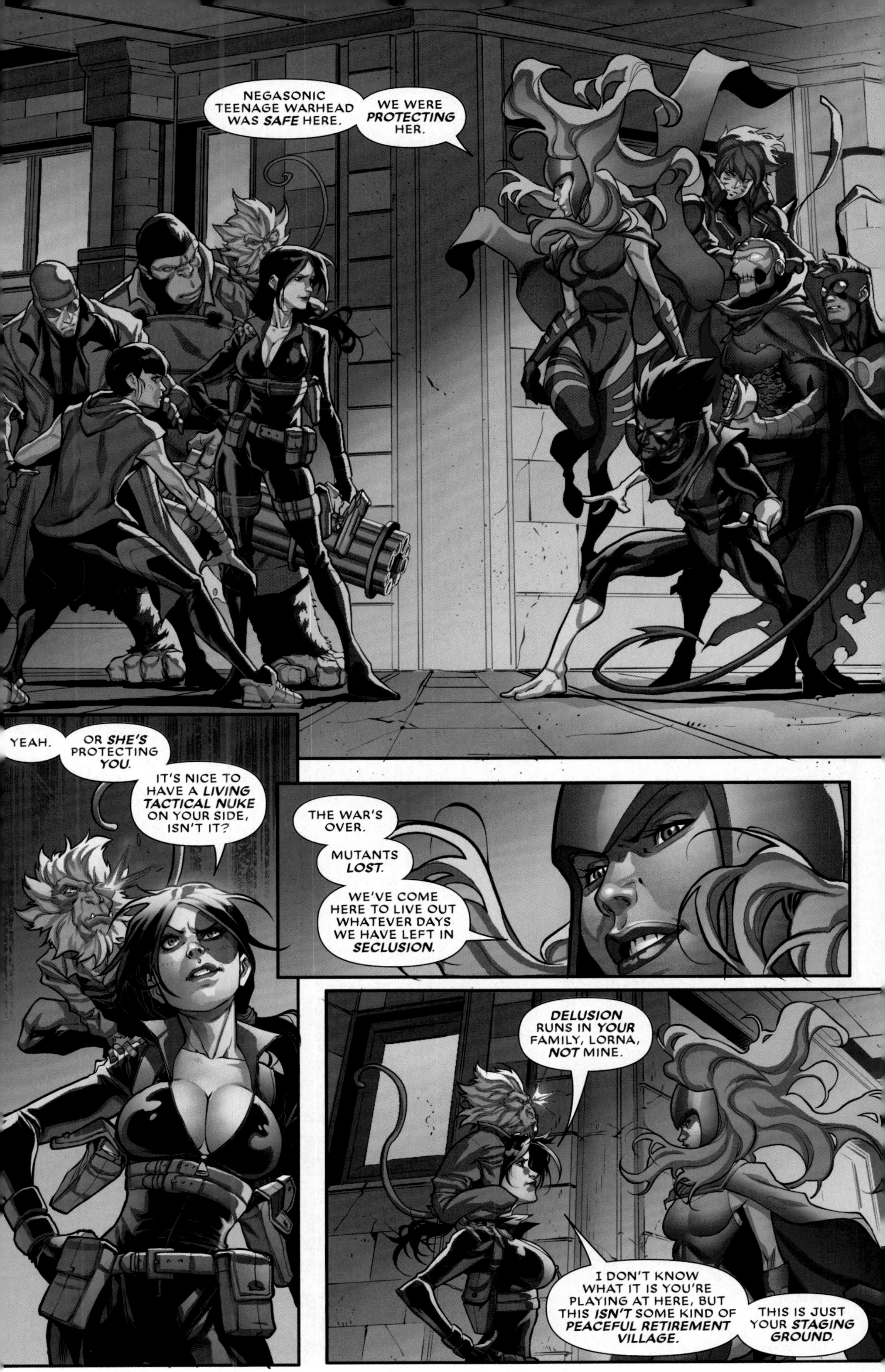
NEGASONIC TEENAGE WARHEAD WAS SAFE HERE.
WE WERE PROTECTING HER.
YEAH.
OR SHE'S PROTECTING YOU.
IT'S NICE TO HAVE A LIVING TACTICAL NUKE ON YOUR SIDE, ISN'T IT?
THE WAR'S OVER.
MUTANTS LOST.
WE'VE COME HERE TO LIVE OUT WHATEVER DAYS WE HAVE LEFT IN SECLUSION.
DELUSION RUNS IN YOUR FAMILY, LORNA, NOT MINE.
I DON'T KNOW WHAT IT IS YOU'RE PLAYING AT HERE, BUT THIS ISN'T SOME KIND OF PEACEFUL RETIREMENT VILLAGE.
THIS IS JUST YOUR STAGING GROUND.

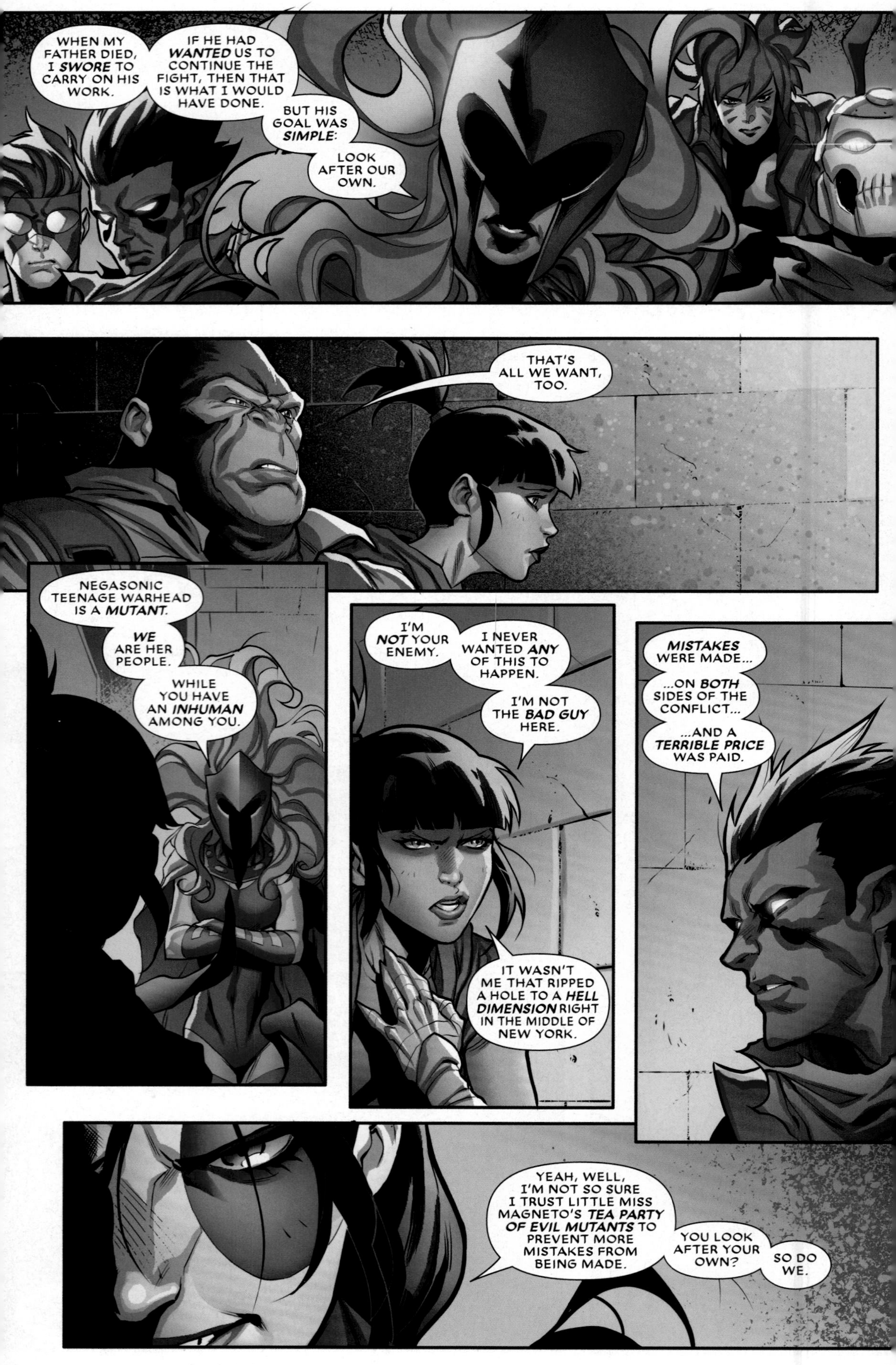
WHEN MY FATHER DIED, I *SWORE* TO CARRY ON HIS WORK.
IF HE HAD *WANTED* US TO CONTINUE THE FIGHT, THEN THAT IS WHAT I WOULD HAVE DONE.
BUT HIS GOAL WAS *SIMPLE*:
LOOK AFTER OUR OWN.
THAT'S ALL WE WANT, TOO.
NEGASONIC TEENAGE WARHEAD IS A *MUTANT*.
WE ARE HER PEOPLE.
WHILE YOU HAVE AN *INHUMAN* AMONG YOU.
I'M *NOT* YOUR ENEMY.
I NEVER WANTED *ANY* OF THIS TO HAPPEN.
I'M NOT THE *BAD GUY* HERE.
IT WASN'T ME THAT RIPPED A HOLE TO A *HELL DIMENSION* RIGHT IN THE MIDDLE OF NEW YORK.
MISTAKES WERE MADE...
...ON *BOTH* SIDES OF THE CONFLICT...
...AND A *TERRIBLE PRICE* WAS PAID.
YEAH, WELL, I'M NOT SO SURE I TRUST LITTLE MISS MAGNETO'S *TEA PARTY OF EVIL MUTANTS* TO PREVENT MORE MISTAKES FROM BEING MADE.
YOU LOOK AFTER YOUR OWN?
SO DO WE.

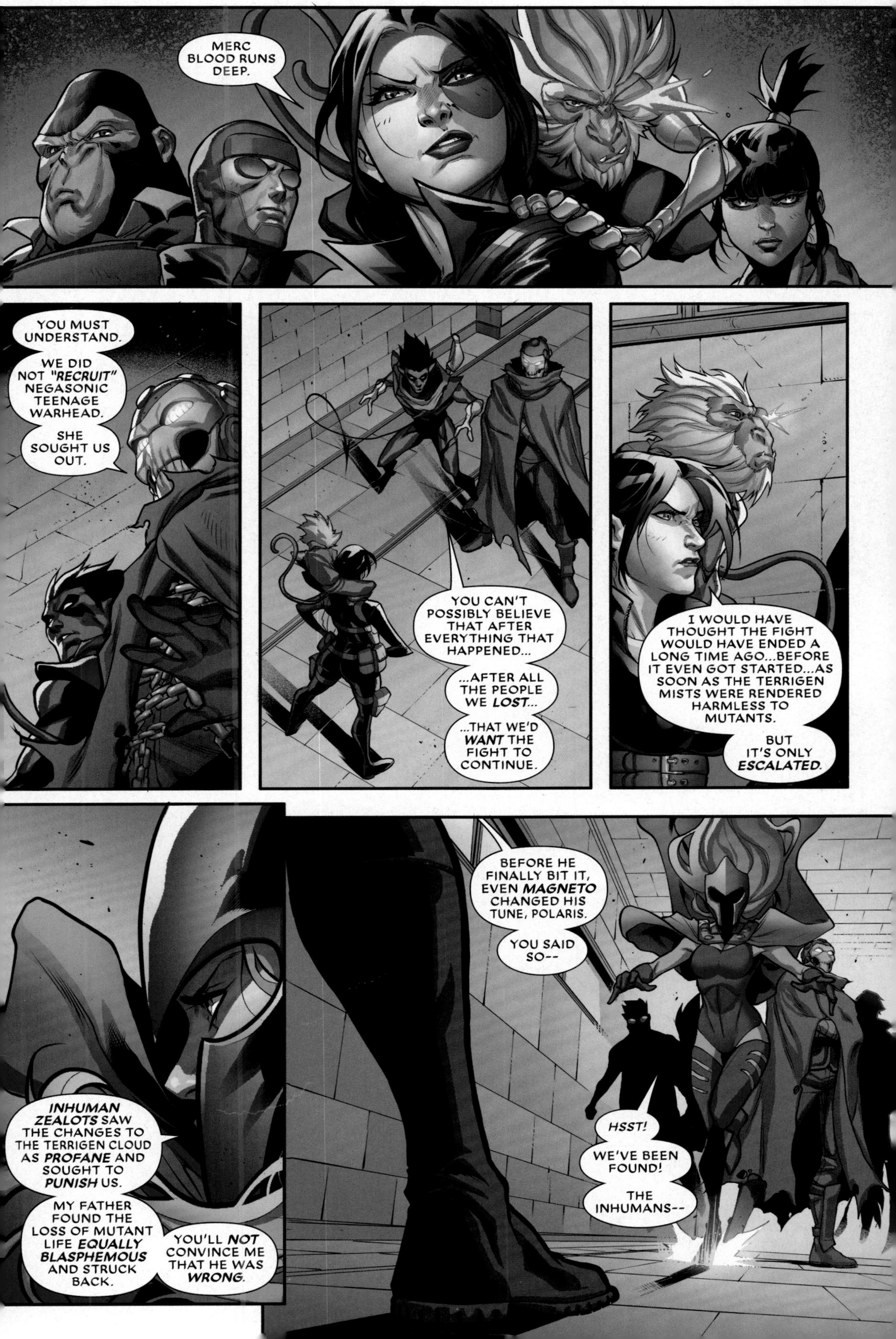

MERC BLOOD RUNS DEEP.
YOU MUST UNDERSTAND.
WE DID NOT "RECRUIT" NEGASONIC TEENAGE WARHEAD.
SHE SOUGHT US OUT.
YOU CAN'T POSSIBLY BELIEVE THAT AFTER EVERYTHING THAT HAPPENED...
...AFTER ALL THE PEOPLE WE LOST...
...THAT WE'D WANT THE FIGHT TO CONTINUE.
I WOULD HAVE THOUGHT THE FIGHT WOULD HAVE ENDED A LONG TIME AGO...BEFORE IT EVEN GOT STARTED...AS SOON AS THE TERRIGEN MISTS WERE RENDERED HARMLESS TO MUTANTS.
BUT IT'S ONLY ESCALATED.
BEFORE HE FINALLY BIT IT, EVEN MAGNETO CHANGED HIS TUNE, POLARIS.
YOU SAID SO--
INHUMAN ZEALOTS SAW THE CHANGES TO THE TERRIGEN CLOUD AS PROFANE AND SOUGHT TO PUNISH US.
MY FATHER FOUND THE LOSS OF MUTANT LIFE EQUALLY BLASPHEMOUS AND STRUCK BACK.
YOU'LL NOT CONVINCE ME THAT HE WAS WRONG.
HSST!
WE'VE BEEN FOUND!
THE INHUMANS--

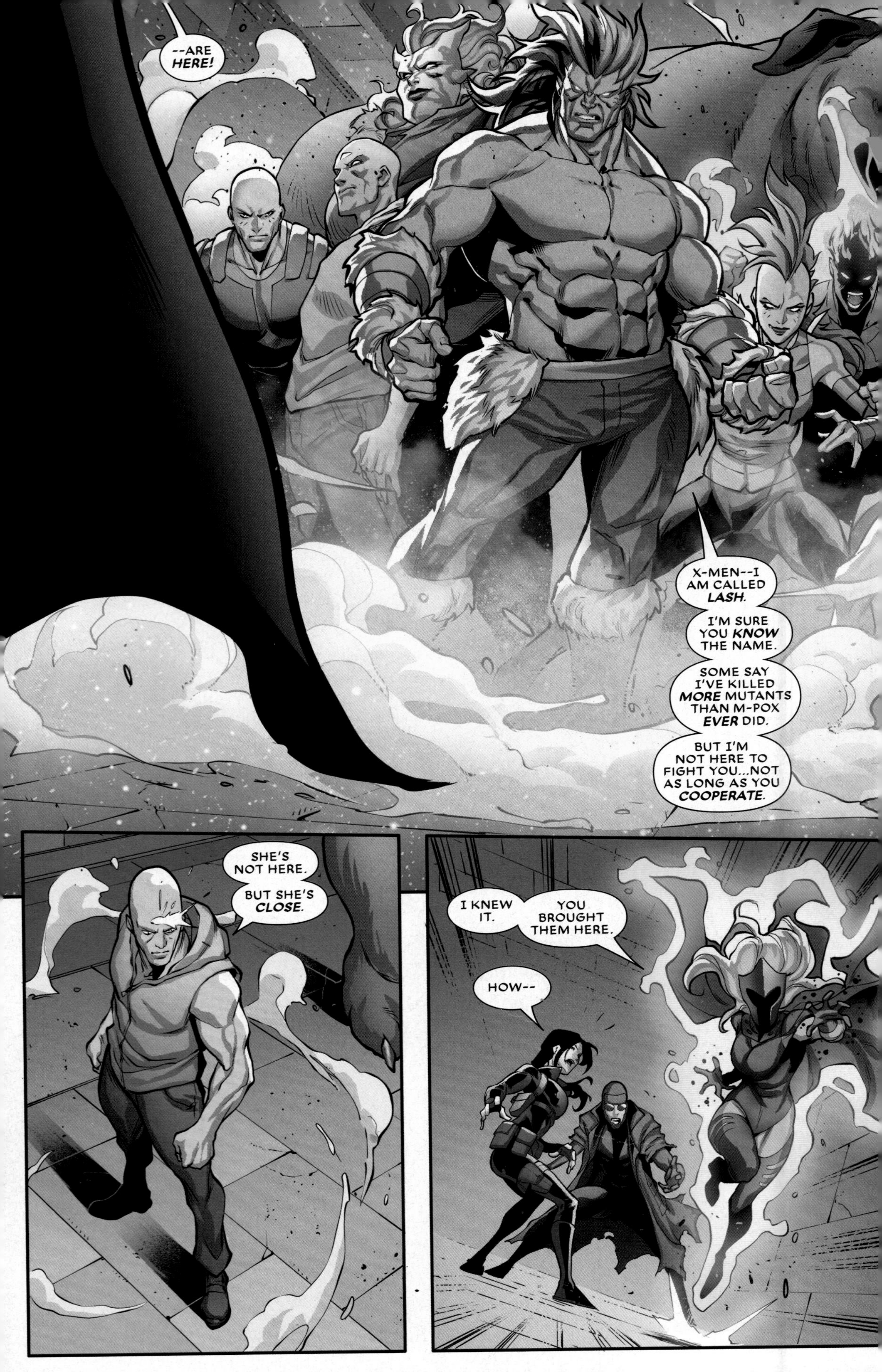
--ARE HERE!
X-MEN--I AM CALLED LASH.
I'M SURE YOU KNOW THE NAME.
SOME SAY I'VE KILLED MORE MUTANTS THAN M-POX EVER DID.
BUT I'M NOT HERE TO FIGHT YOU...NOT AS LONG AS YOU COOPERATE.
SHE'S NOT HERE.
BUT SHE'S CLOSE.
I KNEW IT.
YOU BROUGHT THEM HERE.
HOW--

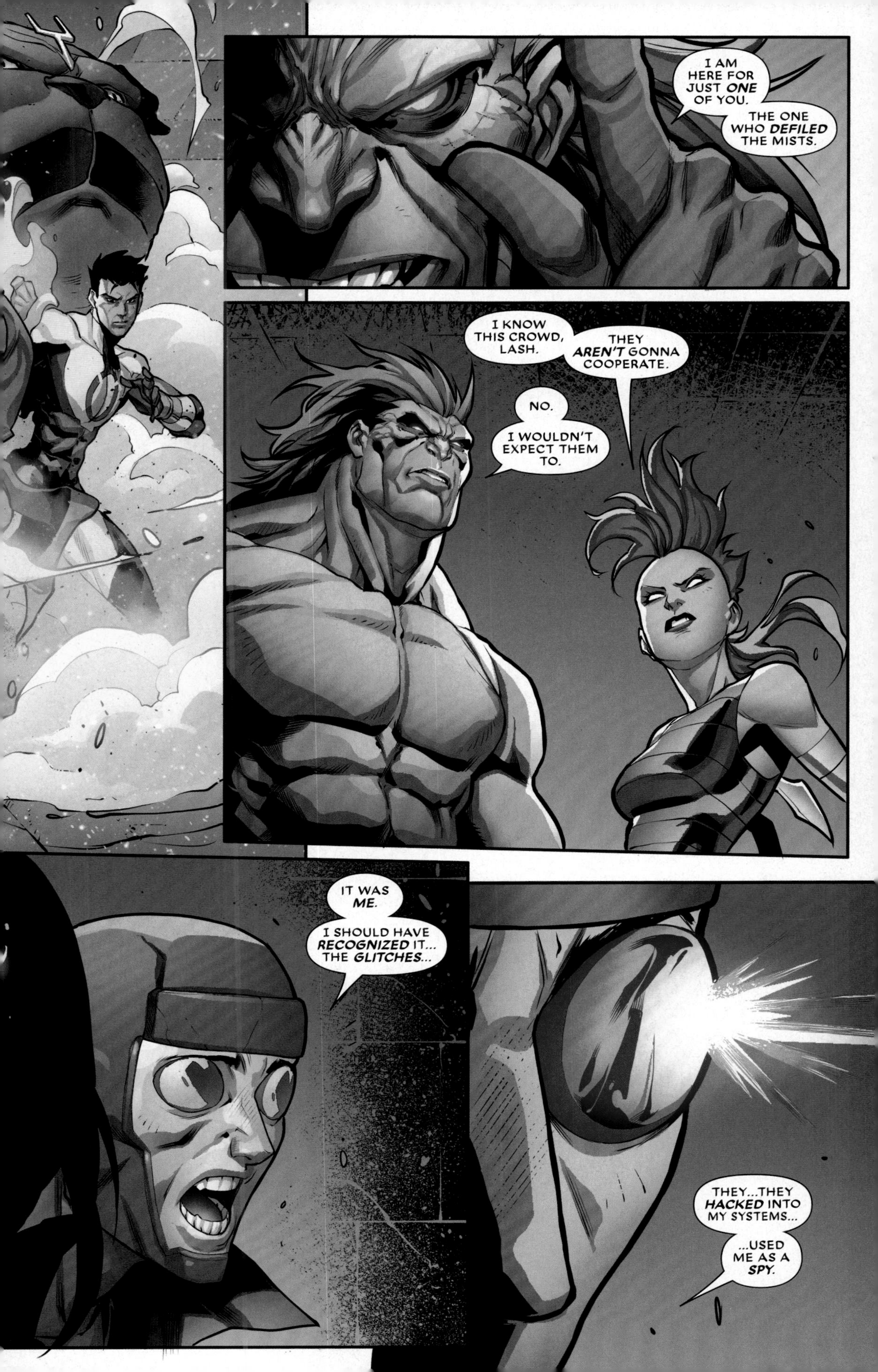
I AM HERE FOR JUST ONE OF YOU.
THE ONE WHO DEFILED THE MISTS.
I KNOW THIS CROWD, LASH.
THEY AREN'T GONNA COOPERATE.
NO.
I WOULDN'T EXPECT THEM TO.
IT WAS ME.
I SHOULD HAVE RECOGNIZED IT... THE GLITCHES...
THEY...THEY HACKED INTO MY SYSTEMS...
...USED ME AS A SPY.

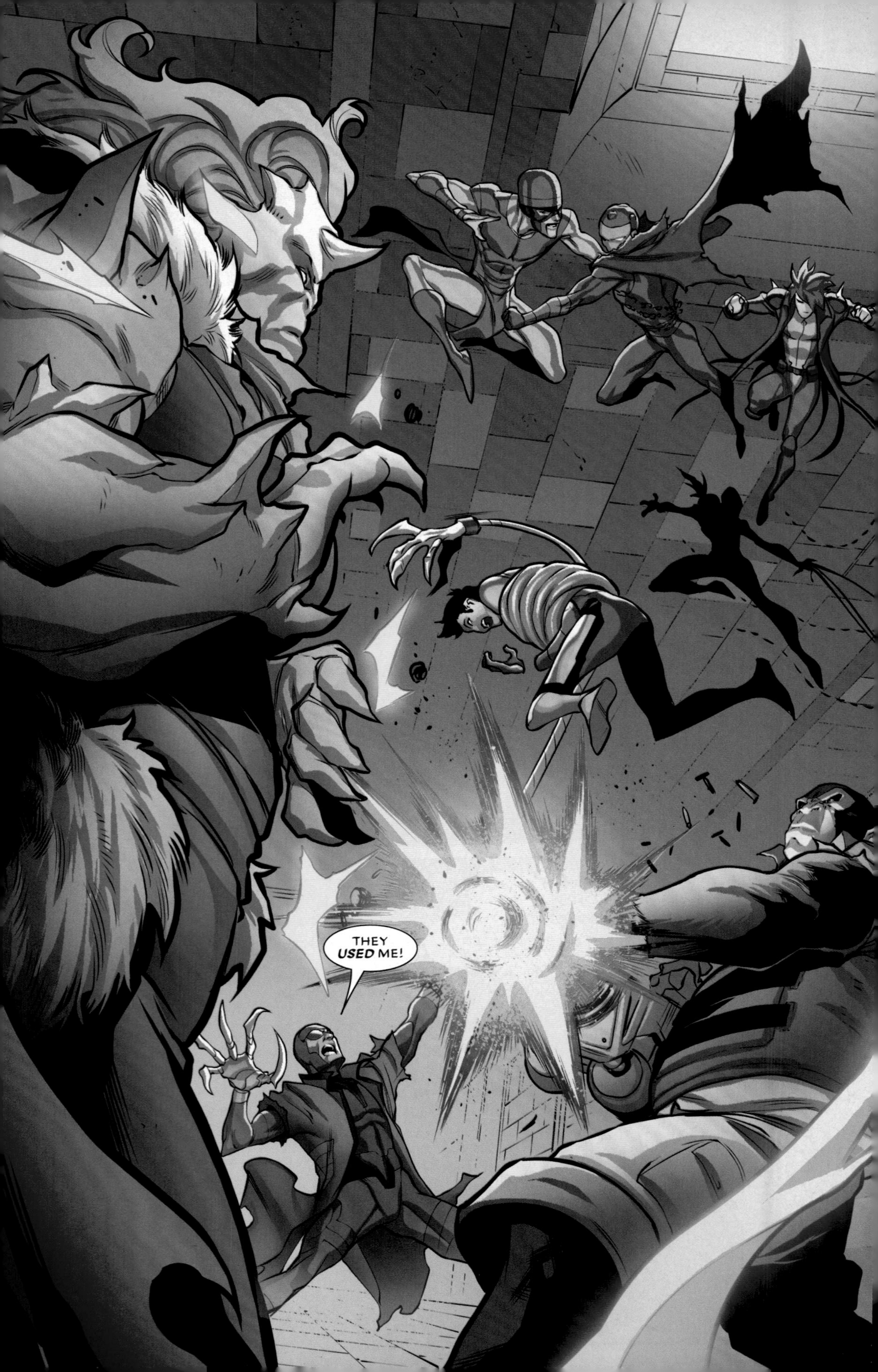
THEY *USED* ME!

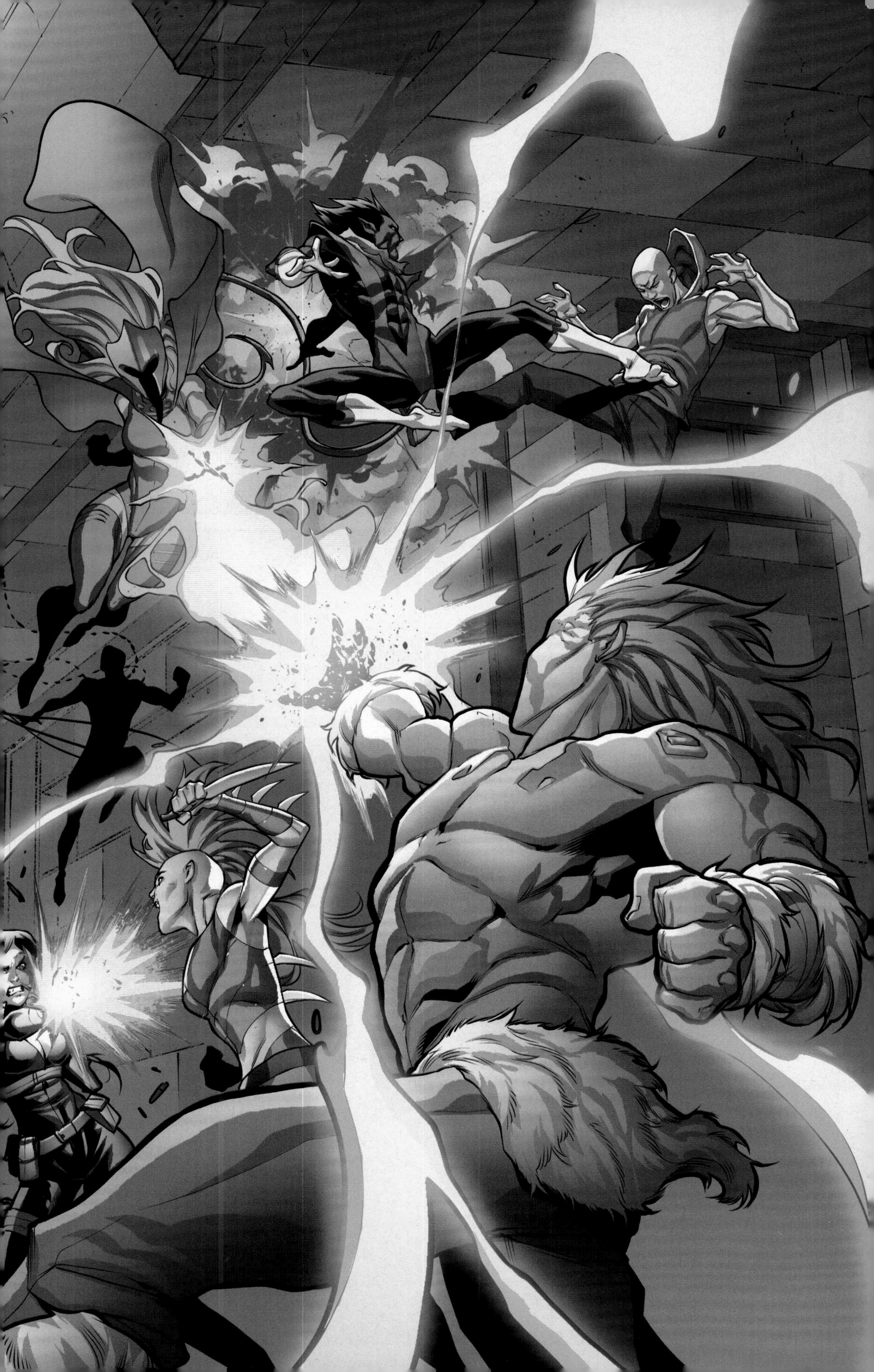

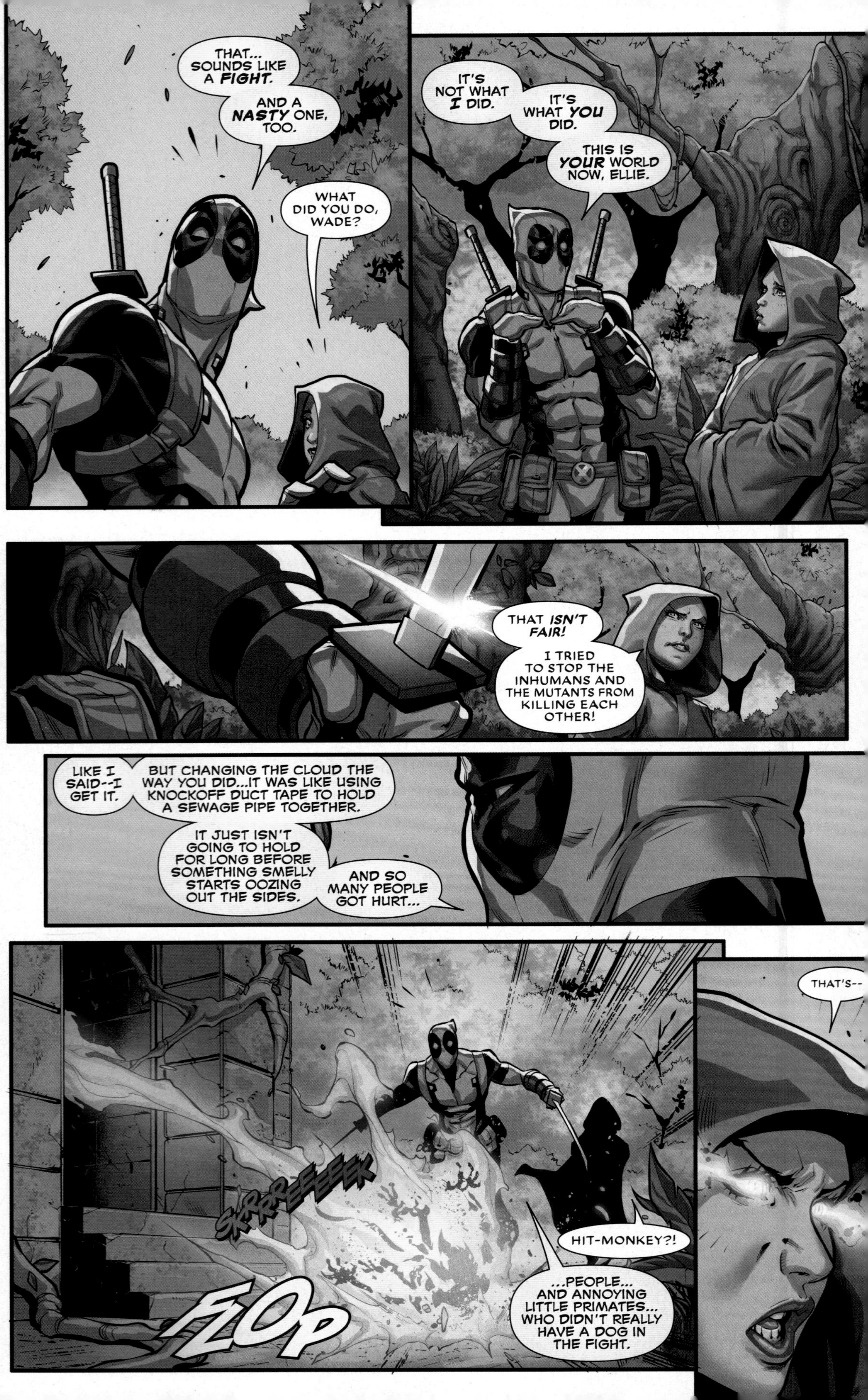
THAT... SOUNDS LIKE A FIGHT.
AND A NASTY ONE, TOO.
WHAT DID YOU DO, WADE?
IT'S NOT WHAT I DID.
IT'S WHAT YOU DID.
THIS IS YOUR WORLD NOW, ELLIE.
THAT ISN'T FAIR!
I TRIED TO STOP THE INHUMANS AND THE MUTANTS FROM KILLING EACH OTHER!
LIKE I SAID--I GET IT.
BUT CHANGING THE CLOUD THE WAY YOU DID...IT WAS LIKE USING KNOCKOFF DUCT TAPE TO HOLD A SEWAGE PIPE TOGETHER.
IT JUST ISN'T GOING TO HOLD FOR LONG BEFORE SOMETHING SMELLY STARTS OOZING OUT THE SIDES.
AND SO MANY PEOPLE GOT HURT...
SKRREEEEEK
FLOP
HIT-MONKEY?!
...PEOPLE... AND ANNOYING LITTLE PRIMATES... WHO DIDN'T REALLY HAVE A DOG IN THE FIGHT.
THAT'S--

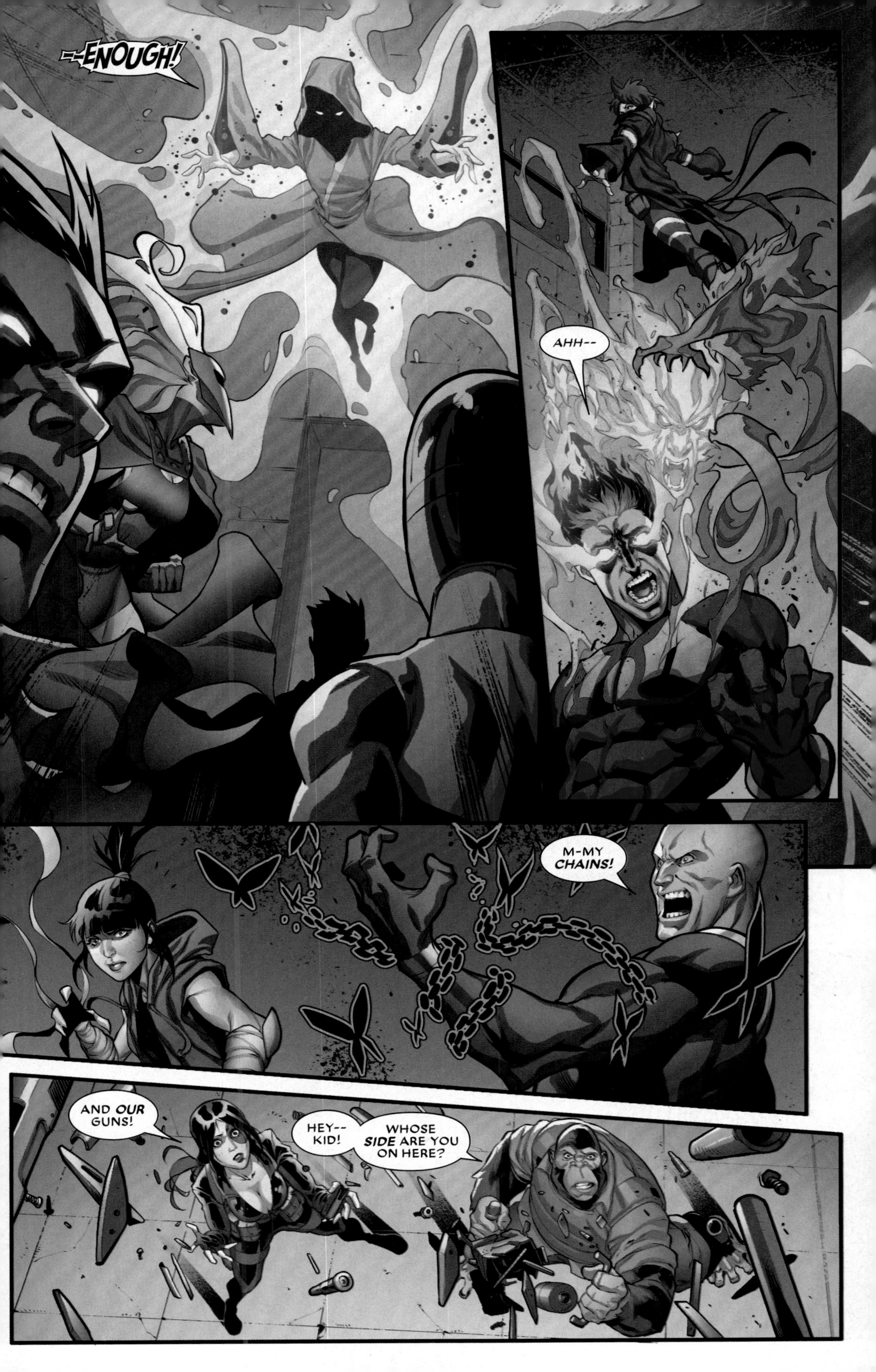
--ENOUGH!
AHH--
M-MY CHAINS!
AND OUR GUNS!
HEY-- KID!
WHOSE SIDE ARE YOU ON HERE?

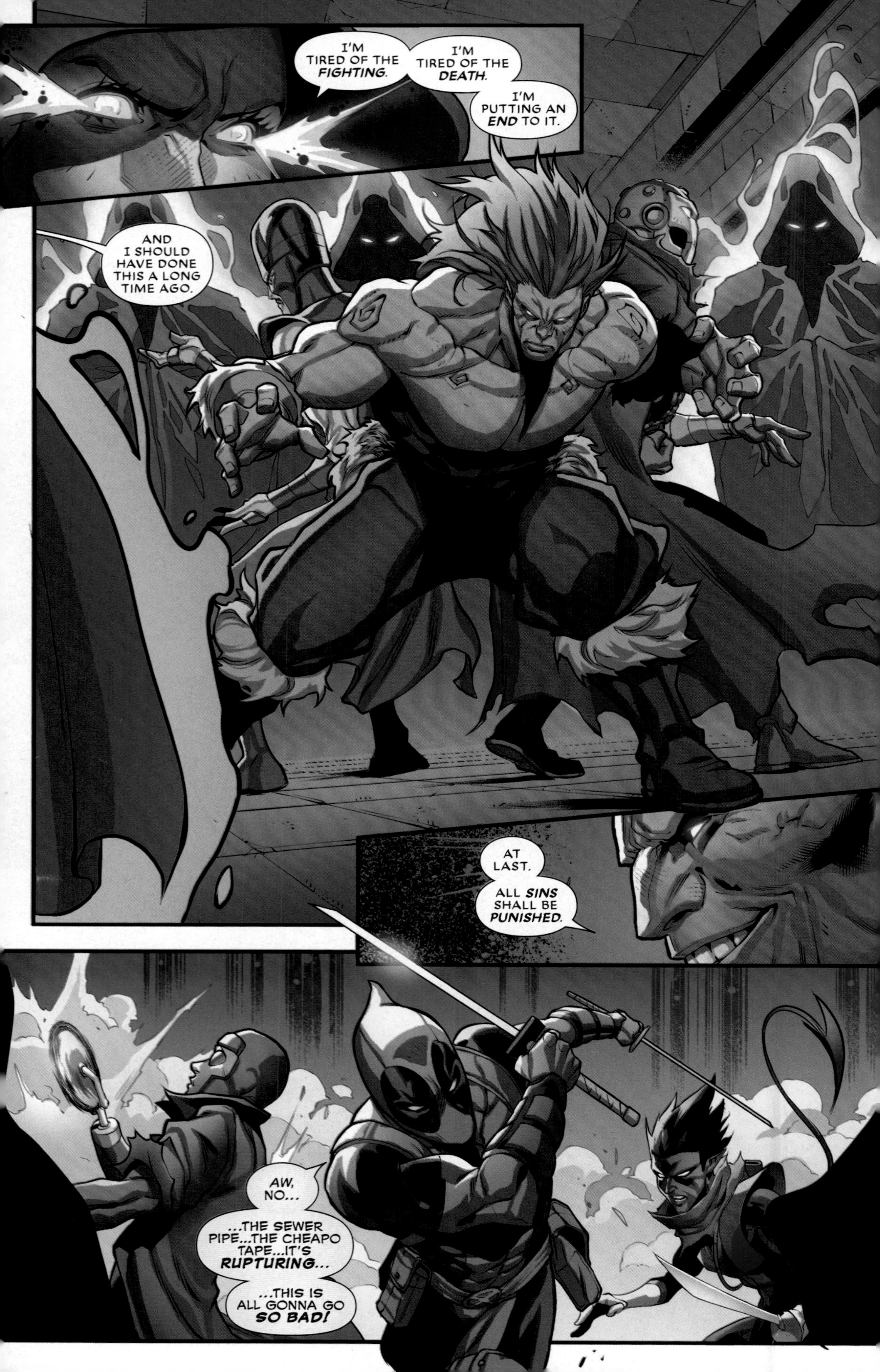
I'M TIRED OF THE FIGHTING.
I'M TIRED OF THE DEATH.
I'M PUTTING AN END TO IT.
AND I SHOULD HAVE DONE THIS A LONG TIME AGO.
AT LAST.
ALL SINS SHALL BE PUNISHED.
AW, NO...
...THE SEWER PIPE...THE CHEAPO TAPE...IT'S RUPTURING...
...THIS IS ALL GONNA GO SO BAD!

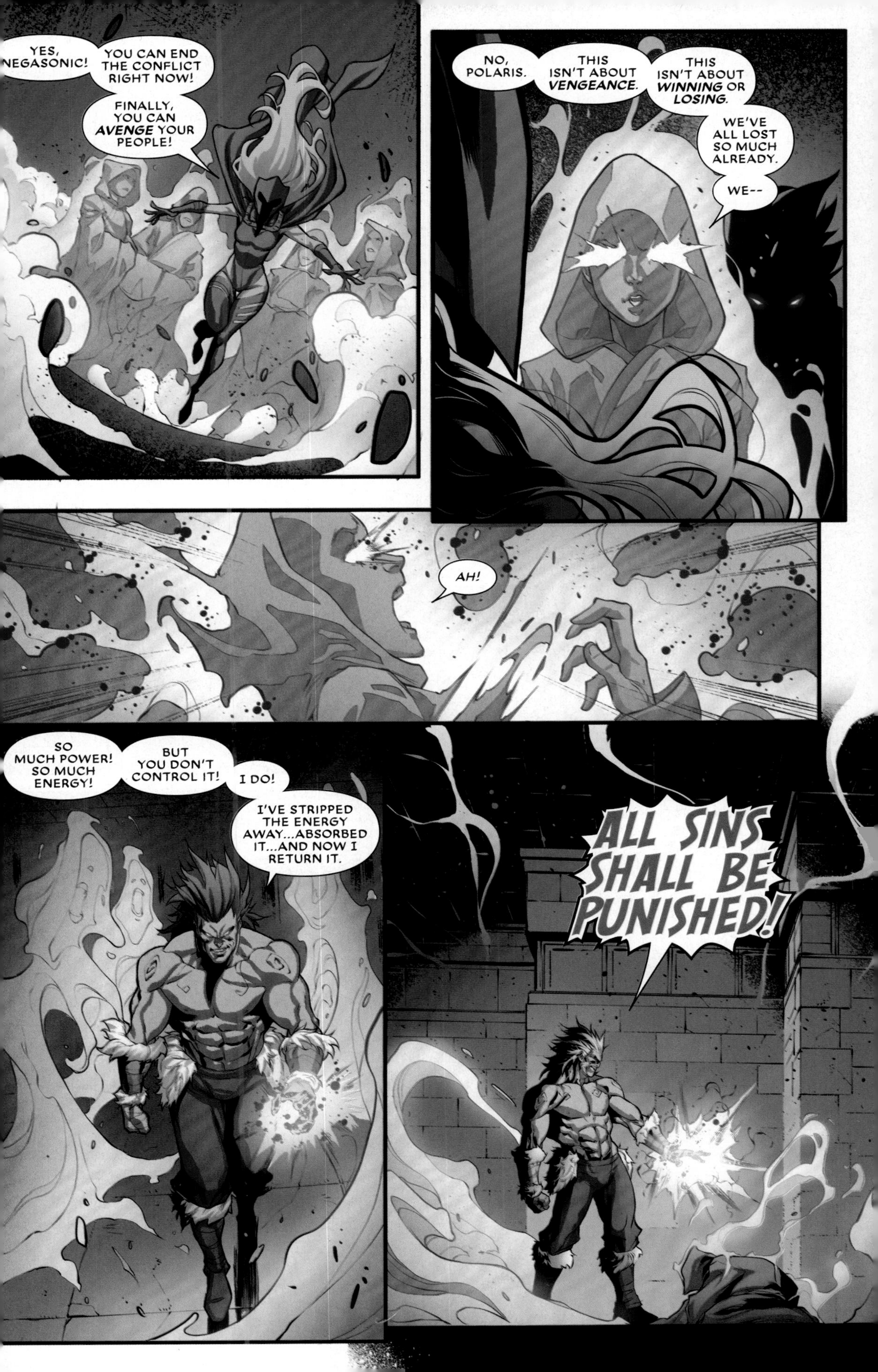
YES, NEGASONIC!
YOU CAN END THE CONFLICT RIGHT NOW!
FINALLY, YOU CAN AVENGE YOUR PEOPLE!
NO, POLARIS.
THIS ISN'T ABOUT VENGEANCE.
THIS ISN'T ABOUT WINNING OR LOSING.
WE'VE ALL LOST SO MUCH ALREADY.
WE--
AH!
SO MUCH POWER! SO MUCH ENERGY!
BUT YOU DON'T CONTROL IT!
I DO!
I'VE STRIPPED THE ENERGY AWAY...ABSORBED IT...AND NOW I RETURN IT.
ALL SINS SHALL BE PUNISHED!

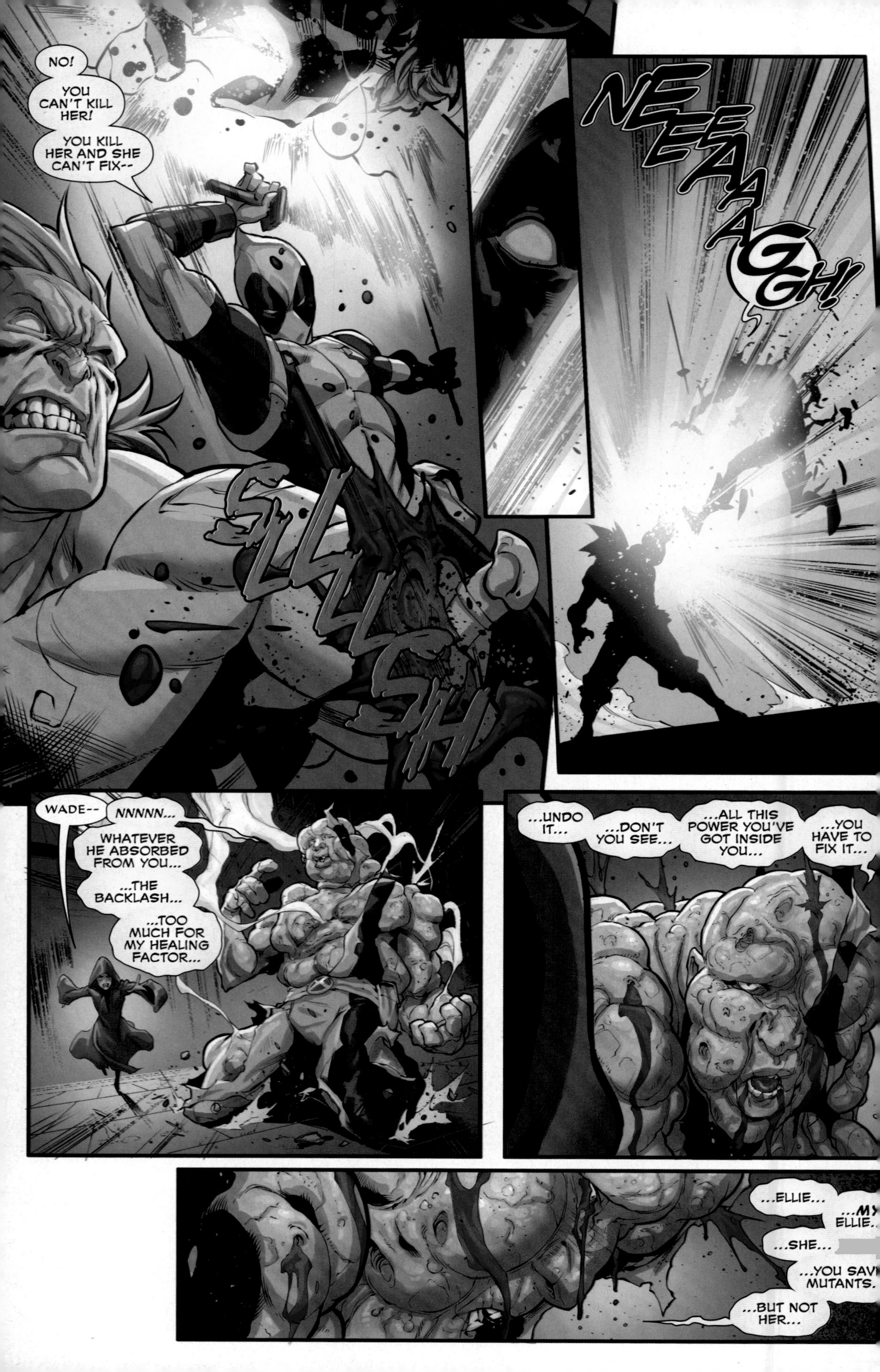
NO!
YOU CAN'T KILL HER!
YOU KILL HER AND SHE CAN'T FIX--
NEEEAAAGGH!
SHLLLSHH
WADE--
NNNNN...
WHATEVER HE ABSORBED FROM YOU...
...THE BACKLASH...
...TOO MUCH FOR MY HEALING FACTOR...
...UNDO IT...
...DON'T YOU SEE...
...ALL THIS POWER YOU'VE GOT INSIDE YOU...
...YOU HAVE TO FIX IT...
...ELLIE...
...MY ELLIE...
...SHE...
...YOU SAV
MUTANTS.
...BUT NOT HER...

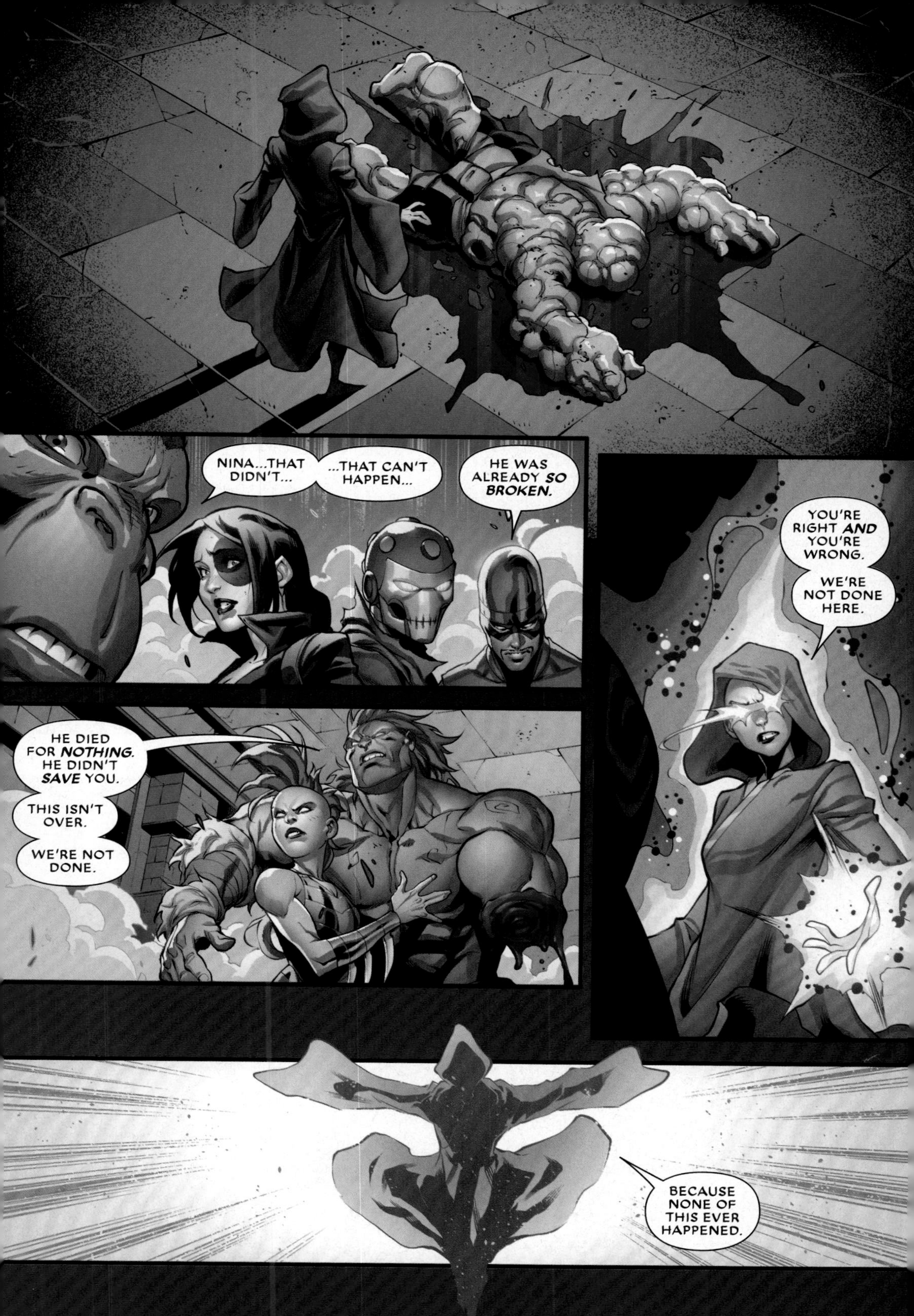

NINA...THAT DIDN'T...
...THAT CAN'T HAPPEN...
HE WAS ALREADY *SO BROKEN.*
YOU'RE RIGHT ***AND*** YOU'RE WRONG.
WE'RE NOT DONE HERE.
HE DIED FOR ***NOTHING***. HE DIDN'T ***SAVE*** YOU.
THIS ISN'T OVER.
WE'RE NOT DONE.
BECAUSE NONE OF THIS EVER HAPPENED.

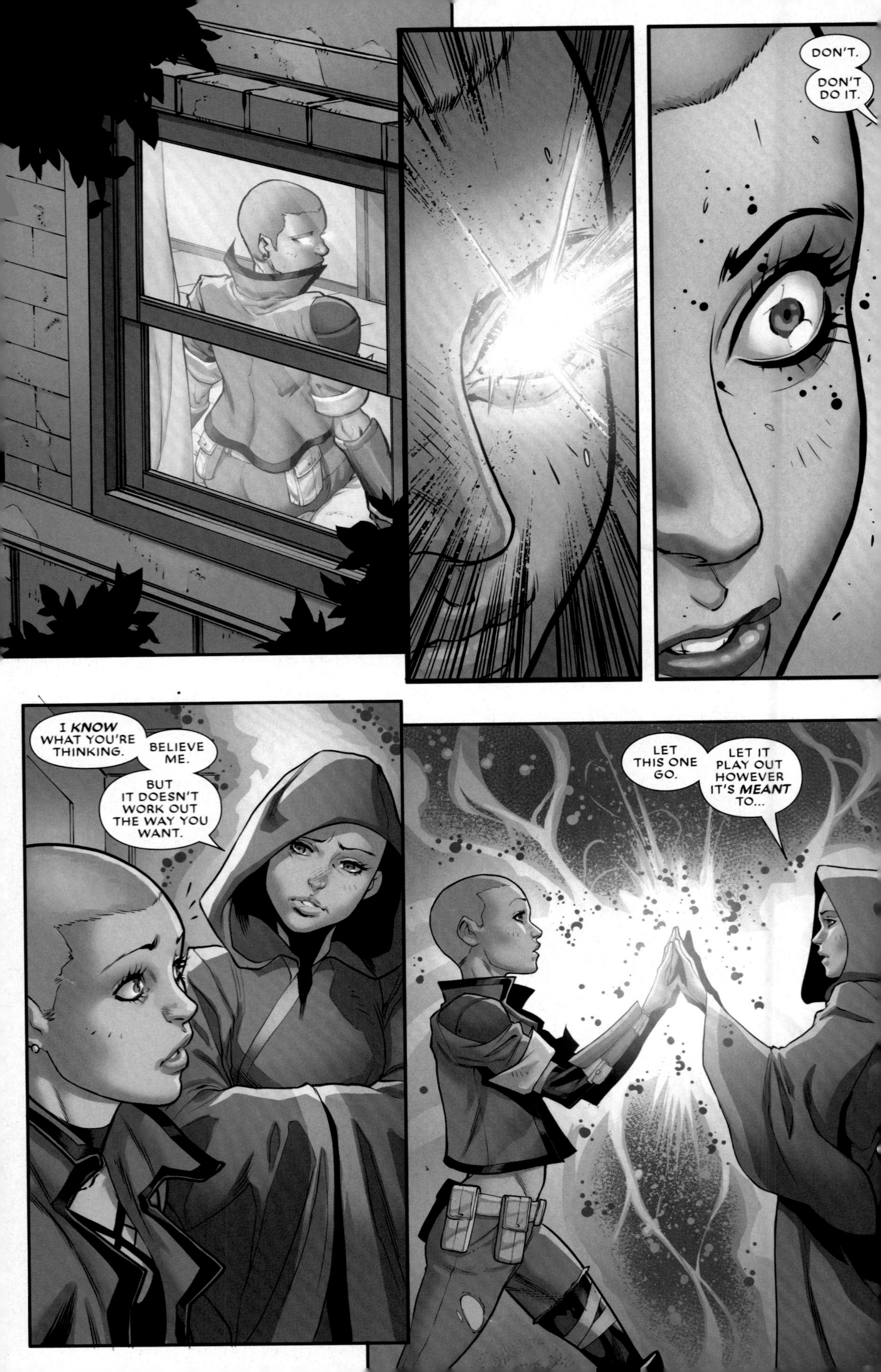
DON'T.
DON'T DO IT.
I *KNOW* WHAT YOU'RE THINKING.
BELIEVE ME.
BUT IT DOESN'T WORK OUT THE WAY YOU WANT.
LET THIS ONE GO.
LET IT PLAY OUT HOWEVER IT'S *MEANT* TO...

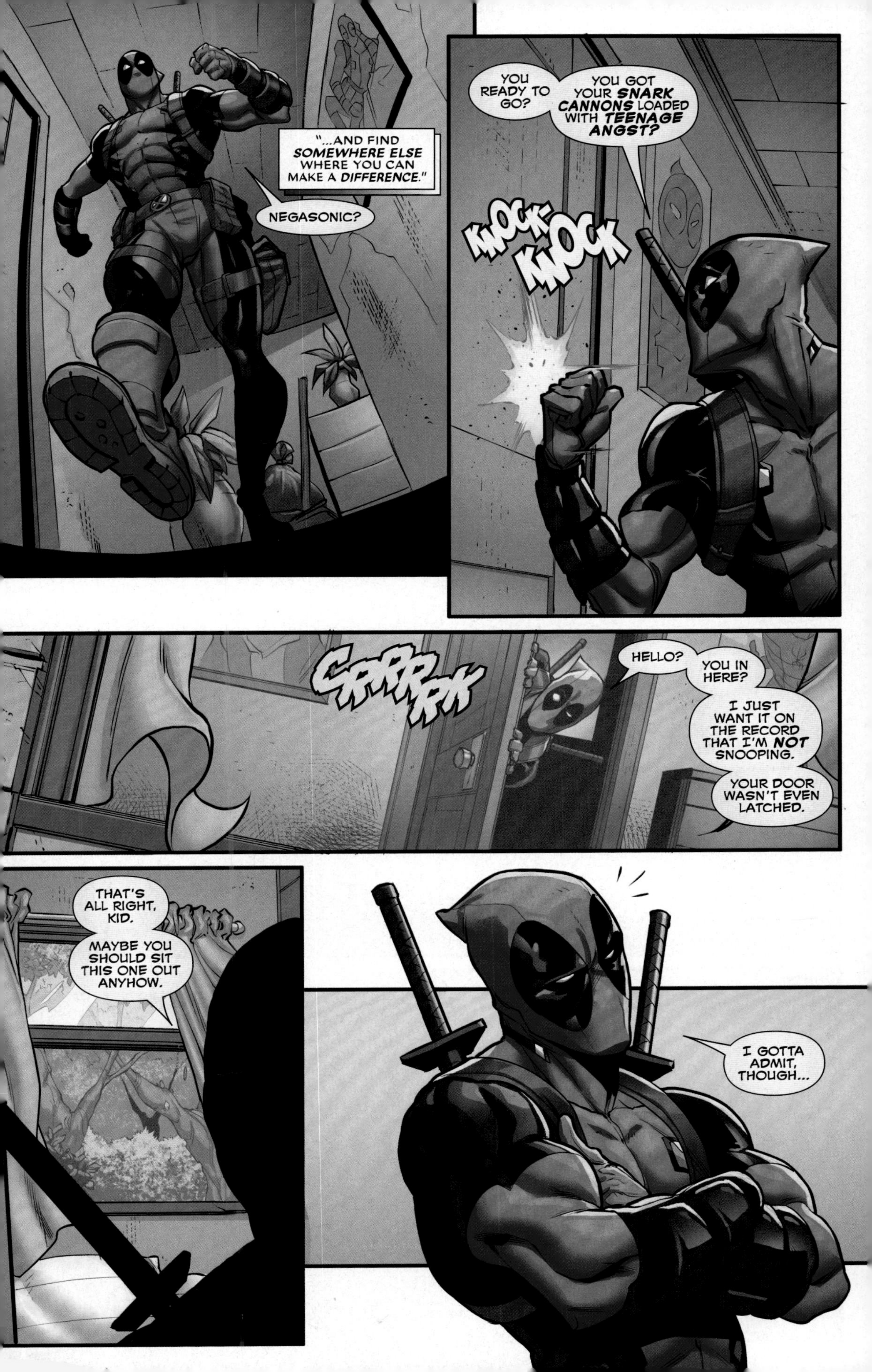
"...AND FIND SOMEWHERE ELSE WHERE YOU CAN MAKE A DIFFERENCE."
NEGASONIC?
YOU READY TO GO?
YOU GOT YOUR SNARK CANNONS LOADED WITH TEENAGE ANGST?
KNOCK KNOCK
CRRRRK
HELLO?
YOU IN HERE?
I JUST WANT IT ON THE RECORD THAT I'M NOT SNOOPING.
YOUR DOOR WASN'T EVEN LATCHED.
THAT'S ALL RIGHT, KID.
MAYBE YOU SHOULD SIT THIS ONE OUT ANYHOW.
I GOTTA ADMIT, THOUGH...

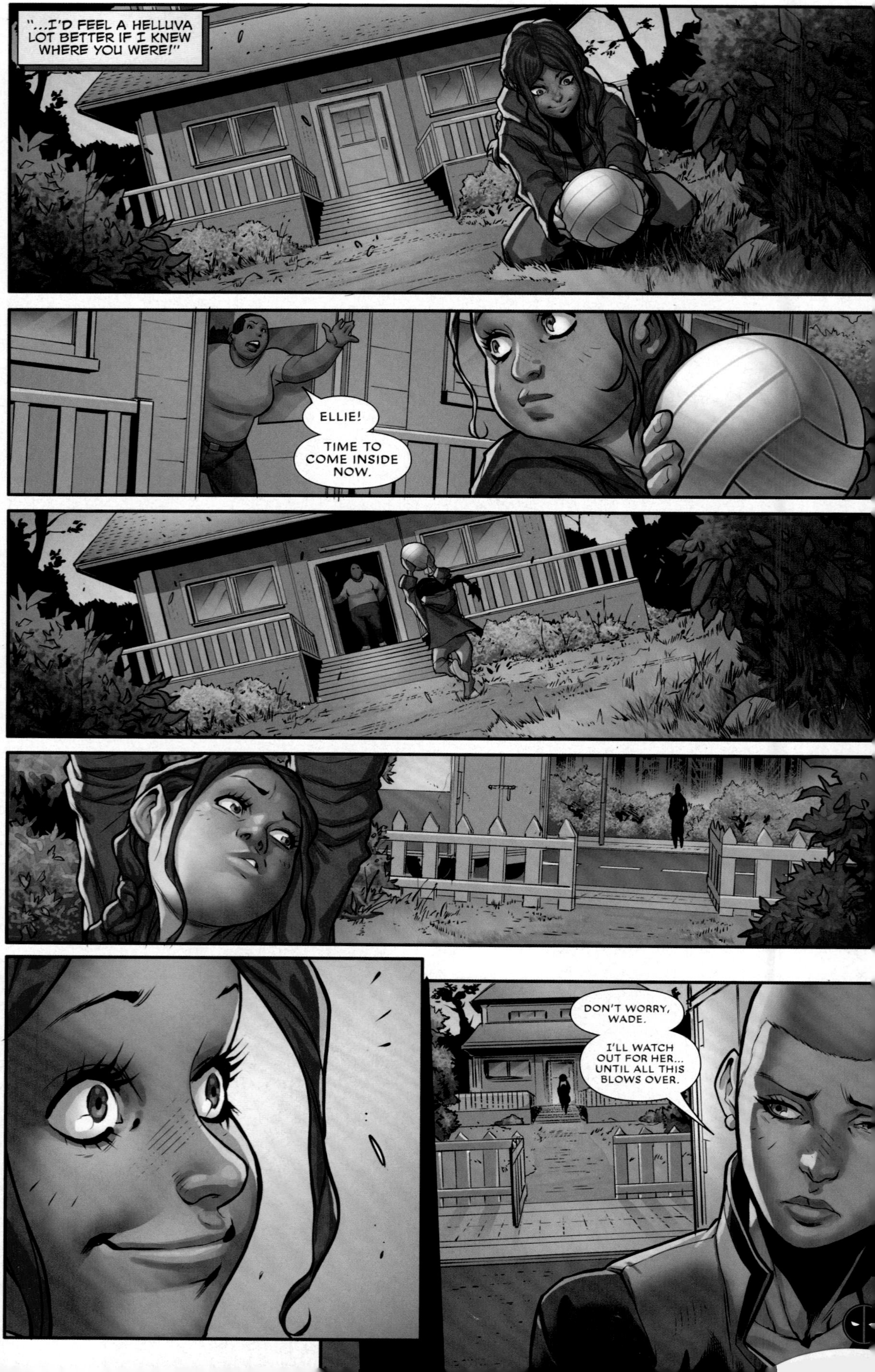
"...I'D FEEL A HELLUVA LOT BETTER IF I KNEW WHERE YOU WERE!"
ELLIE!
TIME TO COME INSIDE NOW.
DON'T WORRY, WADE.
I'LL WATCH OUT FOR HER... UNTIL ALL THIS BLOWS OVER.

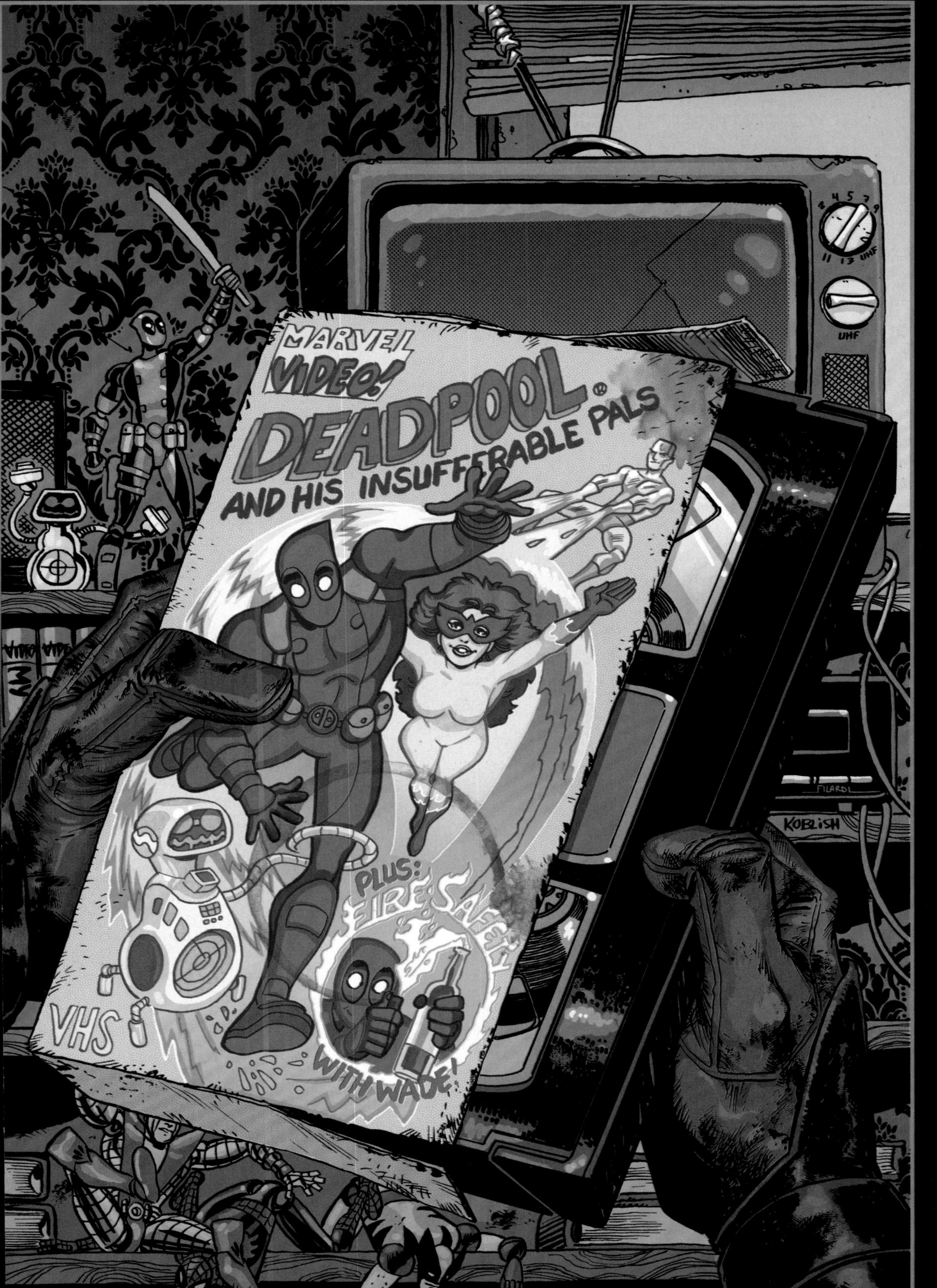
MARVEL VIDEO!
DEADPOOL
AND HIS INSUFFERABLE PALS
PLUS:
WITH WADE!
VHS
FILARDI
KOBLISH

DEADPOOL ANNUAL 1

Possibly the world's most skilled mercenary, definitely the world's most annoying, Wade Wilson was chosen for a top-secret government program that gave him a healing factor allowing him to heal from any wound. Now, Wade makes his way as a gun for hire, shooting his targets' faces off while talking his friends' ears off. Call him the Merc with the Mouth...call him the Regeneratin' Degenerate...call him...

DEADPOOL

HEY THERE, KIDS--IT'S ME, **DEADPOOL!**
ACTUALLY, PLEASE TELL ME THERE ARE NO KIDS READING THIS. I AM A BAD INFLUENCE!
YOU KNOW HOW I KNOW? BECAUSE YOU'RE ABOUT TO WATCH THE PILOT FOR MY CARTOON SHOW, AND THAT'S WHAT THE TV EXECUTIVES SAID ABOUT ME.
I KNOW, I KNOW-- I WAS SHOCKED. I THOUGHT STORIES ABOUT A FOUL-MOUTHED, SEXUALLY-CHARGED MURDERER WHO PLAYS IRRESPONSIBLY WITH FIREARMS AND SHOWS NO REGARD FOR THE SAFETY OF HIMSELF OR OTHERS WOULD BE PERFECT FODDER FOR THE YOUNG MINDS OF THE WORLD.
OH, WELL.
ANYWAY, STRAP YOURSELF IN, AND GRAB YOUR PONCHO AS THERE MAY BE A SPLASH ZONE AS YOU ENJOY...

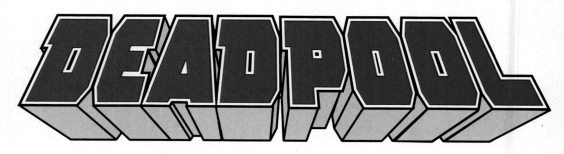

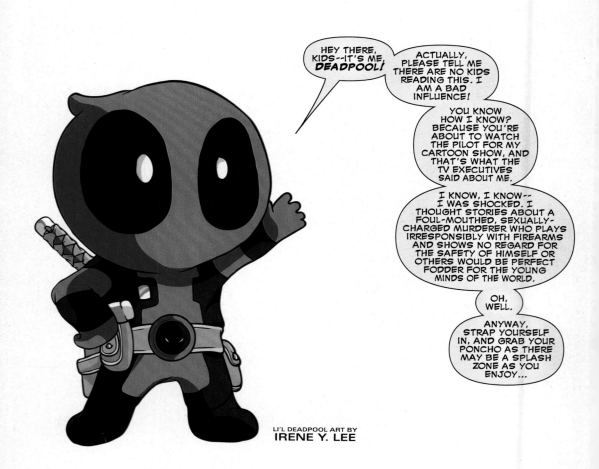

LI'L DEADPOOL ART BY
IRENE Y. LEE

DEADPOOL AND HIS INSUFFERABLE PALS

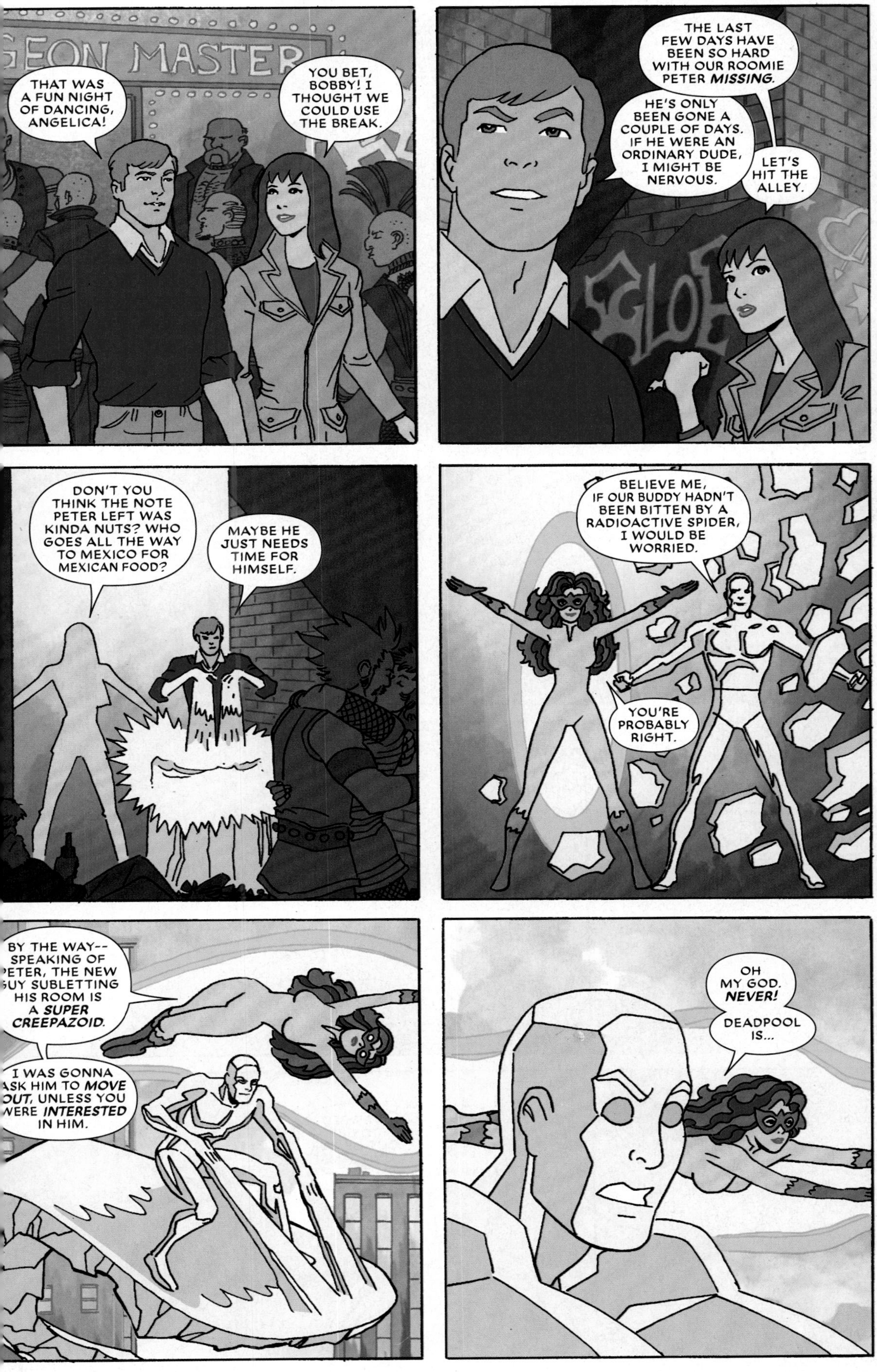
GEON MASTER
THAT WAS A FUN NIGHT OF DANCING, ANGELICA!
YOU BET, BOBBY! I THOUGHT WE COULD USE THE BREAK.
THE LAST FEW DAYS HAVE BEEN SO HARD WITH OUR ROOMIE PETER *MISSING*.
HE'S ONLY BEEN GONE A COUPLE OF DAYS. IF HE WERE AN ORDINARY DUDE, I MIGHT BE NERVOUS.
LET'S HIT THE ALLEY.
DON'T YOU THINK THE NOTE PETER LEFT WAS KINDA NUTS? WHO GOES ALL THE WAY TO MEXICO FOR MEXICAN FOOD?
MAYBE HE JUST NEEDS TIME FOR HIMSELF.
BELIEVE ME, IF OUR BUDDY HADN'T BEEN BITTEN BY A RADIOACTIVE SPIDER, I WOULD BE WORRIED.
YOU'RE PROBABLY RIGHT.
BY THE WAY-- SPEAKING OF PETER, THE NEW GUY SUBLETTING HIS ROOM IS A ***SUPER CREEPAZOID***.
I WAS GONNA ASK HIM TO ***MOVE OUT***, UNLESS YOU WERE ***INTERESTED*** IN HIM.
OH MY GOD. ***NEVER!***
DEADPOOL IS...

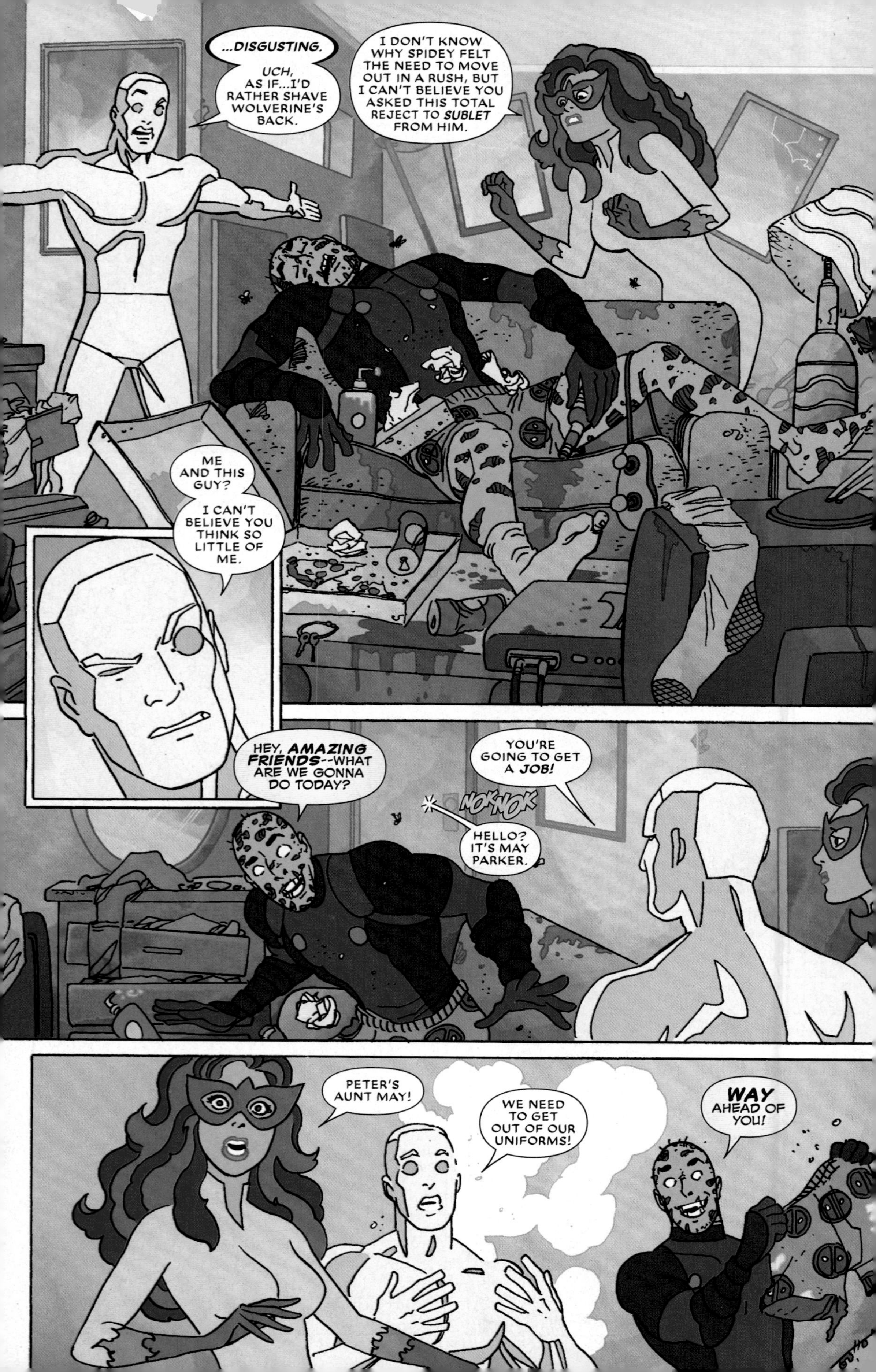
...DISGUSTING.
UCH, AS IF...I'D RATHER SHAVE WOLVERINE'S BACK.
I DON'T KNOW WHY SPIDEY FELT THE NEED TO MOVE OUT IN A RUSH, BUT I CAN'T BELIEVE YOU ASKED THIS TOTAL REJECT TO SUBLET FROM HIM.
ME AND THIS GUY?
I CAN'T BELIEVE YOU THINK SO LITTLE OF ME.
HEY, AMAZING FRIENDS--WHAT ARE WE GONNA DO TODAY?
YOU'RE GOING TO GET A JOB!
NOKNOK
HELLO? IT'S MAY PARKER.
PETER'S AUNT MAY!
WE NEED TO GET OUT OF OUR UNIFORMS!
WAY AHEAD OF YOU!

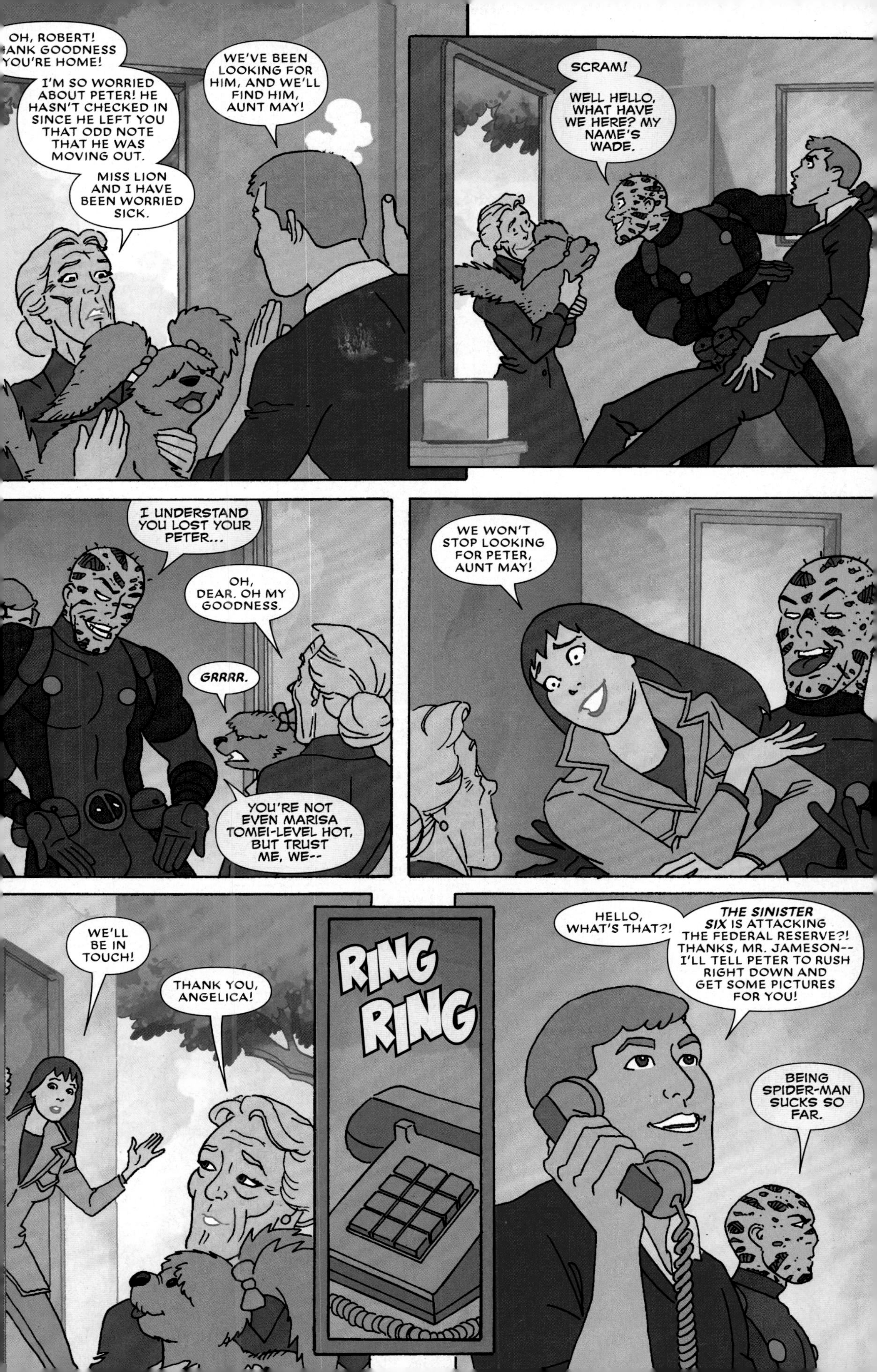
OH, ROBERT! HANK GOODNESS YOU'RE HOME!
I'M SO WORRIED ABOUT PETER! HE HASN'T CHECKED IN SINCE HE LEFT YOU THAT ODD NOTE THAT HE WAS MOVING OUT.
MISS LION AND I HAVE BEEN WORRIED SICK.
WE'VE BEEN LOOKING FOR HIM, AND WE'LL FIND HIM, AUNT MAY!
SCRAM!
WELL HELLO, WHAT HAVE WE HERE? MY NAME'S WADE.
I UNDERSTAND YOU LOST YOUR PETER...
OH, DEAR. OH MY GOODNESS.
GRRRR.
YOU'RE NOT EVEN MARISA TOMEI-LEVEL HOT, BUT TRUST ME, WE--
WE WON'T STOP LOOKING FOR PETER, AUNT MAY!
WE'LL BE IN TOUCH!
THANK YOU, ANGELICA!
RING RING
HELLO, WHAT'S THAT?!
THE SINISTER SIX IS ATTACKING THE FEDERAL RESERVE?! THANKS, MR. JAMESON-- I'LL TELL PETER TO RUSH RIGHT DOWN AND GET SOME PICTURES FOR YOU!
BEING SPIDER-MAN SUCKS SO FAR.

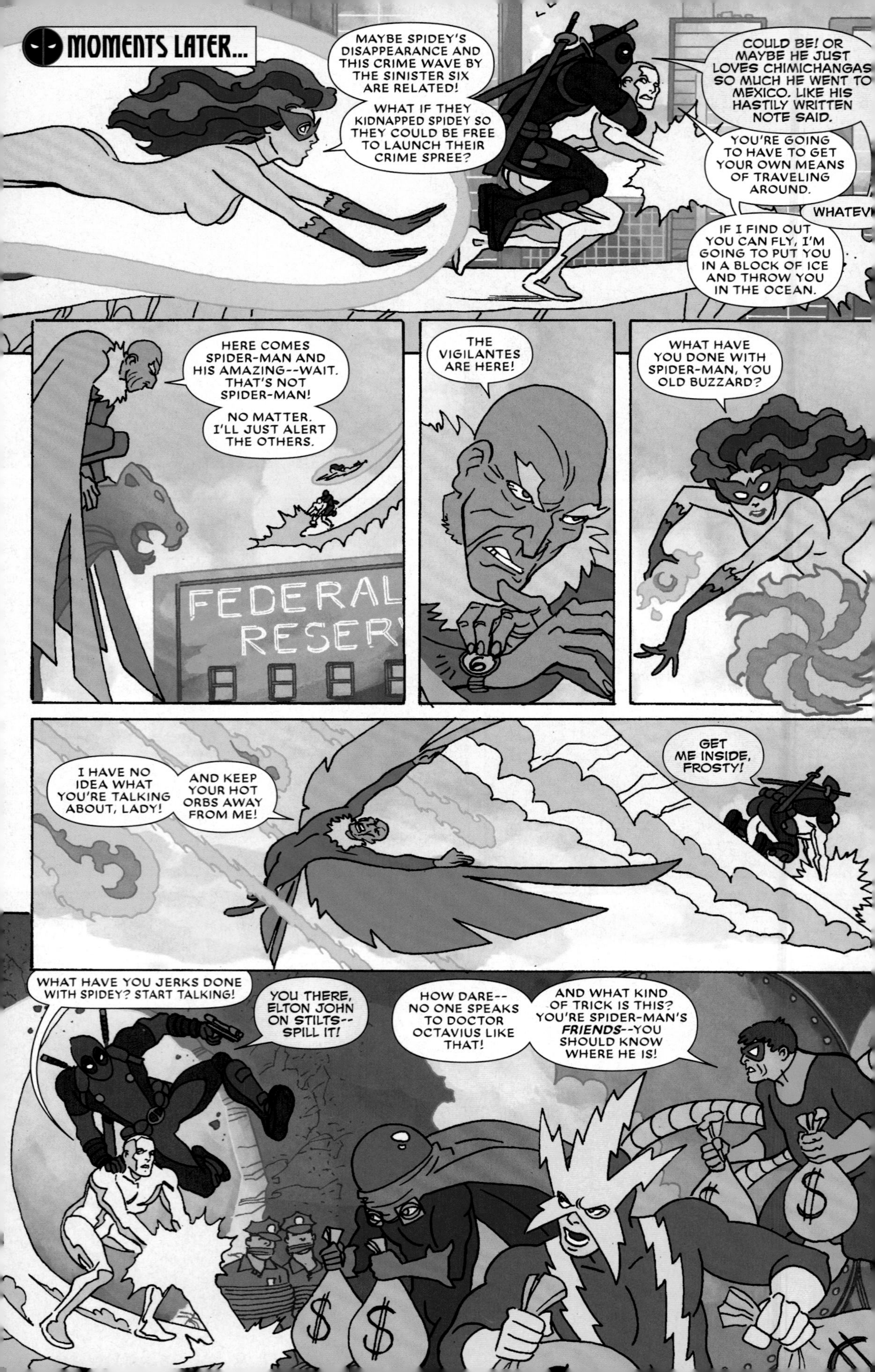

MOMENTS LATER...
MAYBE SPIDEY'S DISAPPEARANCE AND THIS CRIME WAVE BY THE SINISTER SIX ARE RELATED!
WHAT IF THEY KIDNAPPED SPIDEY SO THEY COULD BE FREE TO LAUNCH THEIR CRIME SPREE?
COULD BE! OR MAYBE HE JUST LOVES CHIMICHANGAS SO MUCH HE WENT TO MEXICO. LIKE HIS HASTILY WRITTEN NOTE SAID.
YOU'RE GOING TO HAVE TO GET YOUR OWN MEANS OF TRAVELING AROUND.
WHATEV
IF I FIND OUT YOU CAN FLY, I'M GOING TO PUT YOU IN A BLOCK OF ICE AND THROW YOU IN THE OCEAN.
HERE COMES SPIDER-MAN AND HIS AMAZING--WAIT. THAT'S NOT SPIDER-MAN!
NO MATTER. I'LL JUST ALERT THE OTHERS.
FEDERAL RESER
THE VIGILANTES ARE HERE!
WHAT HAVE YOU DONE WITH SPIDER-MAN, YOU OLD BUZZARD?
I HAVE NO IDEA WHAT YOU'RE TALKING ABOUT, LADY!
AND KEEP YOUR HOT ORBS AWAY FROM ME!
GET ME INSIDE, FROSTY!
WHAT HAVE YOU JERKS DONE WITH SPIDEY? START TALKING!
YOU THERE, ELTON JOHN ON STILTS-- SPILL IT!
HOW DARE-- NO ONE SPEAKS TO DOCTOR OCTAVIUS LIKE THAT!
AND WHAT KIND OF TRICK IS THIS? YOU'RE SPIDER-MAN'S *FRIENDS*--YOU SHOULD KNOW WHERE HE IS!

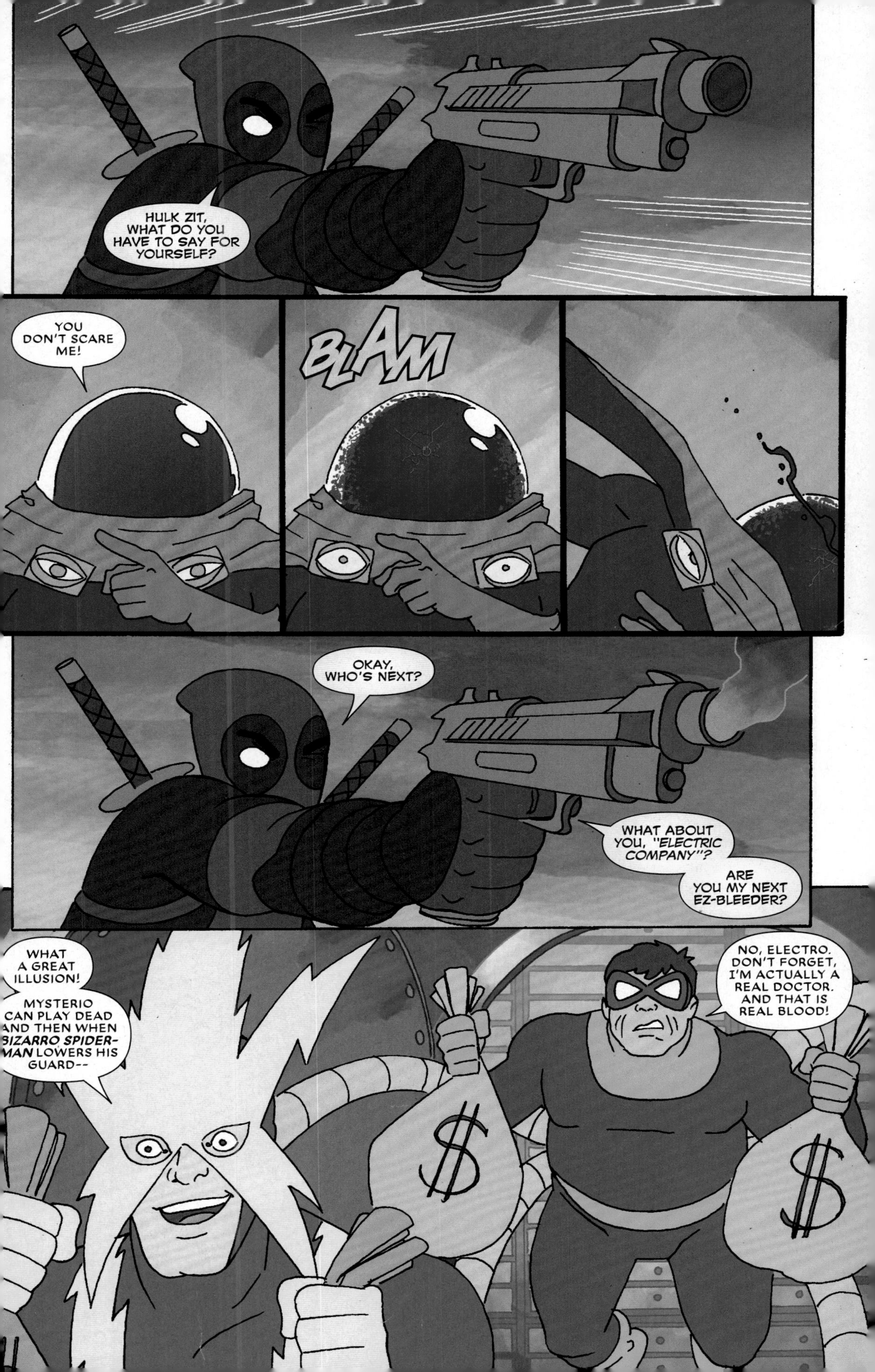
HULK ZIT, WHAT DO YOU HAVE TO SAY FOR YOURSELF?
YOU DON'T SCARE ME!
BLAM
OKAY, WHO'S NEXT?
WHAT ABOUT YOU, "ELECTRIC COMPANY"?
ARE YOU MY NEXT EZ-BLEEDER?
WHAT A GREAT ILLUSION!
MYSTERIO CAN PLAY DEAD AND THEN WHEN BIZARRO SPIDER-MAN LOWERS HIS GUARD--
NO, ELECTRO. DON'T FORGET, I'M ACTUALLY A REAL DOCTOR. AND THAT IS REAL BLOOD!

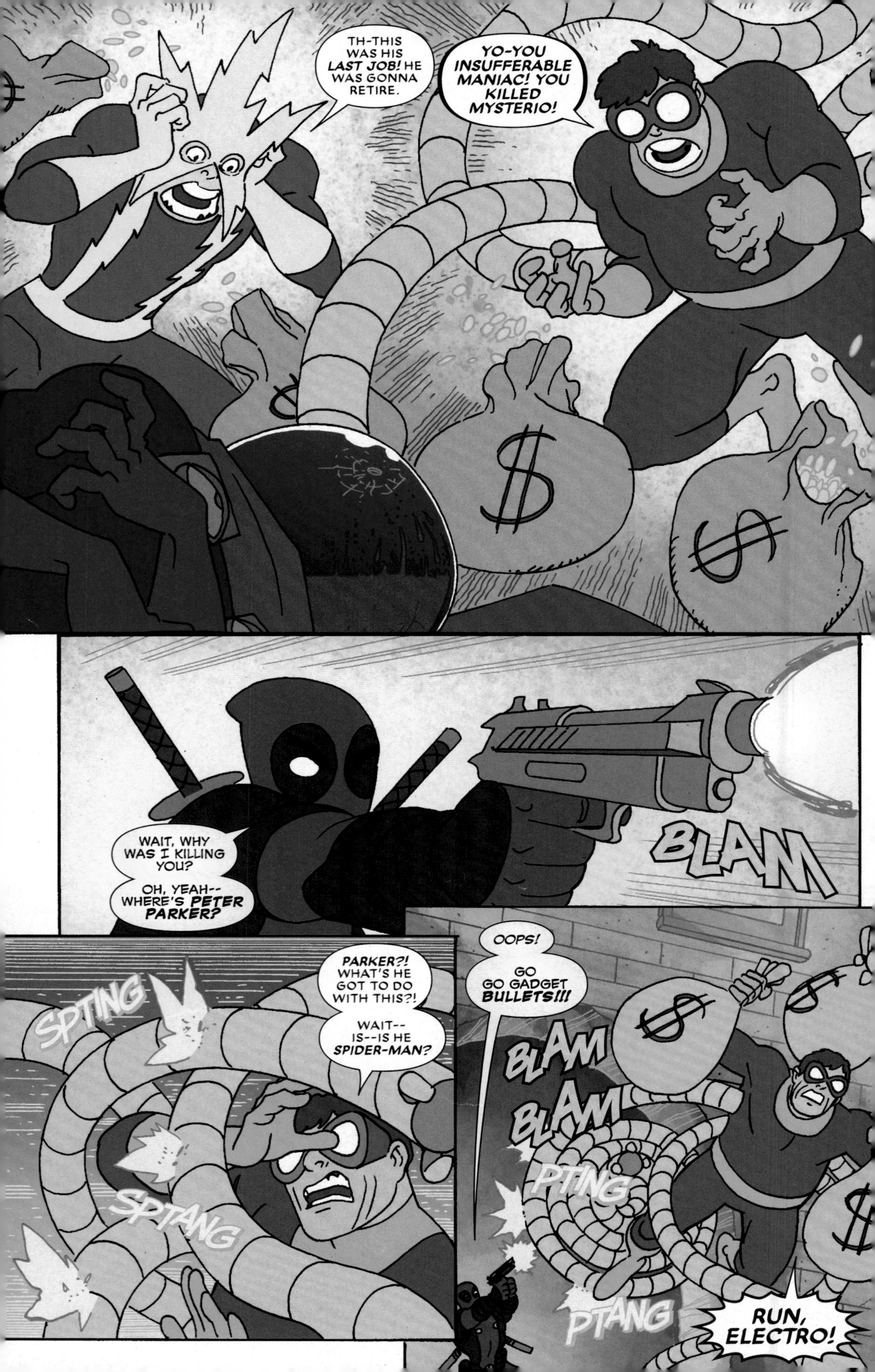
TH-THIS WAS HIS LAST JOB! HE WAS GONNA RETIRE.
YO-YOU INSUFFERABLE MANIAC! YOU KILLED MYSTERIO!
BLAM
WAIT, WHY WAS I KILLING YOU?
OH, YEAH-- WHERE'S PETER PARKER?
SPTING
PARKER?! WHAT'S HE GOT TO DO WITH THIS?!
WAIT-- IS--IS HE SPIDER-MAN?
SPTANG
OOPS!
GO GO GADGET BULLETS!!!
BLAM
BLAM
PTING
PTANG
RUN, ELECTRO!

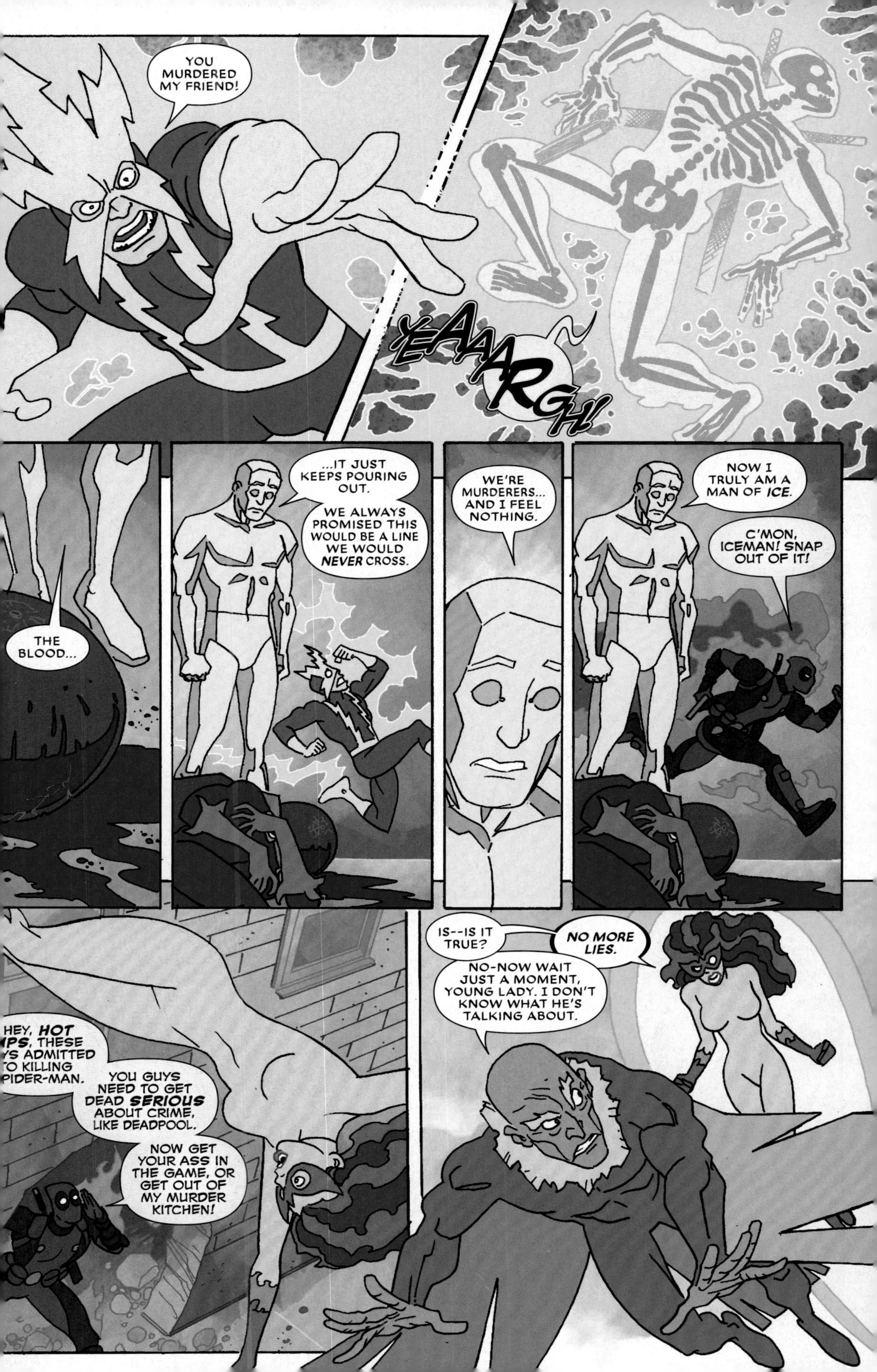
YOU MURDERED MY FRIEND!
YEAAAARGH!
THE BLOOD...
...IT JUST KEEPS POURING OUT.
WE ALWAYS PROMISED THIS WOULD BE A LINE WE WOULD NEVER CROSS.
WE'RE MURDERERS... AND I FEEL NOTHING.
NOW I TRULY AM A MAN OF ICE.
C'MON, ICEMAN! SNAP OUT OF IT!
HEY, HOT IPS, THESE YS ADMITTED TO KILLING PIDER-MAN.
YOU GUYS NEED TO GET DEAD SERIOUS ABOUT CRIME, LIKE DEADPOOL.
NOW GET YOUR ASS IN THE GAME, OR GET OUT OF MY MURDER KITCHEN!
IS--IS IT TRUE?
NO MORE LIES.
NO-NOW WAIT JUST A MOMENT, YOUNG LADY. I DON'T KNOW WHAT HE'S TALKING ABOUT.

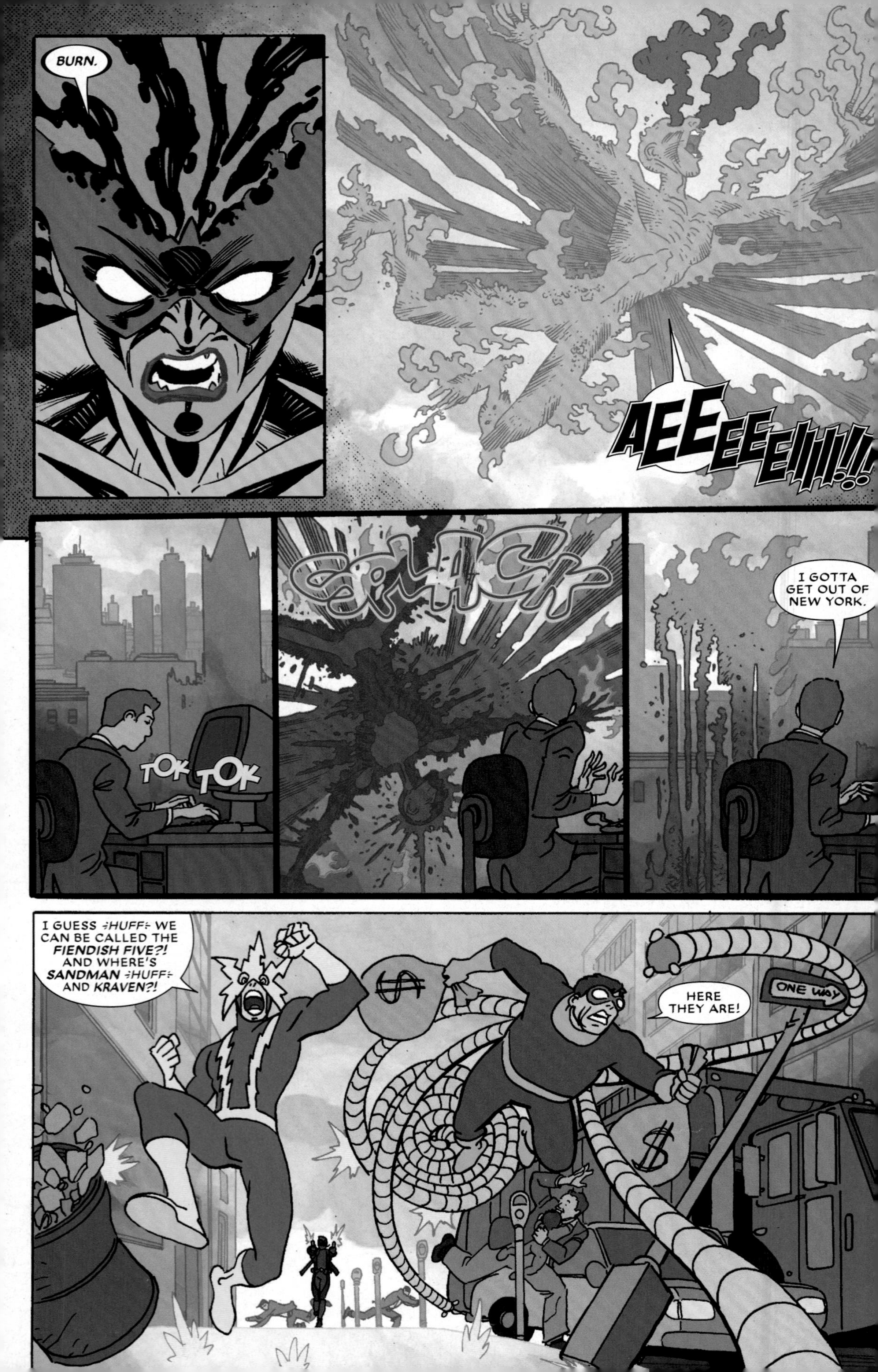
BURN.
AEEEEEEIIIIIII!!!
TOK TOK
SPLACK
I GOTTA GET OUT OF NEW YORK.
I GUESS ÷HUFF÷ WE CAN BE CALLED THE FIENDISH FIVE?! AND WHERE'S SANDMAN ÷HUFF÷ AND KRAVEN?!
HERE THEY ARE!
ONE WAY

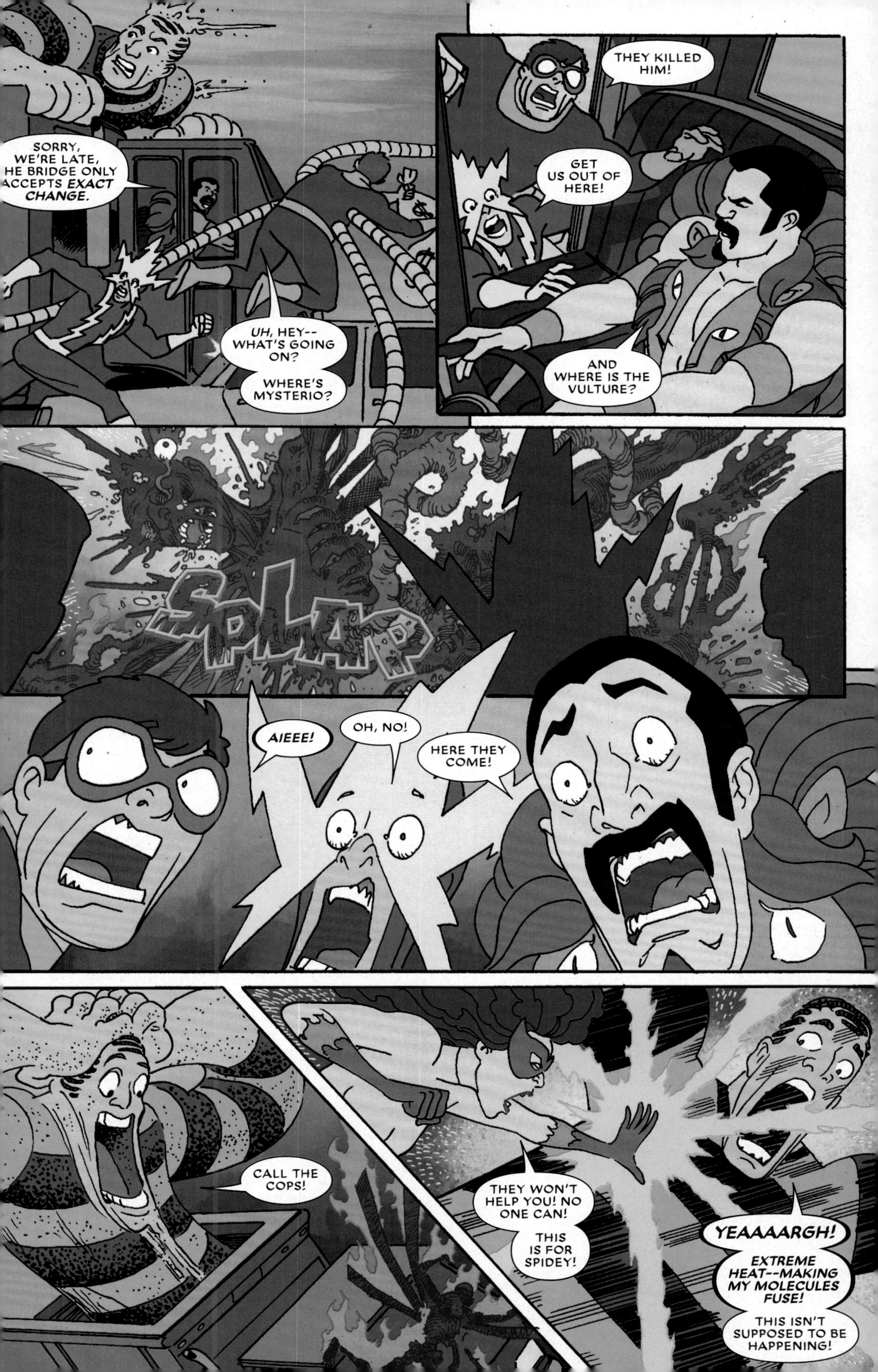
SORRY, WE'RE LATE, HE BRIDGE ONLY ACCEPTS *EXACT CHANGE.*
UH, HEY-- WHAT'S GOING ON?
WHERE'S MYSTERIO?
THEY KILLED HIM!
GET US OUT OF HERE!
AND WHERE IS THE VULTURE?
SPLAAP
AIEEE!
OH, NO!
HERE THEY COME!
CALL THE COPS!
THEY WON'T HELP YOU! NO ONE CAN!
THIS IS FOR SPIDEY!
YEAAAARGH!
EXTREME HEAT--MAKING MY MOLECULES FUSE!
THIS ISN'T SUPPOSED TO BE HAPPENING!

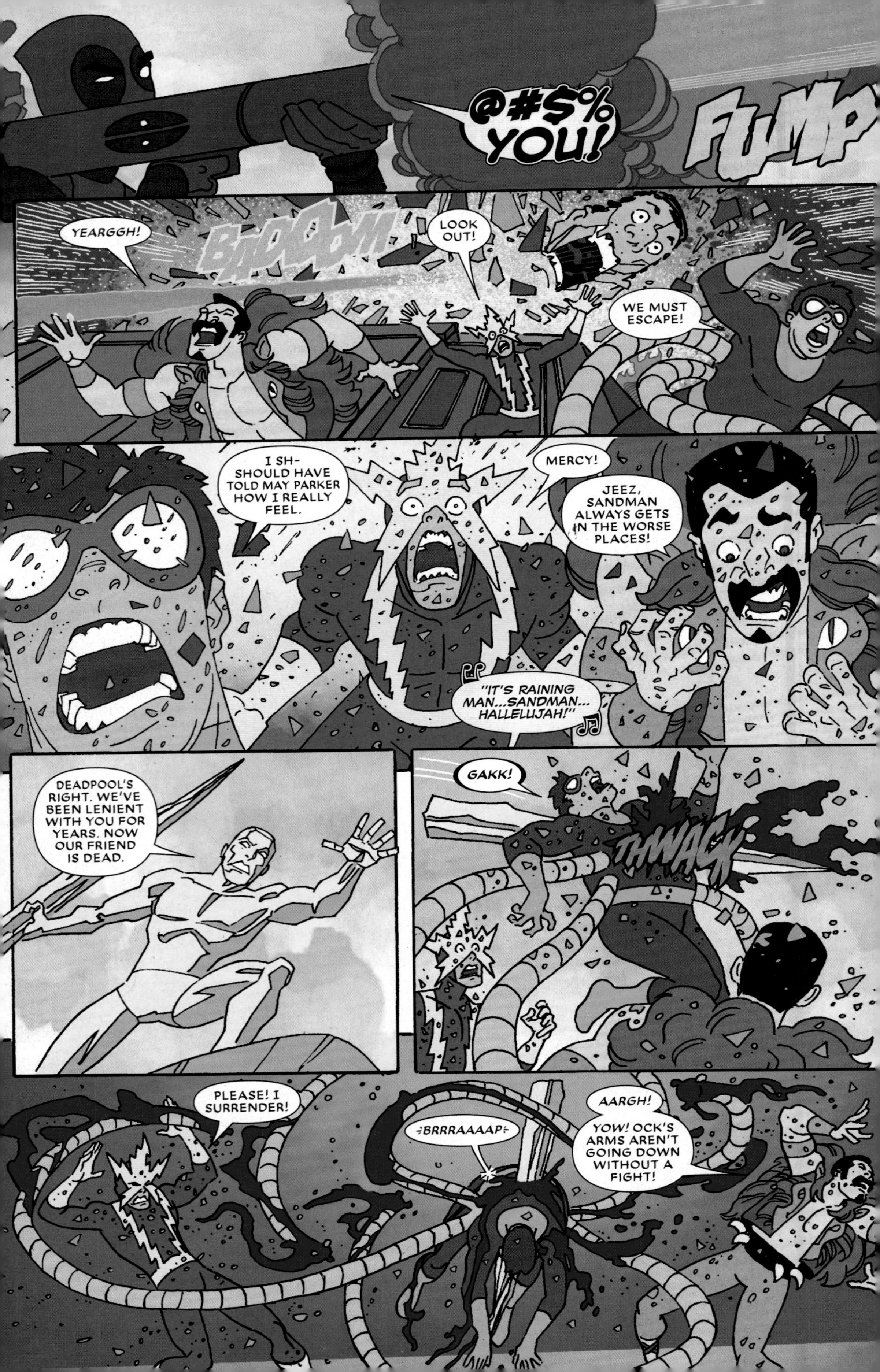
@#$% YOU!
FUMP
YEARGGH!
BADOOM
LOOK OUT!
WE MUST ESCAPE!
I SH- SHOULD HAVE TOLD MAY PARKER HOW I REALLY FEEL.
MERCY!
JEEZ, SANDMAN ALWAYS GETS IN THE WORSE PLACES!
"IT'S RAINING MAN...SANDMAN... HALLELUJAH!"
DEADPOOL'S RIGHT. WE'VE BEEN LENIENT WITH YOU FOR YEARS. NOW OUR FRIEND IS DEAD.
GAKK!
THWACK
PLEASE! I SURRENDER!
BRRRAAAAP
AARGH!
YOW! OCK'S ARMS AREN'T GOING DOWN WITHOUT A FIGHT!

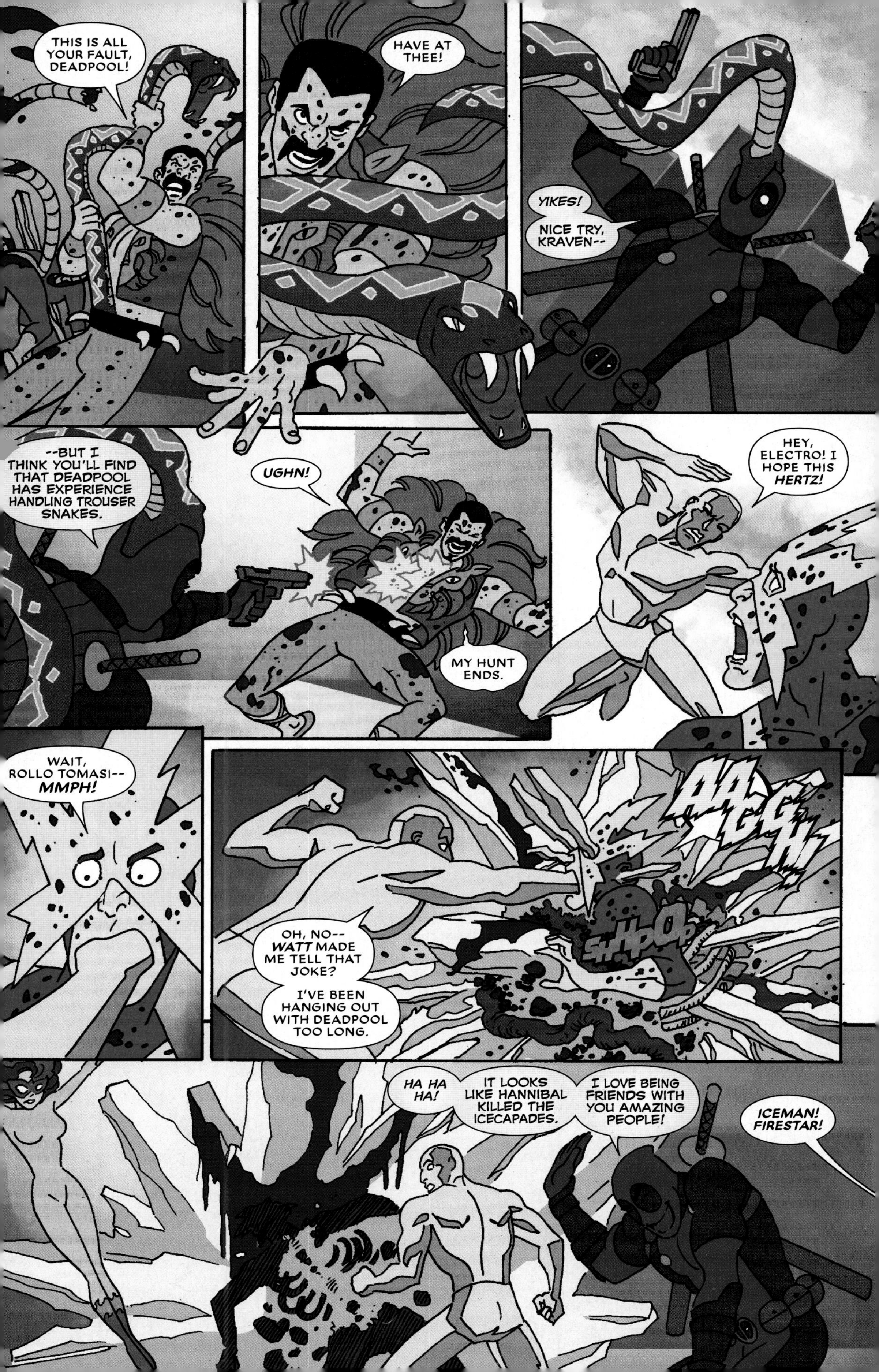
THIS IS ALL YOUR FAULT, DEADPOOL!
HAVE AT THEE!
YIKES!
NICE TRY, KRAVEN--
--BUT I THINK YOU'LL FIND THAT DEADPOOL HAS EXPERIENCE HANDLING TROUSER SNAKES.
UGHN!
MY HUNT ENDS.
HEY, ELECTRO! I HOPE THIS HERTZ!
WAIT, ROLLO TOMASI-- MMPH!
OH, NO-- WATT MADE ME TELL THAT JOKE?
I'VE BEEN HANGING OUT WITH DEADPOOL TOO LONG.
HA HA HA!
IT LOOKS LIKE HANNIBAL KILLED THE ICECAPADES.
I LOVE BEING FRIENDS WITH YOU AMAZING PEOPLE!
ICEMAN! FIRESTAR!

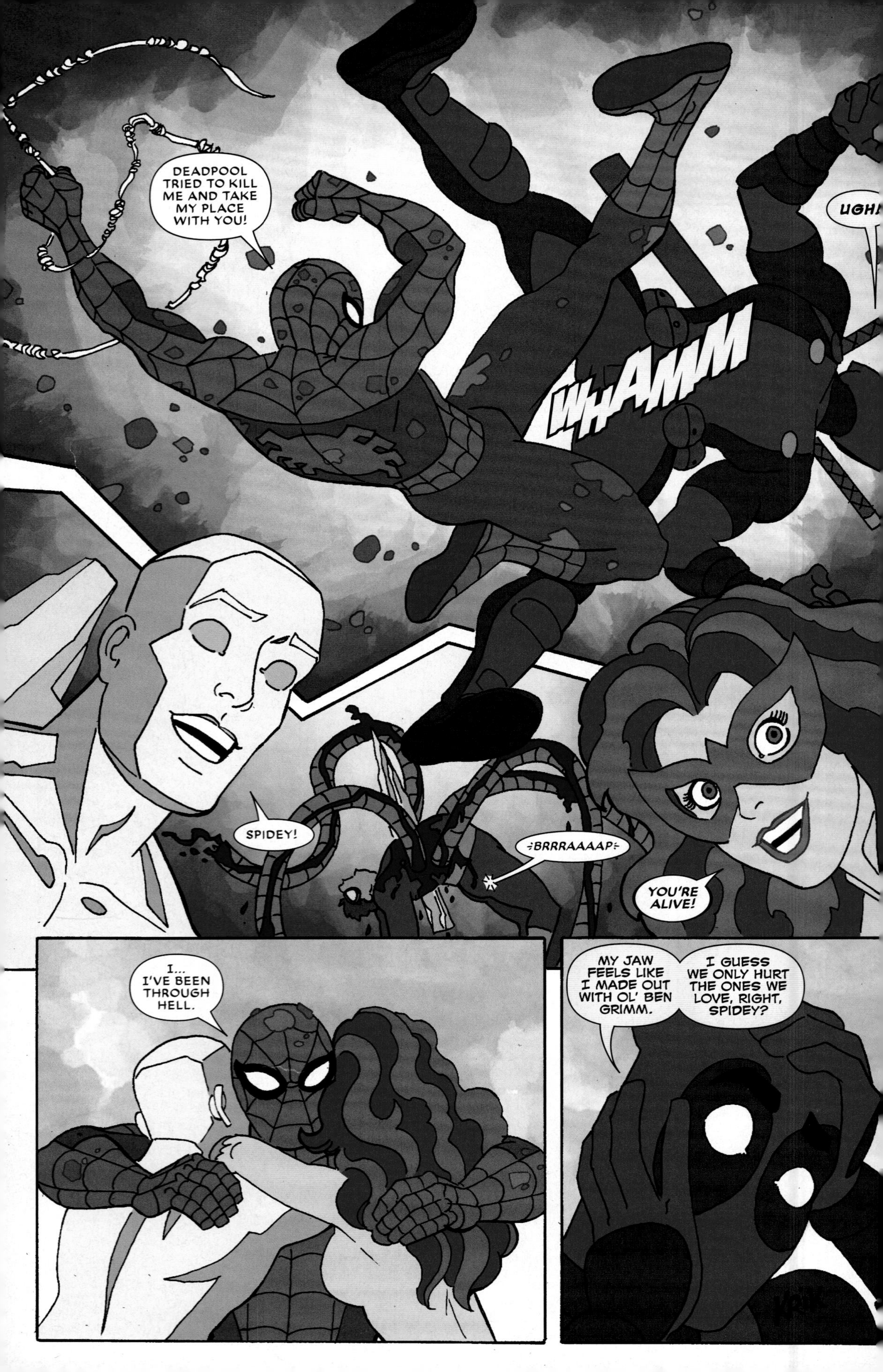
DEADPOOL TRIED TO KILL ME AND TAKE MY PLACE WITH YOU!
UGH
WHAMM
SPIDEY!
BRRRAAAAP
YOU'RE ALIVE!
I... I'VE BEEN THROUGH HELL.
MY JAW FEELS LIKE I MADE OUT WITH OL' BEN GRIMM.
I GUESS WE ONLY HURT THE ONES WE LOVE, RIGHT, SPIDEY?

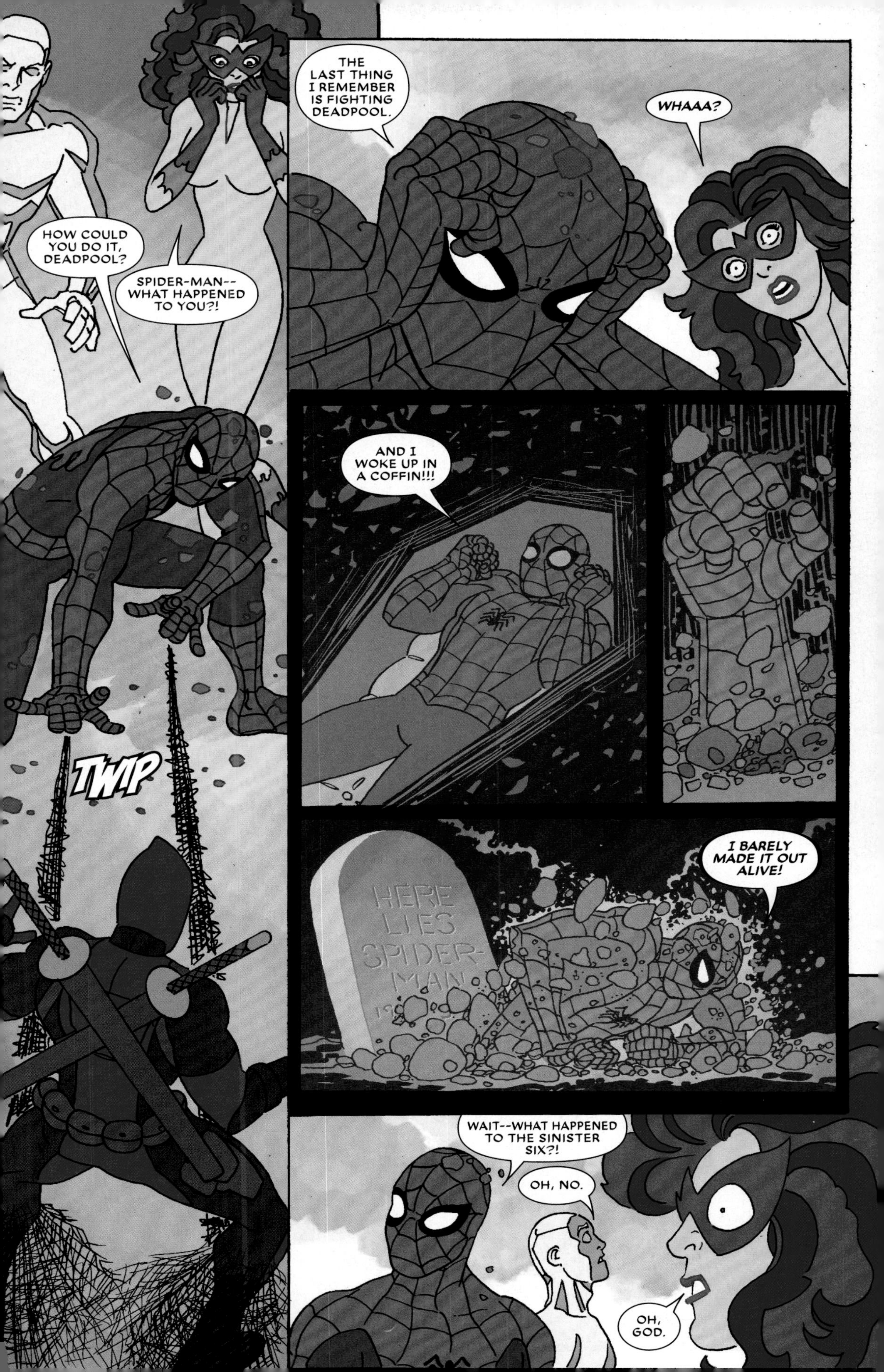
HOW COULD YOU DO IT, DEADPOOL?
SPIDER-MAN-- WHAT HAPPENED TO YOU?!
TWIP
THE LAST THING I REMEMBER IS FIGHTING DEADPOOL.
WHAAA?
AND I WOKE UP IN A COFFIN!!!
HERE LIES SPIDER-MAN
I BARELY MADE IT OUT ALIVE!
WAIT--WHAT HAPPENED TO THE SINISTER SIX?!
OH, NO.
OH, GOD.

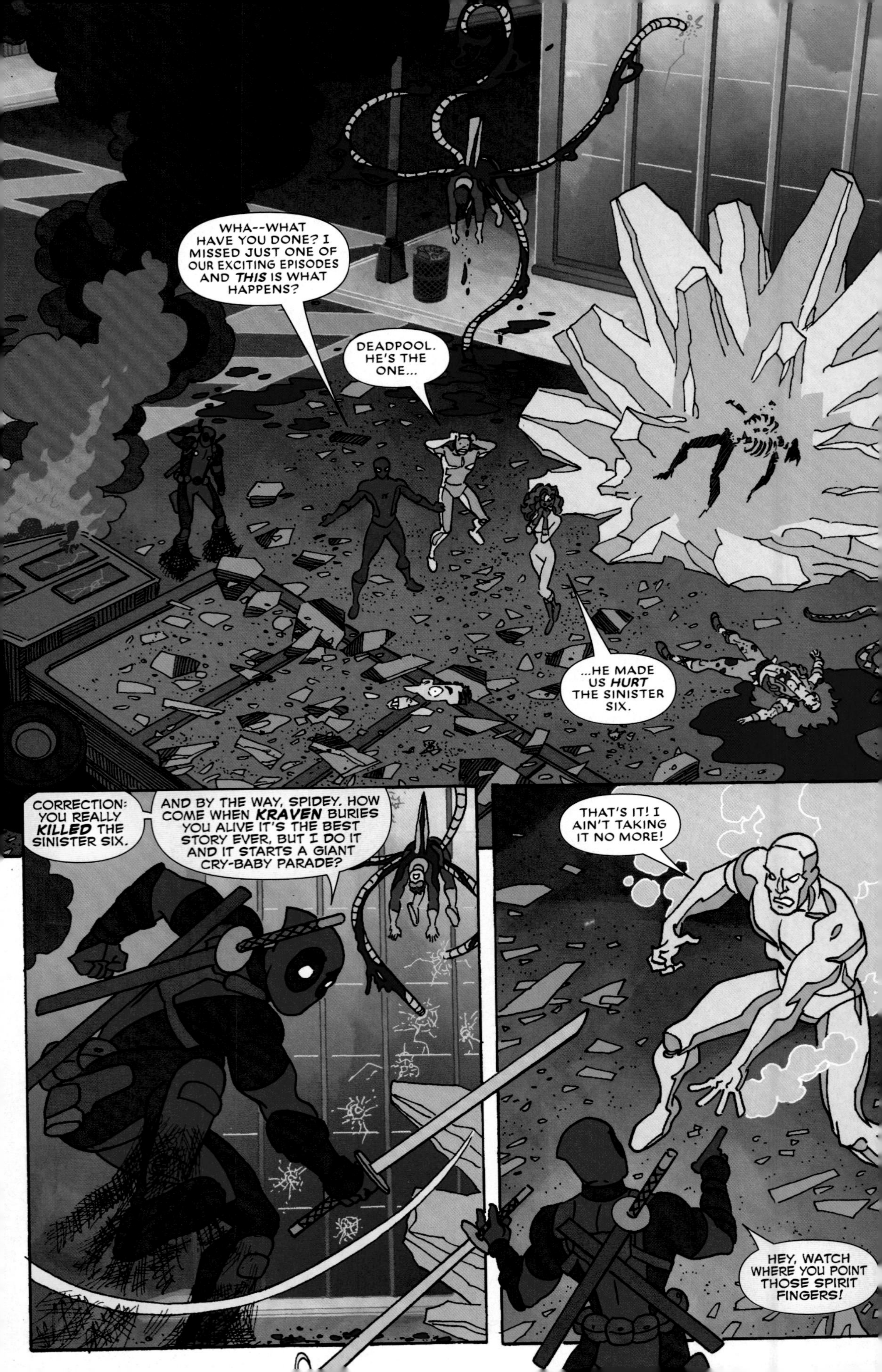
WHA--WHAT HAVE YOU DONE? I MISSED JUST ONE OF OUR EXCITING EPISODES AND *THIS* IS WHAT HAPPENS?
DEADPOOL. HE'S THE ONE...
...HE MADE US *HURT* THE SINISTER SIX.
CORRECTION: YOU REALLY ***KILLED*** THE SINISTER SIX.
AND BY THE WAY, SPIDEY. HOW COME WHEN ***KRAVEN*** BURIES YOU ALIVE IT'S THE BEST STORY EVER, BUT I DO IT AND IT STARTS A GIANT CRY-BABY PARADE?
THAT'S IT! I AIN'T TAKING IT NO MORE!
HEY, WATCH WHERE YOU POINT THOSE SPIRIT FINGERS!

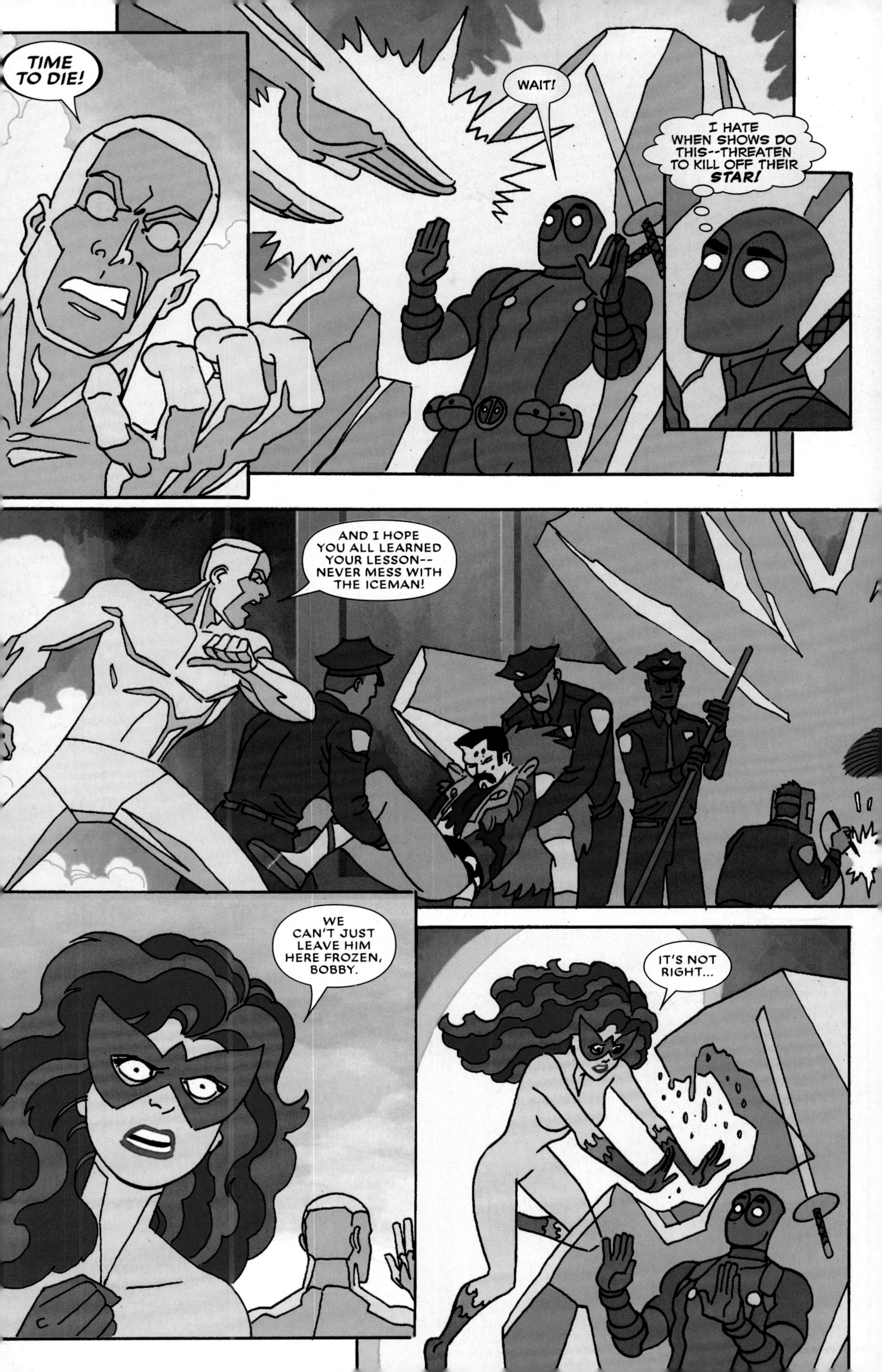
TIME TO DIE!
WAIT!
I HATE WHEN SHOWS DO THIS--THREATEN TO KILL OFF THEIR STAR!
AND I HOPE YOU ALL LEARNED YOUR LESSON-- NEVER MESS WITH THE ICEMAN!
WE CAN'T JUST LEAVE HIM HERE FROZEN, BOBBY.
IT'S NOT RIGHT...

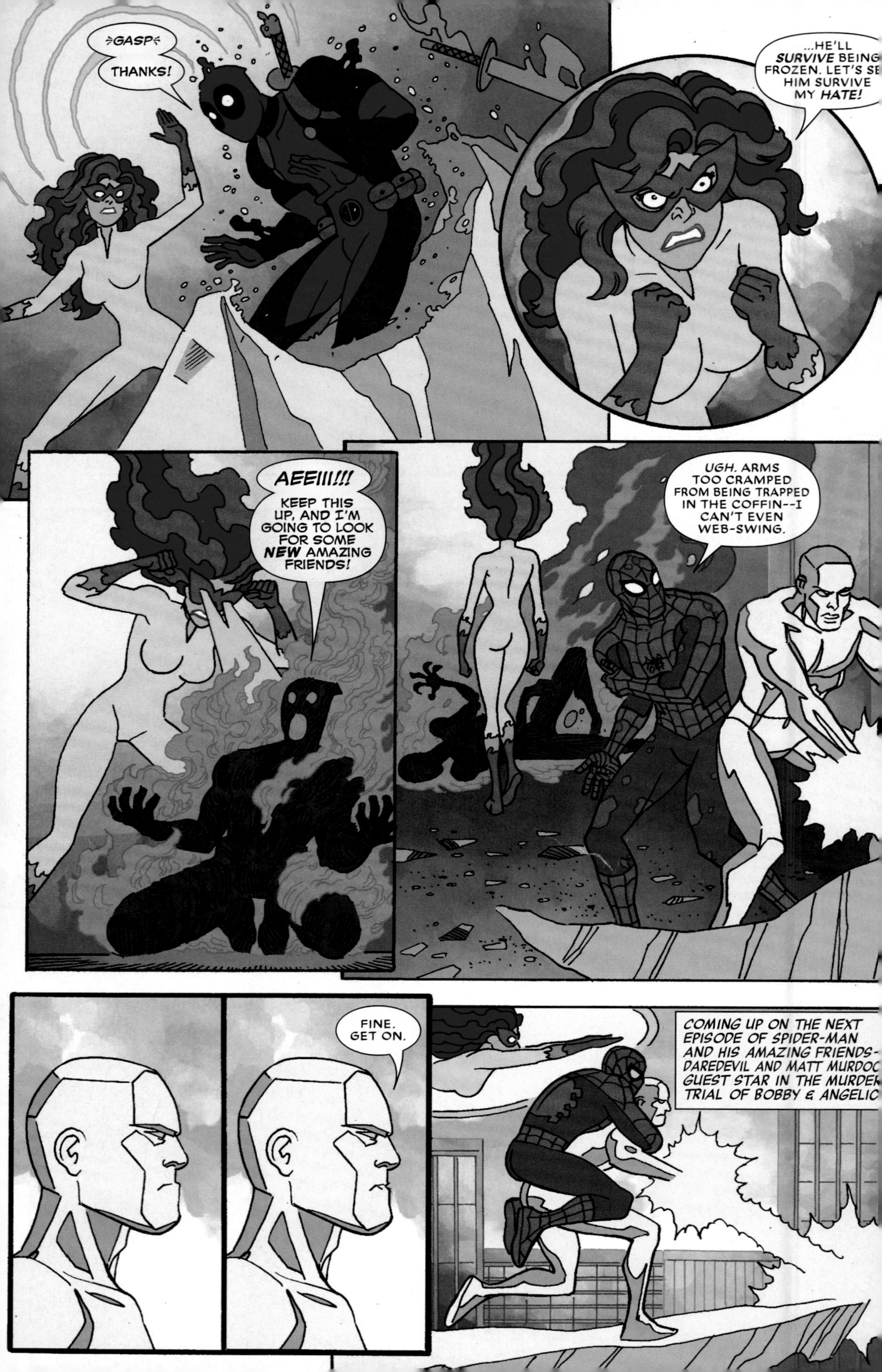

GASP
THANKS!
...HE'LL SURVIVE BEING FROZEN. LET'S SE HIM SURVIVE MY HATE!
AEEIIII!!!
KEEP THIS UP, AND I'M GOING TO LOOK FOR SOME NEW AMAZING FRIENDS!
UGH. ARMS TOO CRAMPED FROM BEING TRAPPED IN THE COFFIN--I CAN'T EVEN WEB-SWING.
FINE. GET ON.
COMING UP ON THE NEXT EPISODE OF SPIDER-MAN AND HIS AMAZING FRIENDS- DAREDEVIL AND MATT MURDOC GUEST STAR IN THE MURDER TRIAL OF BOBBY & ANGELIC

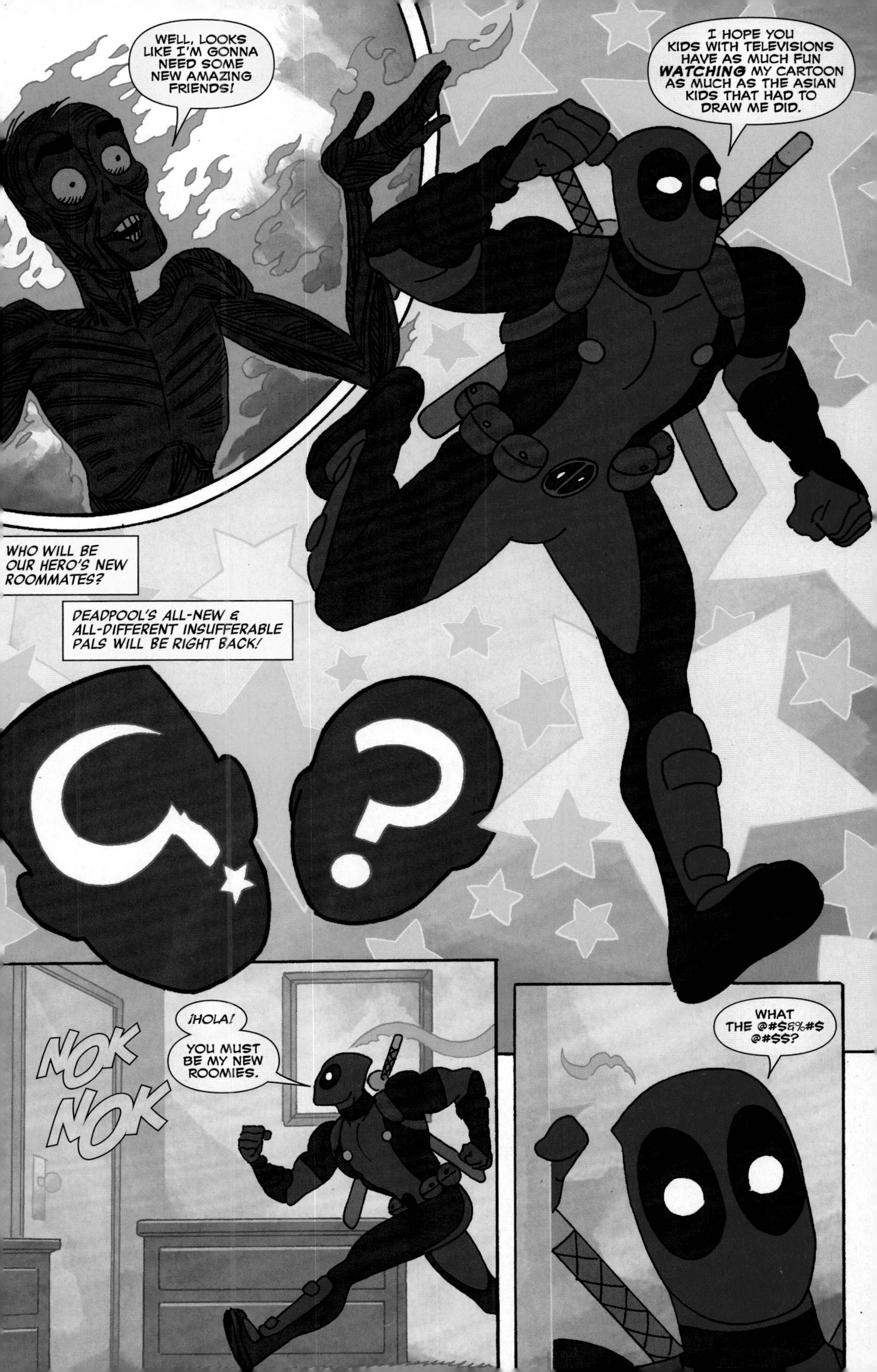
WELL, LOOKS LIKE I'M GONNA NEED SOME NEW AMAZING FRIENDS!
I HOPE YOU KIDS WITH TELEVISIONS HAVE AS MUCH FUN WATCHING MY CARTOON AS MUCH AS THE ASIAN KIDS THAT HAD TO DRAW ME DID.
WHO WILL BE OUR HERO'S NEW ROOMMATES?
DEADPOOL'S ALL-NEW & ALL-DIFFERENT INSUFFERABLE PALS WILL BE RIGHT BACK!
NOK NOK
¡HOLA!
YOU MUST BE MY NEW ROOMIES.
WHAT THE @#$&%#$ @#$$?

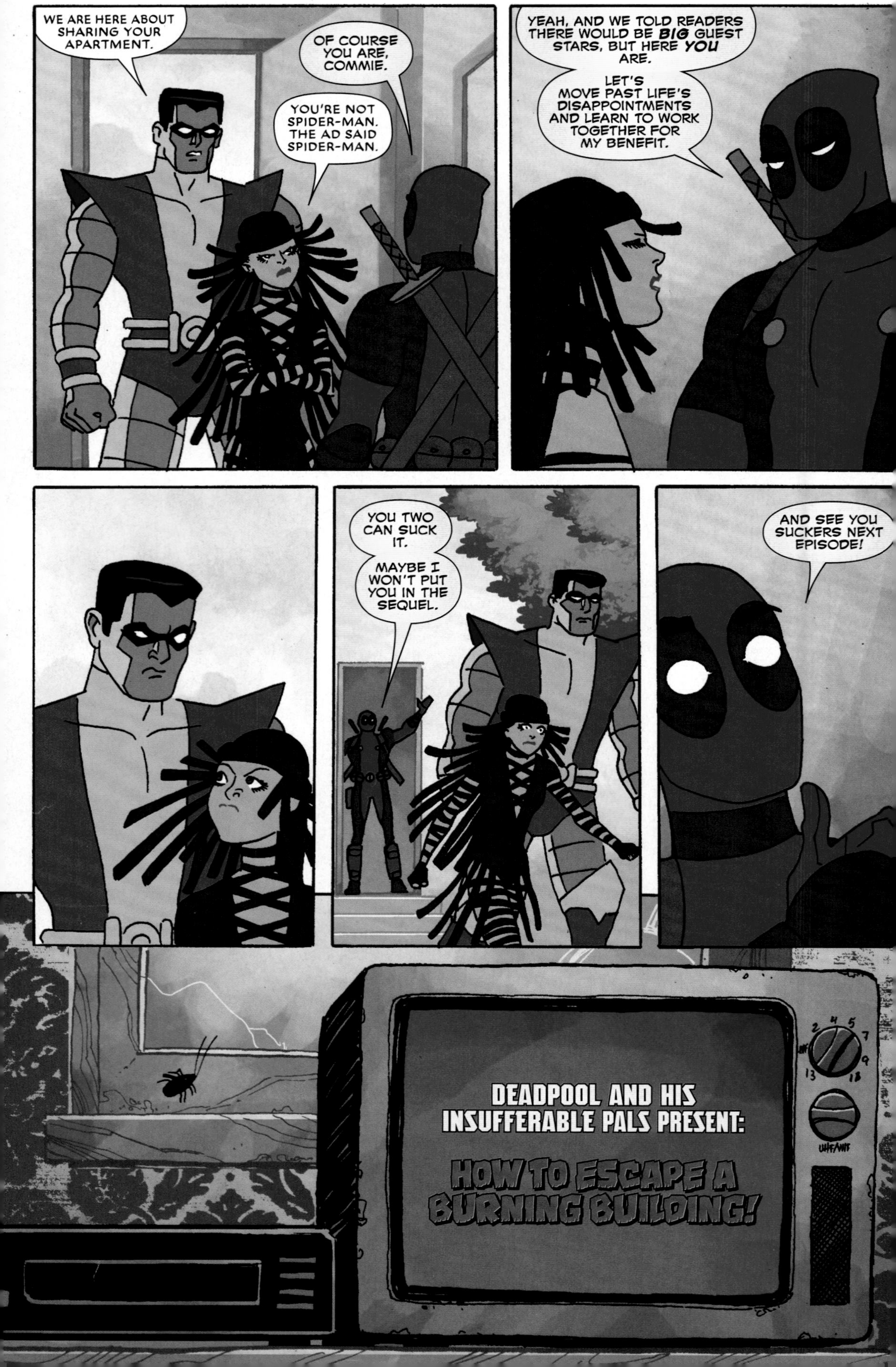
WE ARE HERE ABOUT SHARING YOUR APARTMENT.
OF COURSE YOU ARE, COMMIE.
YOU'RE NOT SPIDER-MAN. THE AD SAID SPIDER-MAN.
YEAH, AND WE TOLD READERS THERE WOULD BE BIG GUEST STARS, BUT HERE YOU ARE.
LET'S MOVE PAST LIFE'S DISAPPOINTMENTS AND LEARN TO WORK TOGETHER FOR MY BENEFIT.
YOU TWO CAN SUCK IT.
MAYBE I WON'T PUT YOU IN THE SEQUEL.
AND SEE YOU SUCKERS NEXT EPISODE!
DEADPOOL AND HIS INSUFFERABLE PALS PRESENT:
HOW TO ESCAPE A BURNING BUILDING!

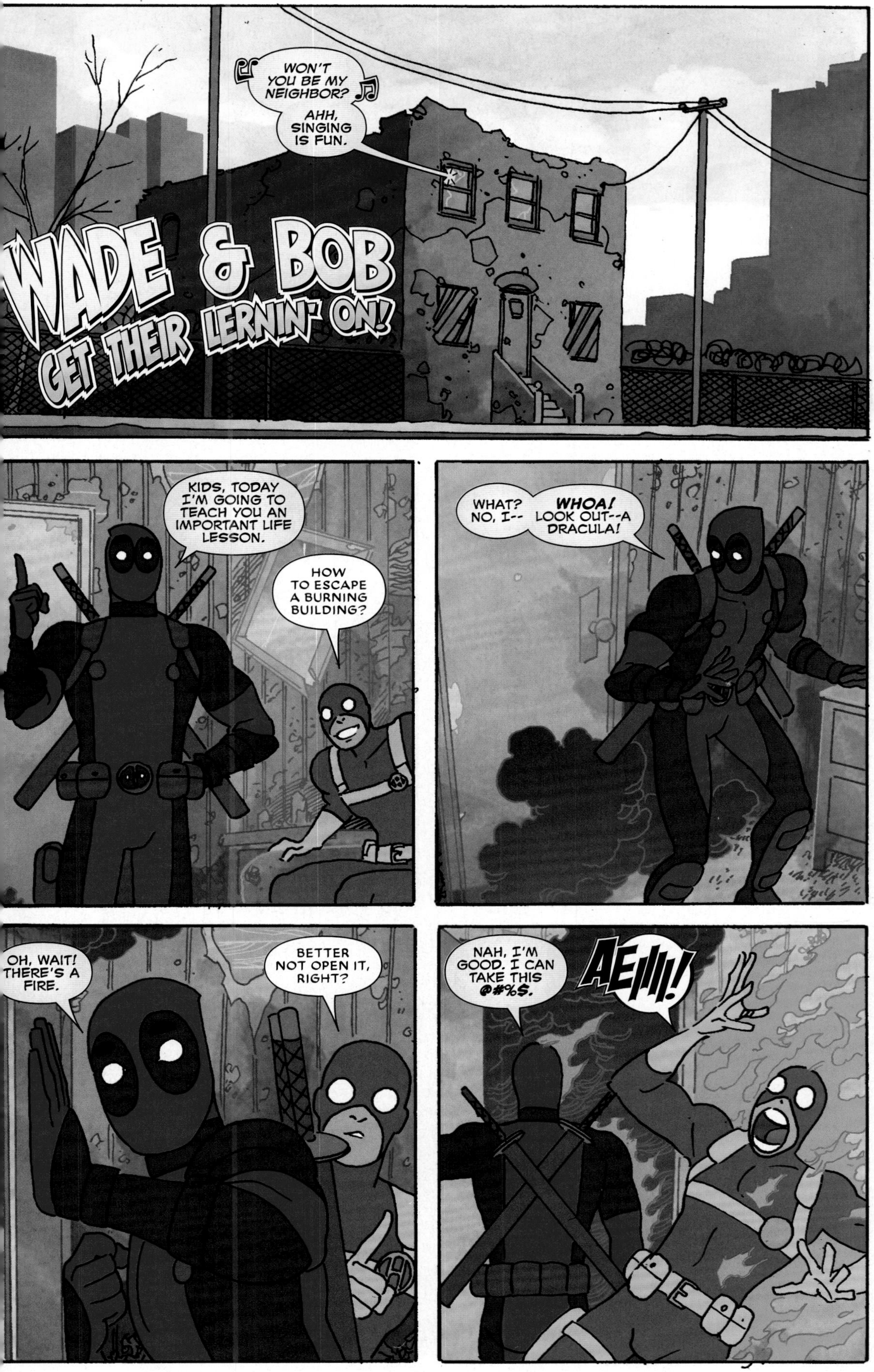

WON'T YOU BE MY NEIGHBOR?
AHH, SINGING IS FUN.
WADE & BOB GET THEIR LERNIN' ON!
KIDS, TODAY I'M GOING TO TEACH YOU AN IMPORTANT LIFE LESSON.
HOW TO ESCAPE A BURNING BUILDING?
WHAT? NO, I--
WHOA! LOOK OUT--A DRACULA!
OH, WAIT! THERE'S A FIRE.
BETTER NOT OPEN IT, RIGHT?
NAH, I'M GOOD. I CAN TAKE THIS @#%$.
AEIIII!

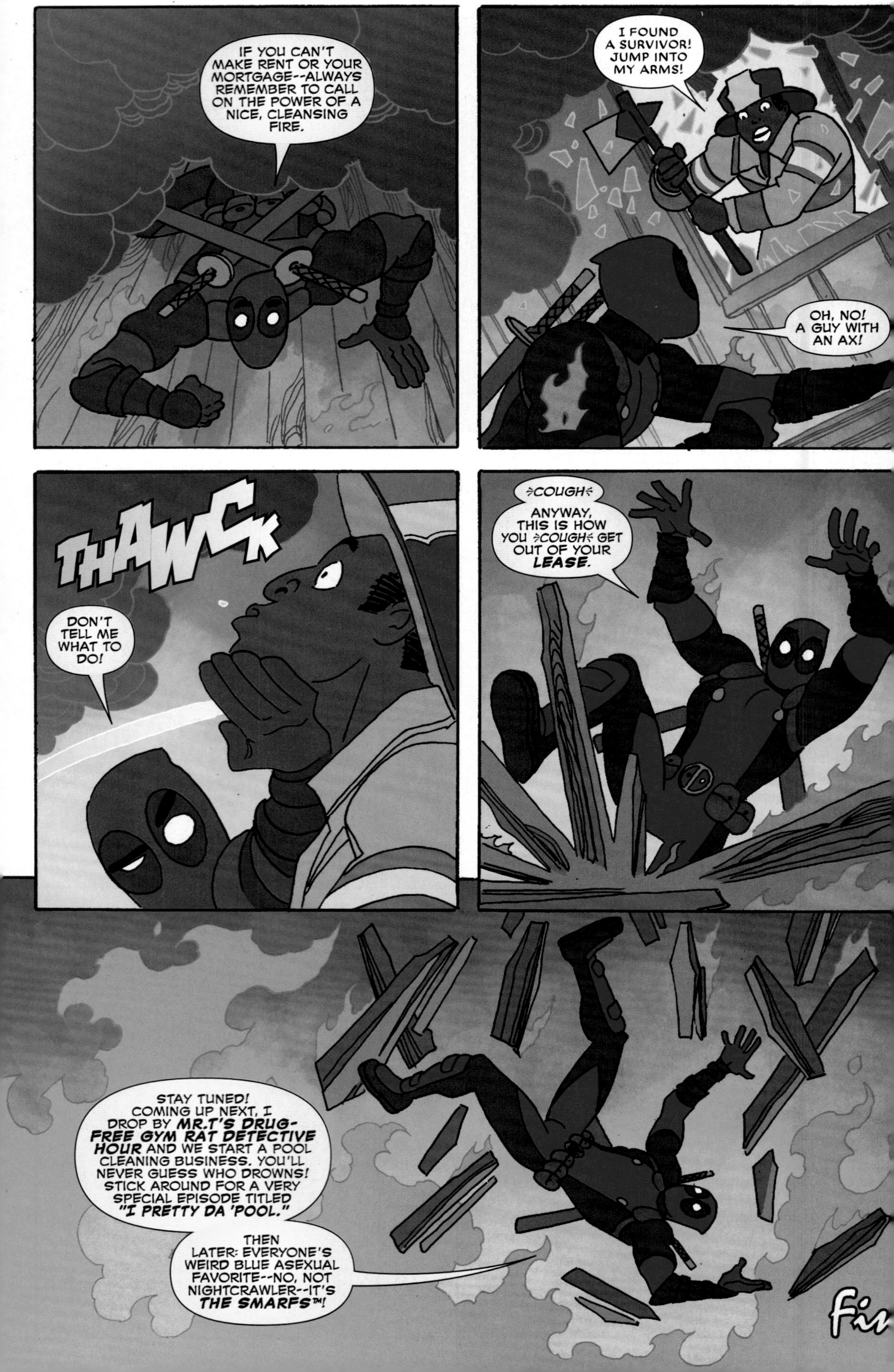
IF YOU CAN'T MAKE RENT OR YOUR MORTGAGE--ALWAYS REMEMBER TO CALL ON THE POWER OF A NICE, CLEANSING FIRE.
I FOUND A SURVIVOR! JUMP INTO MY ARMS!
OH, NO! A GUY WITH AN AX!
THAWCK
DON'T TELL ME WHAT TO DO!
COUGH
ANYWAY, THIS IS HOW YOU COUGH GET OUT OF YOUR LEASE.
STAY TUNED! COMING UP NEXT, I DROP BY MR.T'S DRUG-FREE GYM RAT DETECTIVE HOUR AND WE START A POOL CLEANING BUSINESS. YOU'LL NEVER GUESS WHO DROWNS! STICK AROUND FOR A VERY SPECIAL EPISODE TITLED "I PRETTY DA 'POOL."
THEN LATER: EVERYONE'S WEIRD BLUE ASEXUAL FAVORITE--NO, NOT NIGHTCRAWLER--IT'S THE SMARFS™!

venger...Assassin...Superstar...Smelly person...Possibly the world's most skilled mercenary, definitely he world's most annoying, Wade Wilson was chosen for a top-secret government program that gave im a healing factor allowing him to heal from any wound. Somehow, despite making his money as a un for hire, Wade has become one of the most beloved "heroes" in the world. Call him the Merc with the Mouth...call him the Regeneratin' Degenerate...call him...

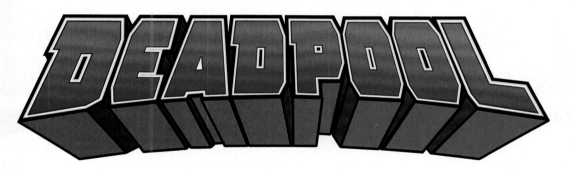

DEADPOOL

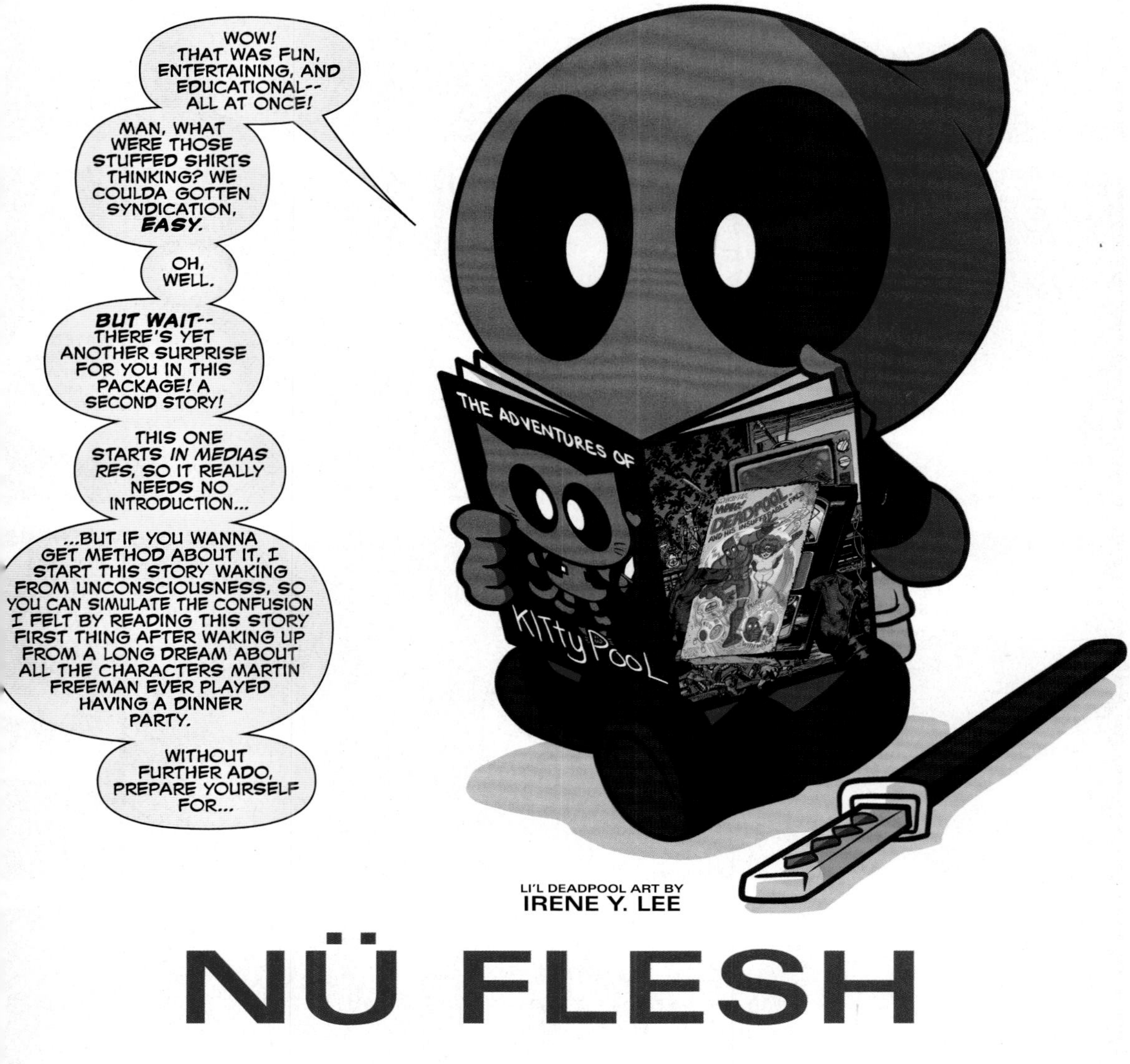
WOW! THAT WAS FUN, ENTERTAINING, AND EDUCATIONAL-- ALL AT ONCE!
MAN, WHAT WERE THOSE STUFFED SHIRTS THINKING? WE COULDA GOTTEN SYNDICATION, *EASY*.
OH, WELL.
BUT WAIT-- THERE'S YET ANOTHER SURPRISE FOR YOU IN THIS PACKAGE! A SECOND STORY!
THIS ONE STARTS *IN MEDIAS RES*, SO IT REALLY NEEDS NO INTRODUCTION...
...BUT IF YOU WANNA GET METHOD ABOUT IT, I START THIS STORY WAKING FROM UNCONSCIOUSNESS, SO YOU CAN SIMULATE THE CONFUSION I FELT BY READING THIS STORY FIRST THING AFTER WAKING UP FROM A LONG DREAM ABOUT ALL THE CHARACTERS MARTIN FREEMAN EVER PLAYED HAVING A DINNER PARTY.
WITHOUT FURTHER ADO, PREPARE YOURSELF FOR...
THE ADVENTURES OF
KittyPooL
DEADPOOL

LI'L DEADPOOL ART BY
IRENE Y. LEE

NÜ FLESH

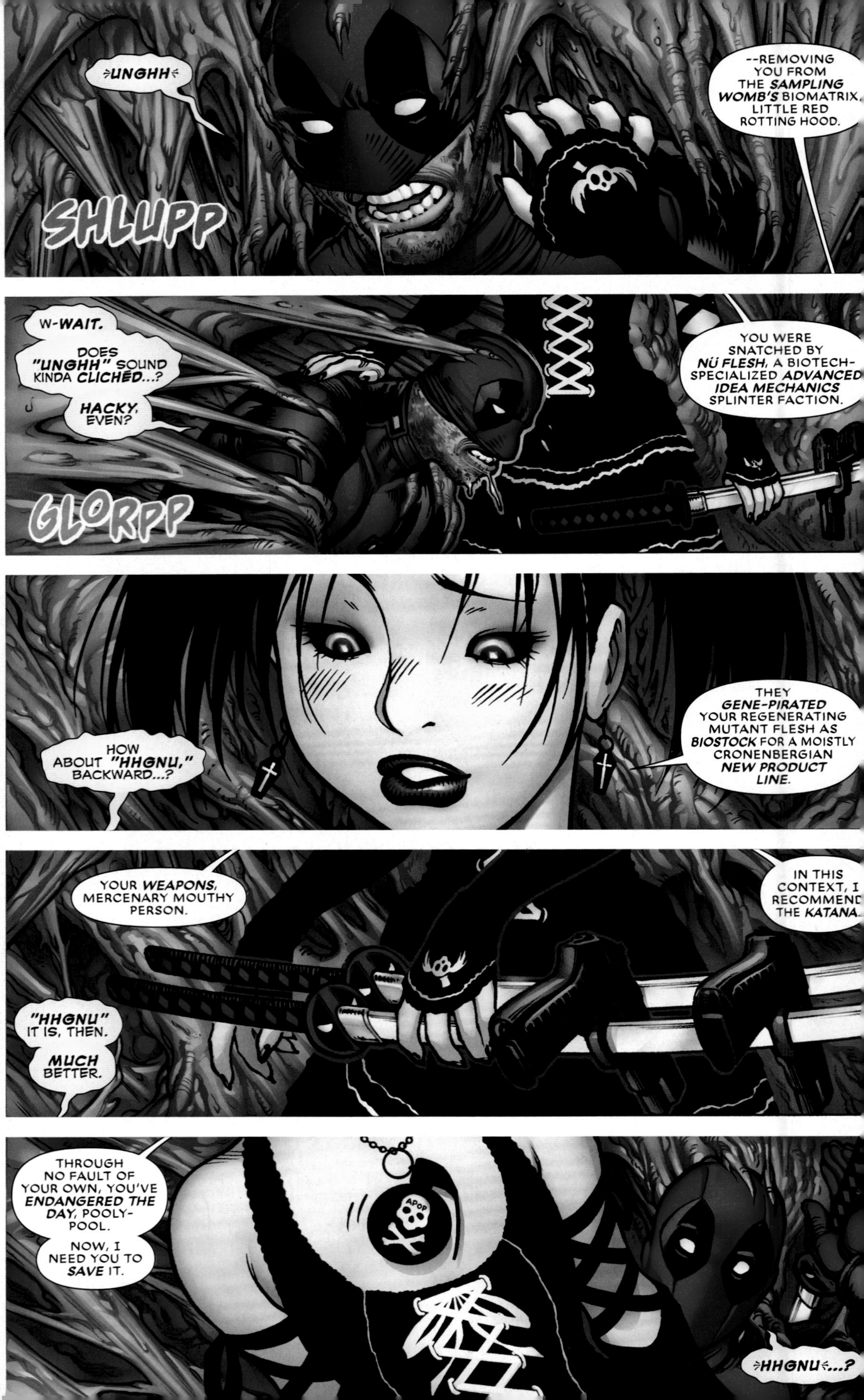

>UNGHH<
--REMOVING YOU FROM THE SAMPLING WOMB'S BIOMATRIX, LITTLE RED ROTTING HOOD.
SHLUPP
W-WAIT.
DOES "UNGHH" SOUND KINDA CLICHÉD...?
HACKY, EVEN?
YOU WERE SNATCHED BY NÜ FLESH, A BIOTECH-SPECIALIZED ADVANCED IDEA MECHANICS SPLINTER FACTION.
GLORPP
HOW ABOUT "HHGNU," BACKWARD...?
THEY GENE-PIRATED YOUR REGENERATING MUTANT FLESH AS BIOSTOCK FOR A MOISTLY CRONENBERGIAN NEW PRODUCT LINE.
YOUR WEAPONS, MERCENARY MOUTHY PERSON.
IN THIS CONTEXT, I RECOMMEND THE KATANA.
"HHGNU" IT IS, THEN.
MUCH BETTER.
THROUGH NO FAULT OF YOUR OWN, YOU'VE ENDANGERED THE DAY, POOLY-POOL.
NOW, I NEED YOU TO SAVE IT.
APOP
>HHGNU<...?

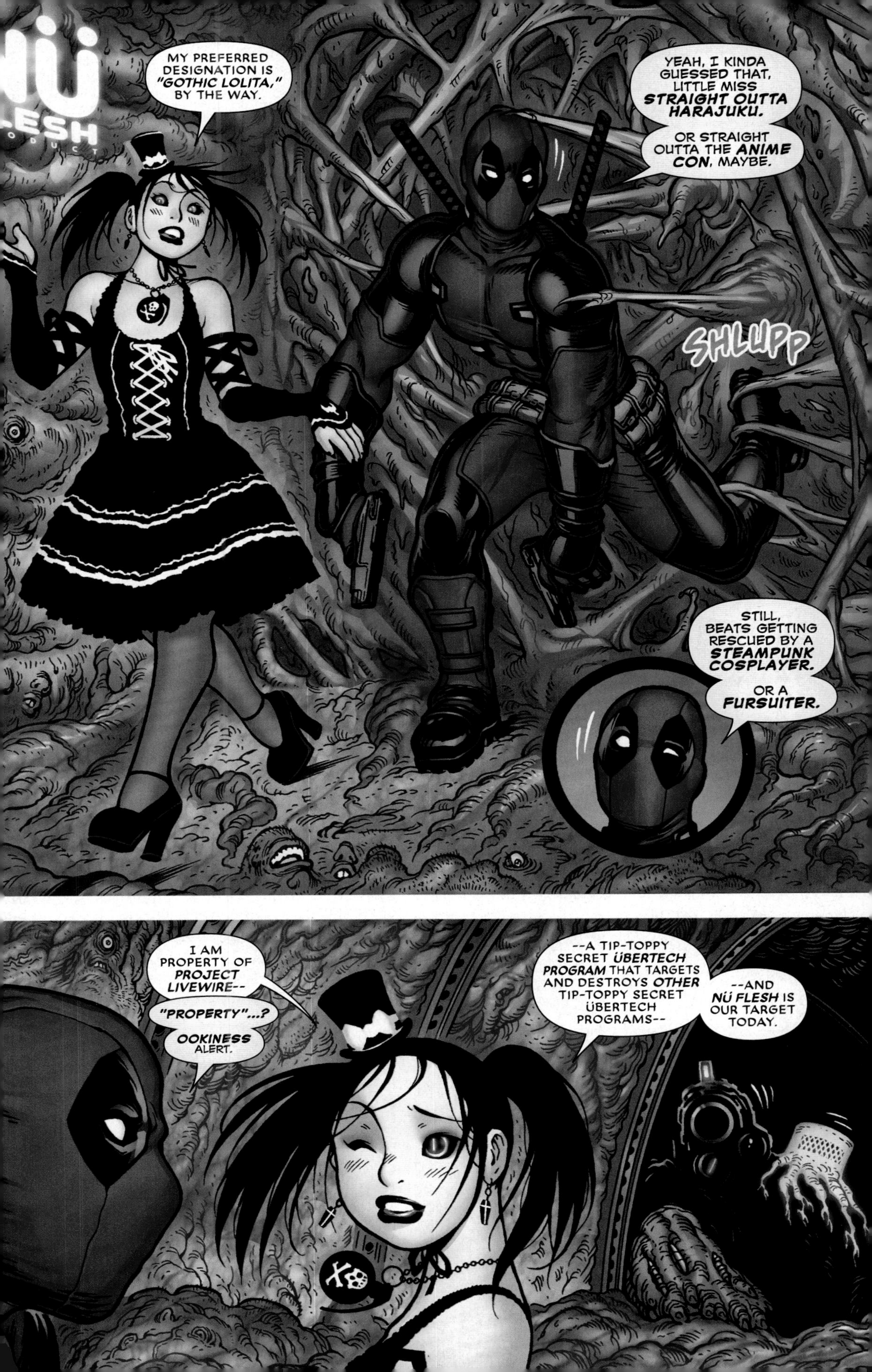

MY PREFERRED DESIGNATION IS "GOTHIC LOLITA," BY THE WAY.
YEAH, I KINDA GUESSED THAT, LITTLE MISS STRAIGHT OUTTA HARAJUKU.
OR STRAIGHT OUTTA THE ANIME CON, MAYBE.
SHLUPP
STILL, BEATS GETTING RESCUED BY A STEAMPUNK COSPLAYER.
OR A FURSUITER.
I AM PROPERTY OF PROJECT LIVEWIRE--
"PROPERTY"...?
OOKINESS ALERT.
--A TIP-TOPPY SECRET ÜBERTECH PROGRAM THAT TARGETS AND DESTROYS OTHER TIP-TOPPY SECRET ÜBERTECH PROGRAMS--
--AND NÜ FLESH IS OUR TARGET TODAY.

NÜ FLESH?

!

LOOK OUT, DARK PETTICOAT!

HOSTILE HATBOX AHOY!

WAIT, DON'T--

NÜ FLESH

I WAS HOPING TO USE YOUR *BIOSIGNATURE* TO TIPPY-TOE PAST THESE *SECURITY BIODRONES*, BUT...

EAT *HOLLOW-POINT*, YOU UNHOLY *ABOMINATION* OF THE NON-*HULK*-RELATED VARIETY!

BKAM

BKAM

BKAM

BKAM

BKAM

BKAM SPAK SPA

HEY!

HEY!

...NO TIPPY-TOEING *TODAY*, APPARENTLY.

BKAM

BKAM

SPAK

SPAK

NÜ

ARE YOU USING MY OWN PIRATED HEALING FACTOR *AGAINST* ME, A.I.M.HOLE?

SHLUPP

BLORPP

FLESH?

BKAM BKAM BKAM

MY *PETARD'S* FEELIN' SERIOUSLY *HOISTED!*

DRAMATIC SIGH.

AND MY *PETARD HATES* THAT!

KRKK

BKAM BKAM

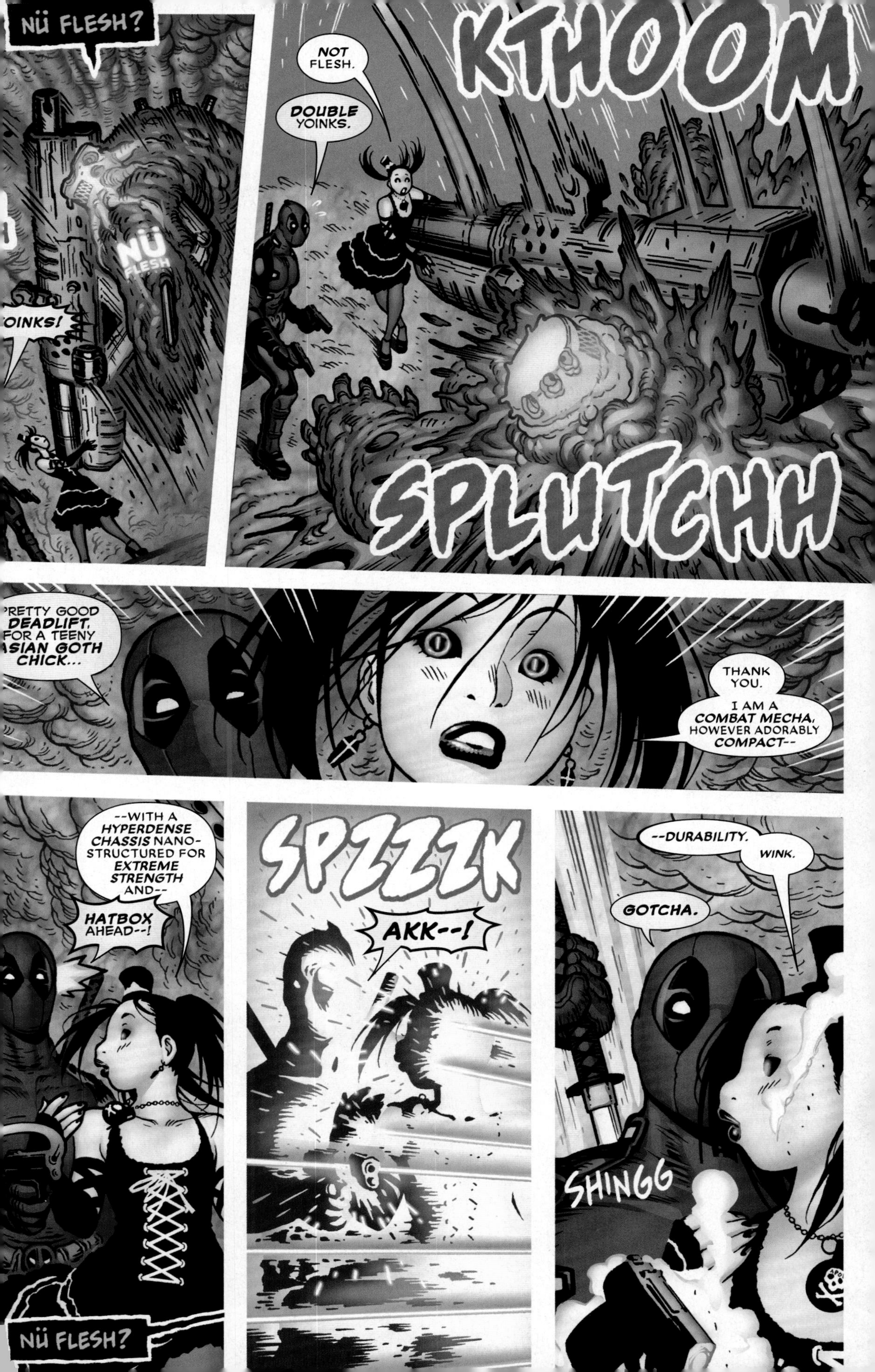
NÜ FLESH?
OINKS!
NÜ FLESH
NOT FLESH.
DOUBLE YOINKS.
KTHOOM
SPLUTCHH
PRETTY GOOD DEADLIFT, FOR A TEENY ASIAN GOTH CHICK...
THANK YOU.
I AM A COMBAT MECHA, HOWEVER ADORABLY COMPACT--
--WITH A HYPERDENSE CHASSIS NANO-STRUCTURED FOR EXTREME STRENGTH AND--
HATBOX AHEAD--!
NÜ FLESH?
SPZZZK
AKK--!
--DURABILITY.
WINK.
GOTCHA.
SHINGG

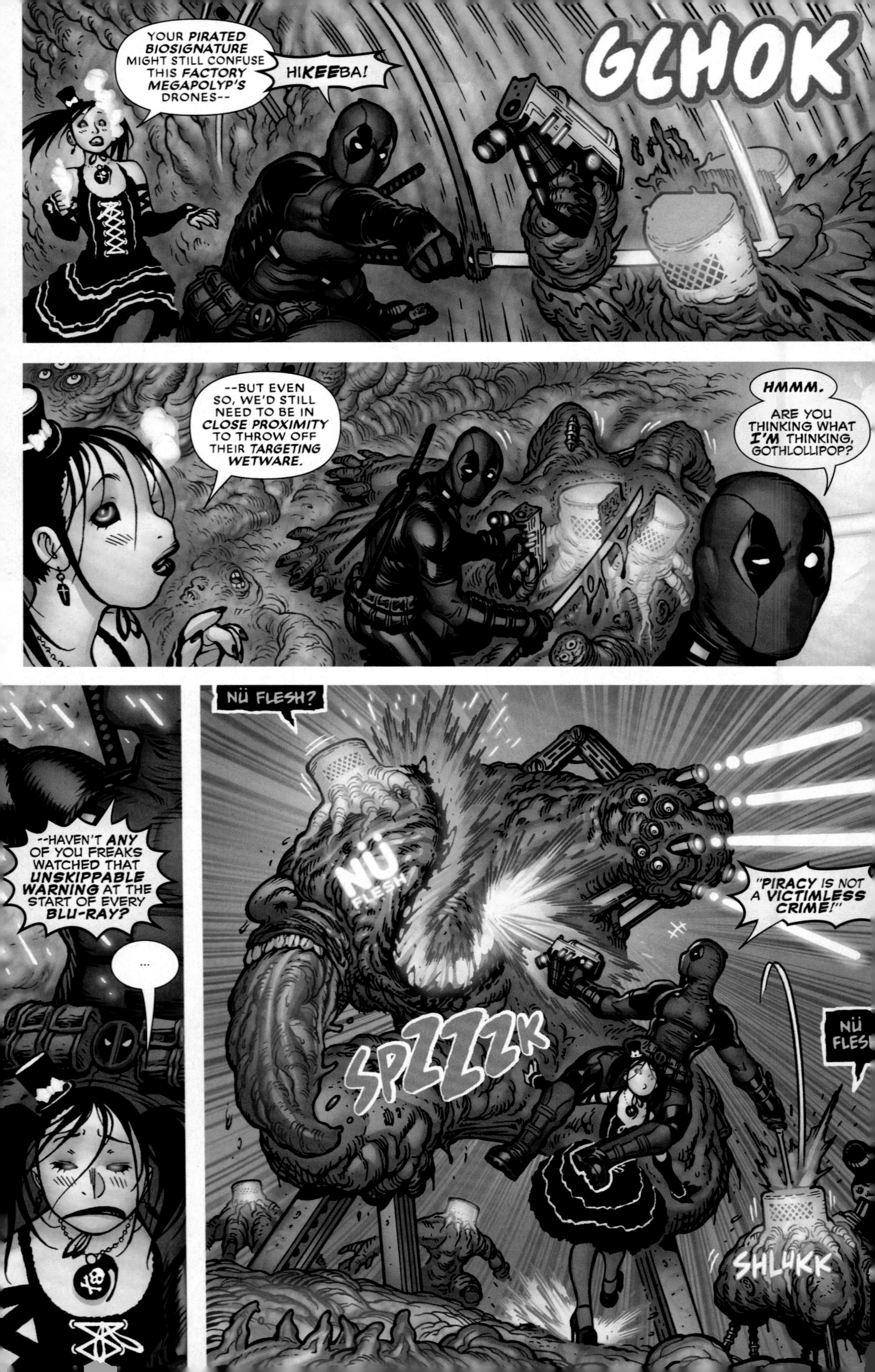
GLCHOK
YOUR PIRATED BIOSIGNATURE MIGHT STILL CONFUSE THIS FACTORY MEGAPOLYP'S DRONES--
HIKEEBA!
--BUT EVEN SO, WE'D STILL NEED TO BE IN CLOSE PROXIMITY TO THROW OFF THEIR TARGETING WETWARE.
HMMM.
ARE YOU THINKING WHAT I'M THINKING, GOTHLOLLIPOP?
NÜ FLESH?
--HAVEN'T ANY OF YOU FREAKS WATCHED THAT UNSKIPPABLE WARNING AT THE START OF EVERY BLU-RAY?
...
NÜ FLESH
"PIRACY IS NOT A VICTIMLESS CRIME!"
SPZZZZK
SHLUKK

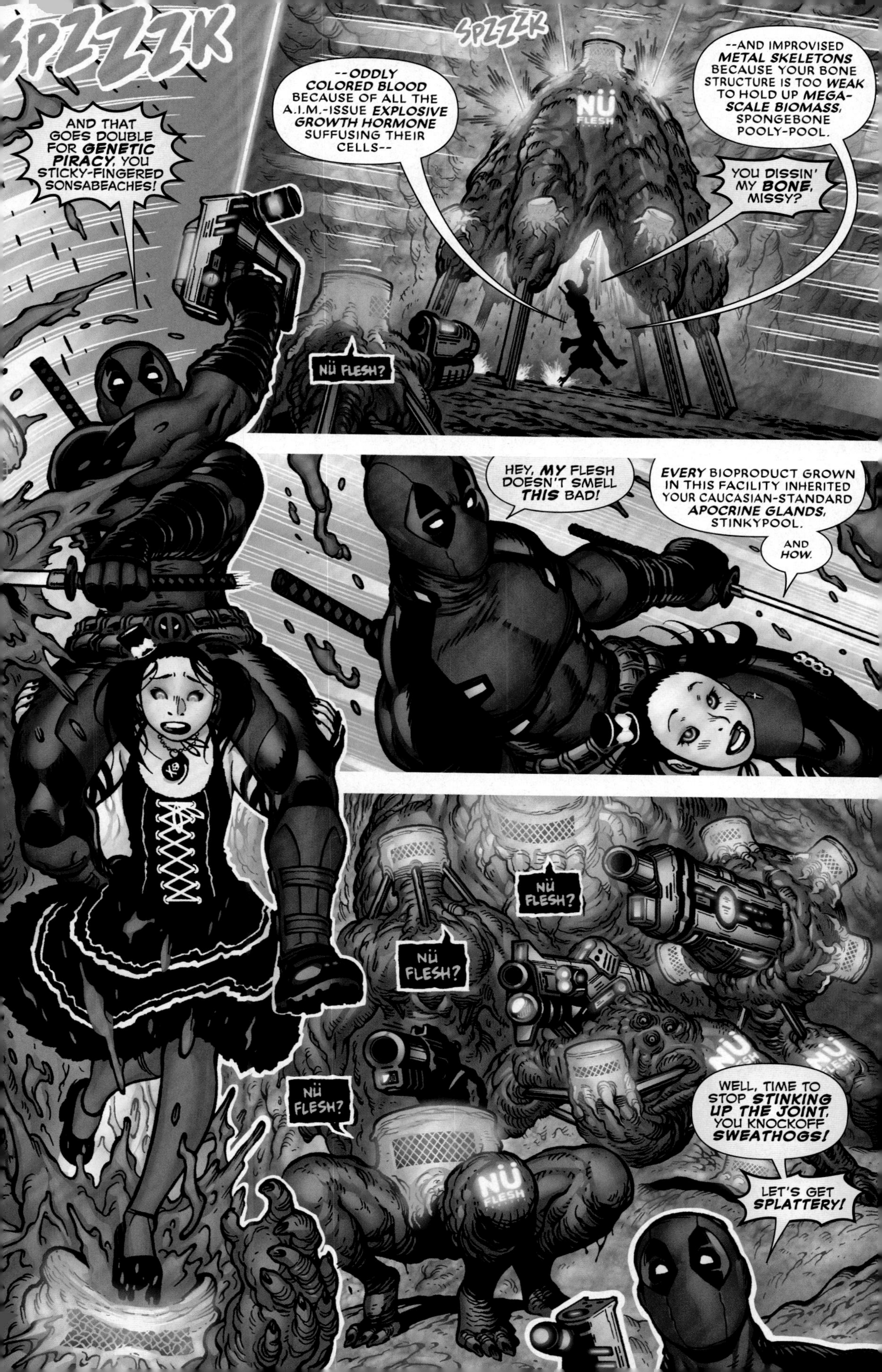
SPZZZK
AND THAT GOES DOUBLE FOR GENETIC PIRACY, YOU STICKY-FINGERED SONSABEACHES!
SPZZZK
--ODDLY COLORED BLOOD BECAUSE OF ALL THE A.I.M.-ISSUE EXPLOSIVE GROWTH HORMONE SUFFUSING THEIR CELLS--
--AND IMPROVISED METAL SKELETONS BECAUSE YOUR BONE STRUCTURE IS TOO WEAK TO HOLD UP MEGA-SCALE BIOMASS, SPONGEBONE POOLY-POOL.
YOU DISSIN' MY BONE, MISSY?
NÜ FLESH
NÜ FLESH?
HEY, MY FLESH DOESN'T SMELL THIS BAD!
EVERY BIOPRODUCT GROWN IN THIS FACILITY INHERITED YOUR CAUCASIAN-STANDARD APOCRINE GLANDS, STINKYPOOL.
AND HOW.
NÜ FLESH?
NÜ FLESH?
NÜ FLESH?
WELL, TIME TO STOP STINKING UP THE JOINT, YOU KNOCKOFF SWEATHOGS!
LET'S GET SPLATTERY!

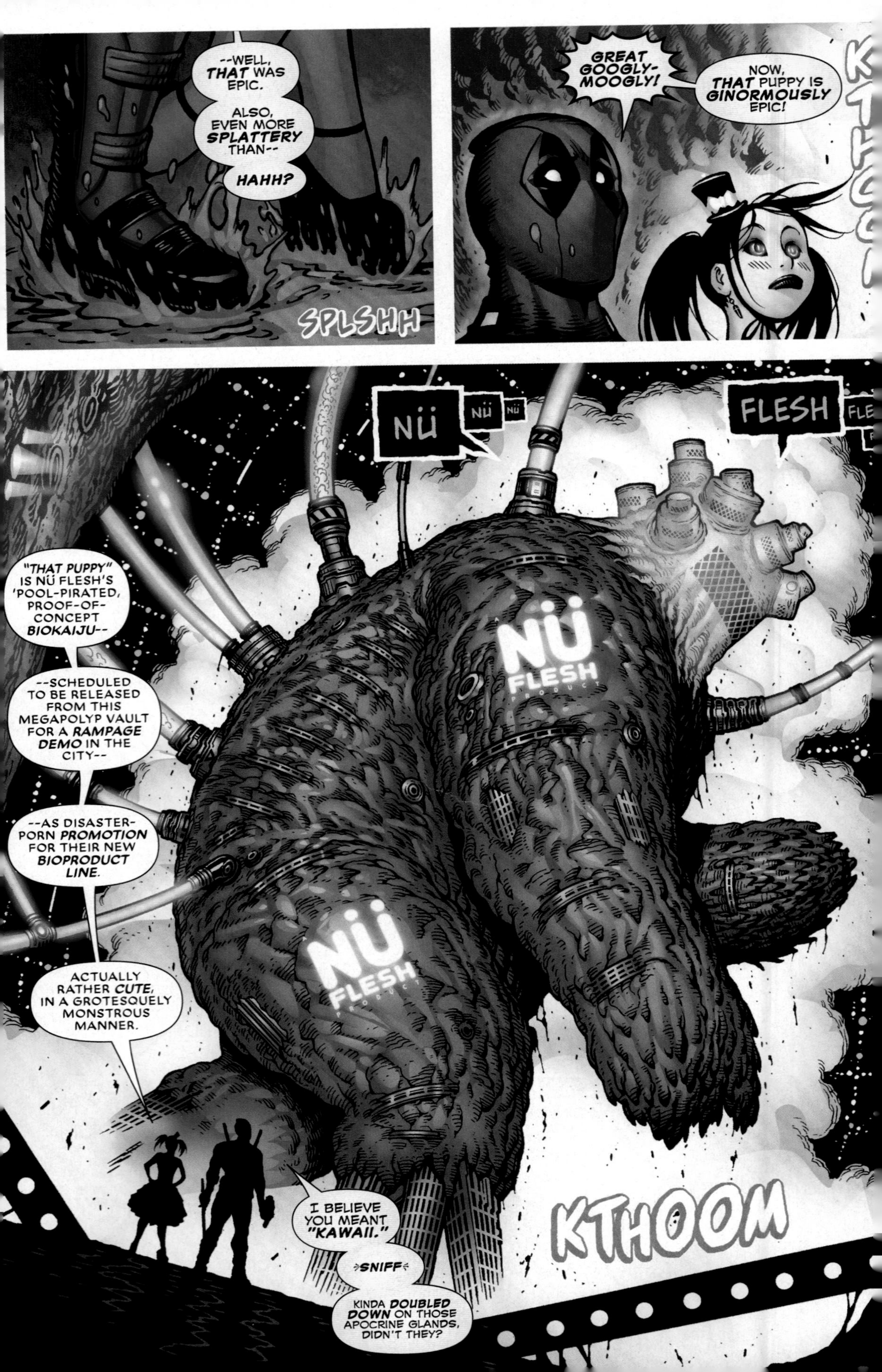
--WELL, THAT WAS EPIC.
ALSO, EVEN MORE SPLATTERY THAN--
HAHH?
SPLSHH
GREAT GOOGLY-MOOGLY!
NOW, THAT PUPPY IS GINORMOUSLY EPIC!
NÜ NÜ NÜ
FLESH
"THAT PUPPY" IS NÜ FLESH'S 'POOL-PIRATED, PROOF-OF-CONCEPT BIOKAIJU--
--SCHEDULED TO BE RELEASED FROM THIS MEGAPOLYP VAULT FOR A RAMPAGE DEMO IN THE CITY--
--AS DISASTER-PORN PROMOTION FOR THEIR NEW BIOPRODUCT LINE.
NÜ FLESH PRODUCT
NÜ FLESH PRODUCT
ACTUALLY RATHER CUTE, IN A GROTESQUELY MONSTROUS MANNER.
I BELIEVE YOU MEANT "KAWAII."
SNIFF
KINDA DOUBLED DOWN ON THOSE APOCRINE GLANDS, DIDN'T THEY?
KTHOOM

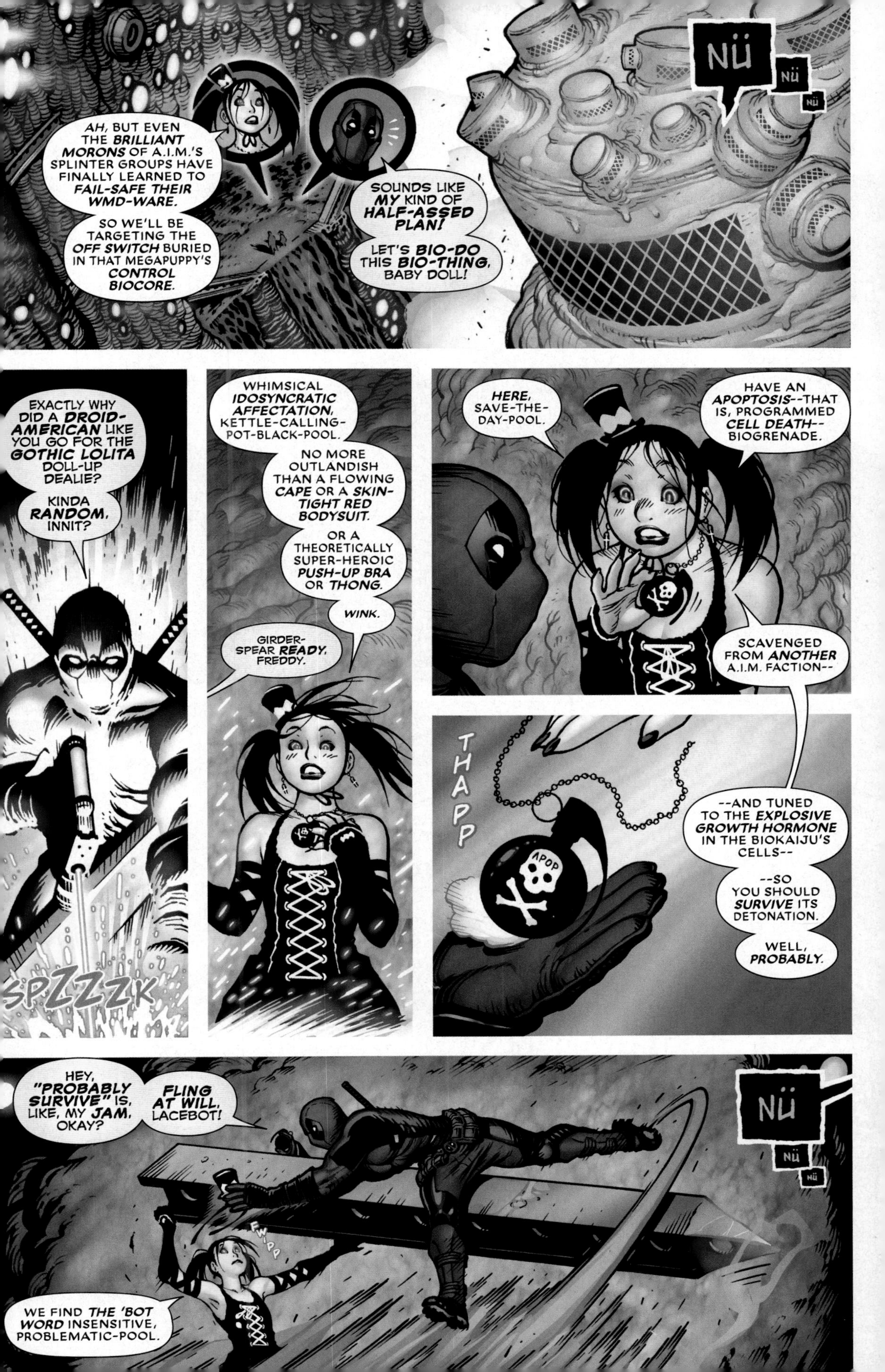
AH, BUT EVEN THE BRILLIANT MORONS OF A.I.M.'S SPLINTER GROUPS HAVE FINALLY LEARNED TO FAIL-SAFE THEIR WMD-WARE.
SO WE'LL BE TARGETING THE OFF SWITCH BURIED IN THAT MEGAPUPPY'S CONTROL BIOCORE.
SOUNDS LIKE MY KIND OF HALF-ASSED PLAN!
LET'S BIO-DO THIS BIO-THING, BABY DOLL!
NÜ
NÜ
NÜ
EXACTLY WHY DID A DROID-AMERICAN LIKE YOU GO FOR THE GOTHIC LOLITA DOLL-UP DEALIE?
KINDA RANDOM, INNIT?
SPZZZK
WHIMSICAL IDOSYNCRATIC AFFECTATION, KETTLE-CALLING-POT-BLACK-POOL.
NO MORE OUTLANDISH THAN A FLOWING CAPE OR A SKIN-TIGHT RED BODYSUIT.
OR A THEORETICALLY SUPER-HEROIC PUSH-UP BRA OR THONG.
WINK.
GIRDER-SPEAR READY, FREDDY.
HERE, SAVE-THE-DAY-POOL.
HAVE AN APOPTOSIS--THAT IS, PROGRAMMED CELL DEATH--BIOGRENADE.
SCAVENGED FROM ANOTHER A.I.M. FACTION--
THAPP
APOP
--AND TUNED TO THE EXPLOSIVE GROWTH HORMONE IN THE BIOKAIJU'S CELLS--
--SO YOU SHOULD SURVIVE ITS DETONATION.
WELL, PROBABLY.
HEY, "PROBABLY SURVIVE" IS, LIKE, MY JAM, OKAY?
FLING AT WILL, LACEBOT!
NÜ
NÜ
NÜ
FWIPP
WE FIND THE 'BOT WORD INSENSITIVE, PROBLEMATIC-POOL.

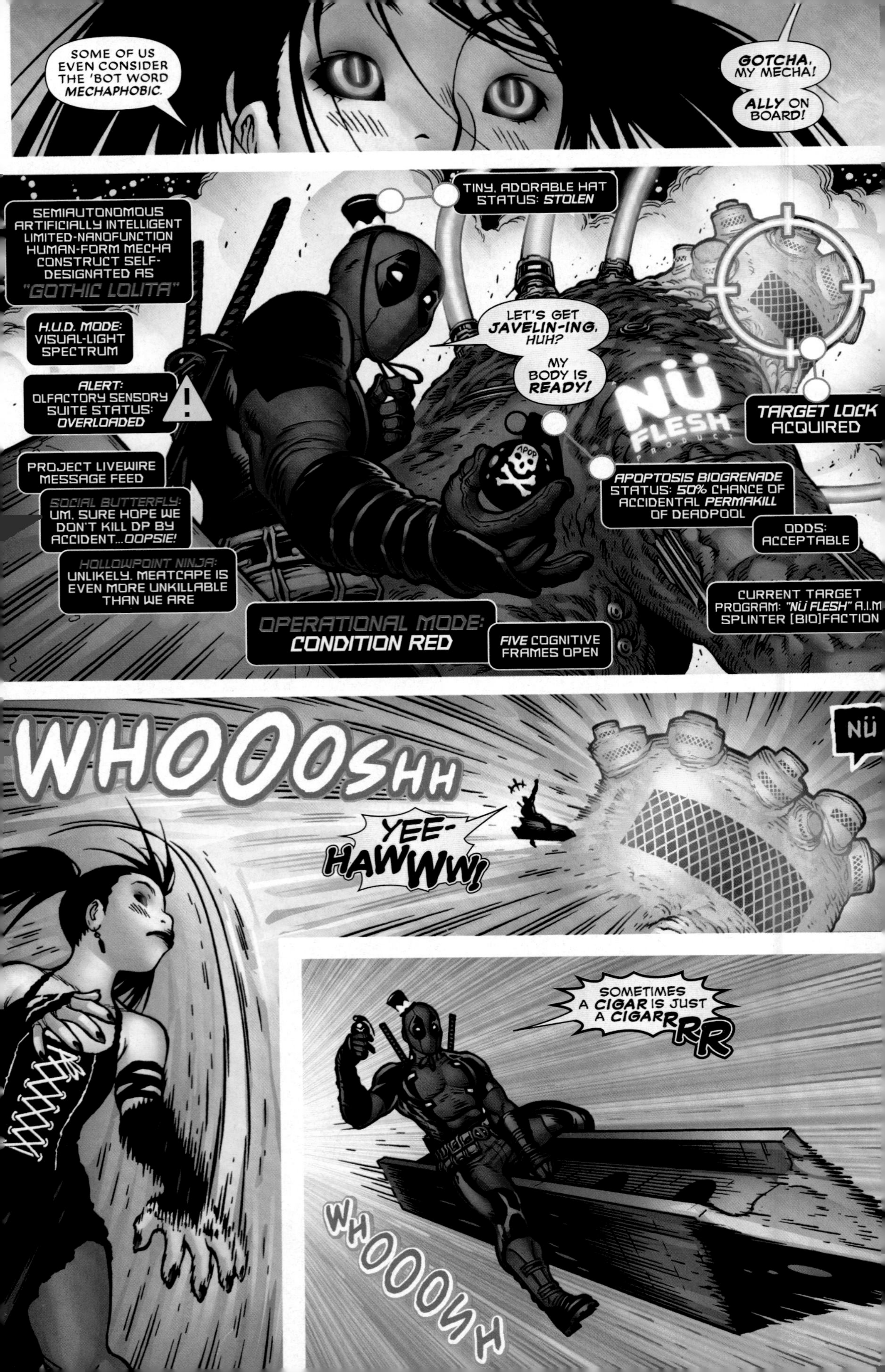

SOME OF US EVEN CONSIDER THE 'BOT WORD MECHAPHOBIC.
GOTCHA, MY MECHA!
ALLY ON BOARD!
SEMIAUTONOMOUS ARTIFICIALLY INTELLIGENT LIMITED-NANOFUNCTION HUMAN-FORM MECHA CONSTRUCT SELF-DESIGNATED AS "GOTHIC LOLITA"
TINY, ADORABLE HAT STATUS: STOLEN
H.U.D. MODE: VISUAL-LIGHT SPECTRUM
LET'S GET JAVELIN-ING, HUH?
MY BODY IS READY!
ALERT: OLFACTORY SENSORY SUITE STATUS: OVERLOADED
NÜ FLESH PRODUCT
TARGET LOCK ACQUIRED
APOP
PROJECT LIVEWIRE MESSAGE FEED
SOCIAL BUTTERFLY: UM, SURE HOPE WE DON'T KILL DP BY ACCIDENT...OOPSIE!
HOLLOWPOINT NINJA: UNLIKELY. MEATCAPE IS EVEN MORE UNKILLABLE THAN WE ARE
APOPTOSIS BIOGRENADE STATUS: 50% CHANCE OF ACCIDENTAL PERMAKILL OF DEADPOOL
ODDS: ACCEPTABLE
CURRENT TARGET PROGRAM: "NÜ FLESH" A.I.M. SPLINTER [BIO]FACTION
OPERATIONAL MODE: CONDITION RED
FIVE COGNITIVE FRAMES OPEN
WHOOOOSHH
NÜ
YEE-HAWWW!
SOMETIMES A CIGAR IS JUST A CIGARRRR
WHOOOOSH

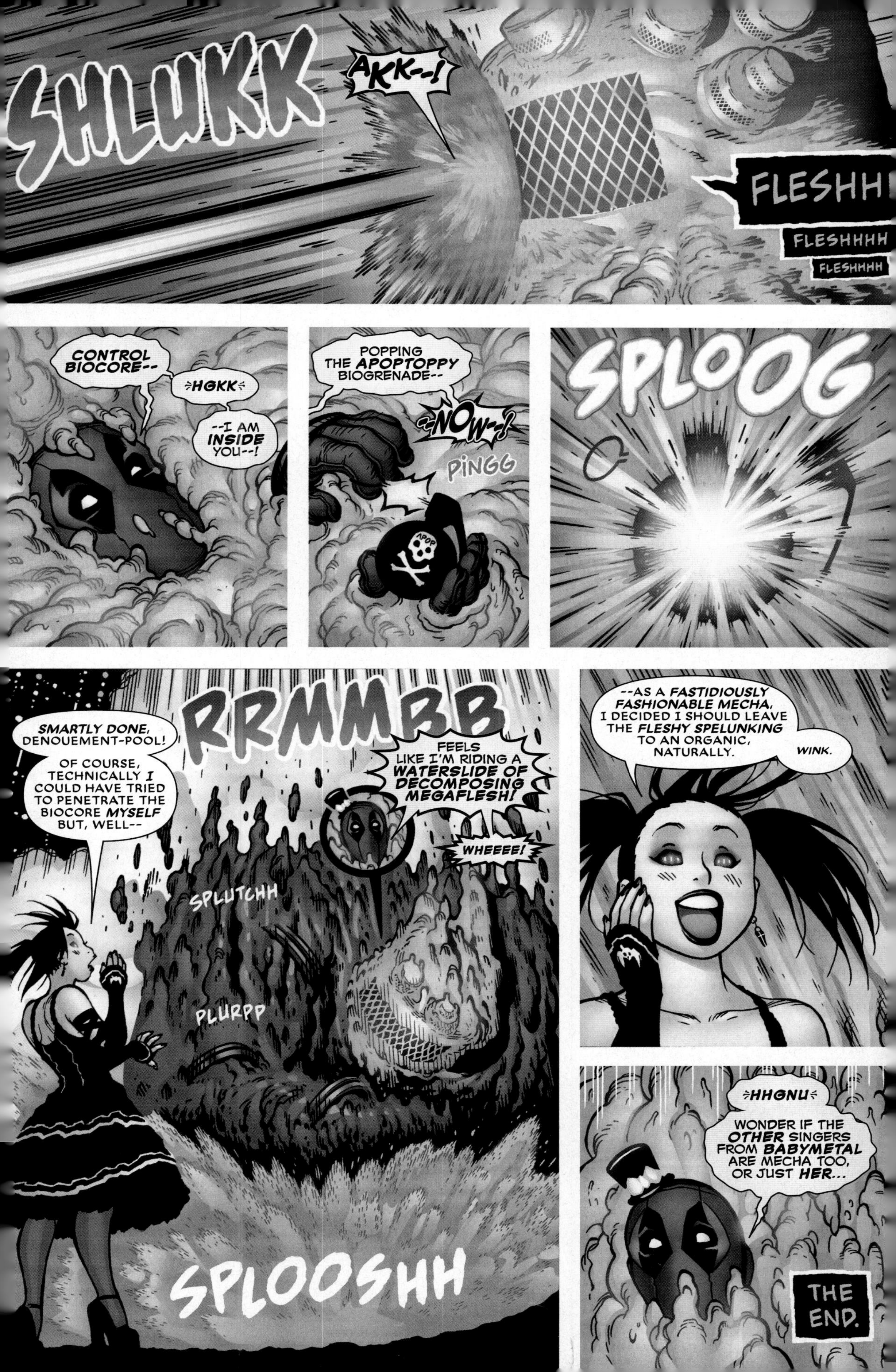
SHLUKK
AKK--!
FLESHH
FLESHHHH
FLESHHHH
CONTROL BIOCORE--
HGKK
--I AM INSIDE YOU--!
POPPING THE APOPTOPPY BIOGRENADE--
--NOW--!
PINGG
APOP
SPLOOG
RRMMBB
SMARTLY DONE, DENOUEMENT-POOL!
OF COURSE, TECHNICALLY I COULD HAVE TRIED TO PENETRATE THE BIOCORE MYSELF BUT, WELL--
FEELS LIKE I'M RIDING A WATERSLIDE OF DECOMPOSING MEGAFLESH!
WHEEEE!
SPLUTCHH
PLURPP
SPLOOSHH
--AS A FASTIDIOUSLY FASHIONABLE MECHA, I DECIDED I SHOULD LEAVE THE FLESHY SPELUNKING TO AN ORGANIC, NATURALLY.
WINK.
HHGNU
WONDER IF THE OTHER SINGERS FROM BABYMETAL ARE MECHA TOO, OR JUST HER...
THE END.

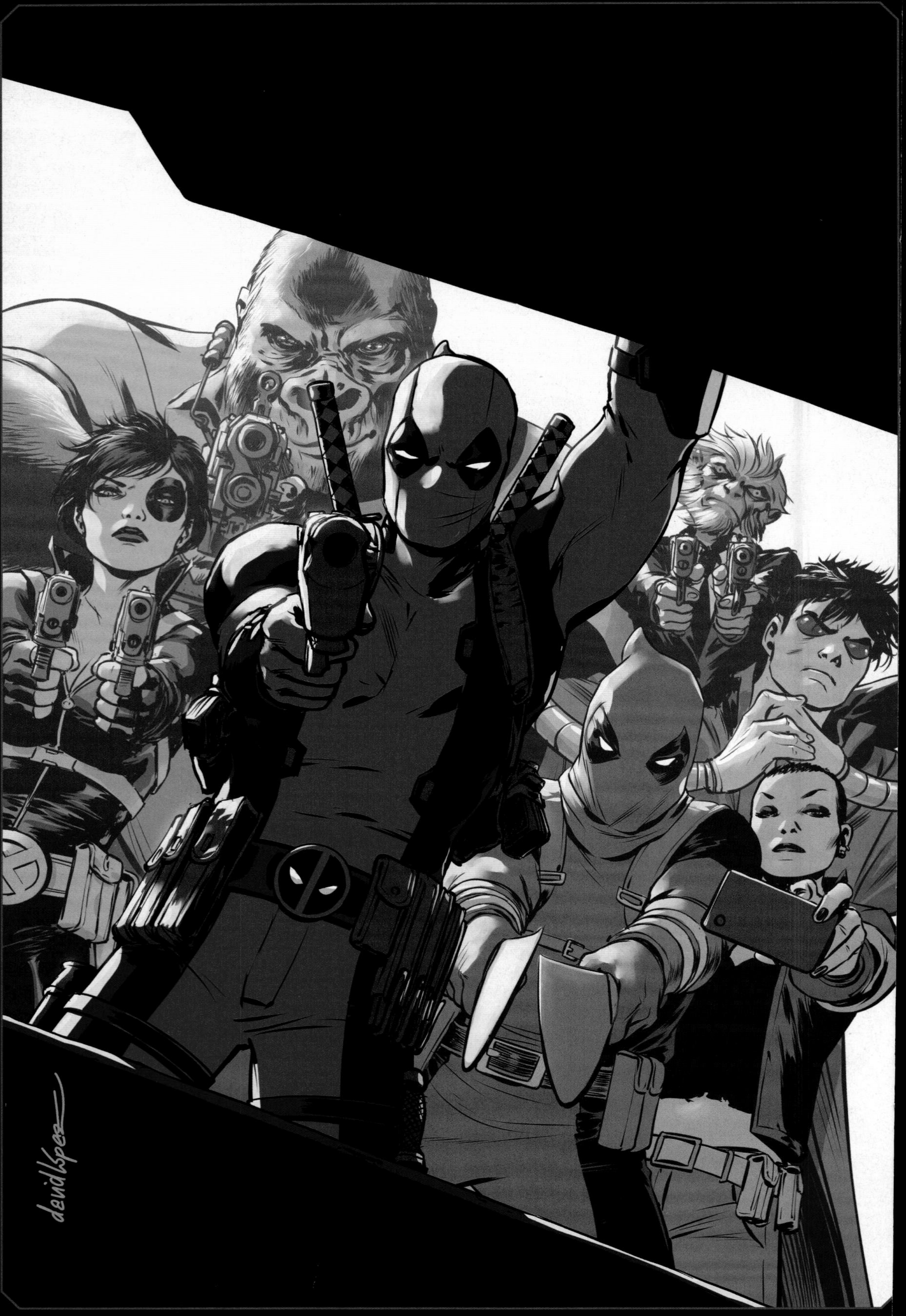

DAVID LOPEZ

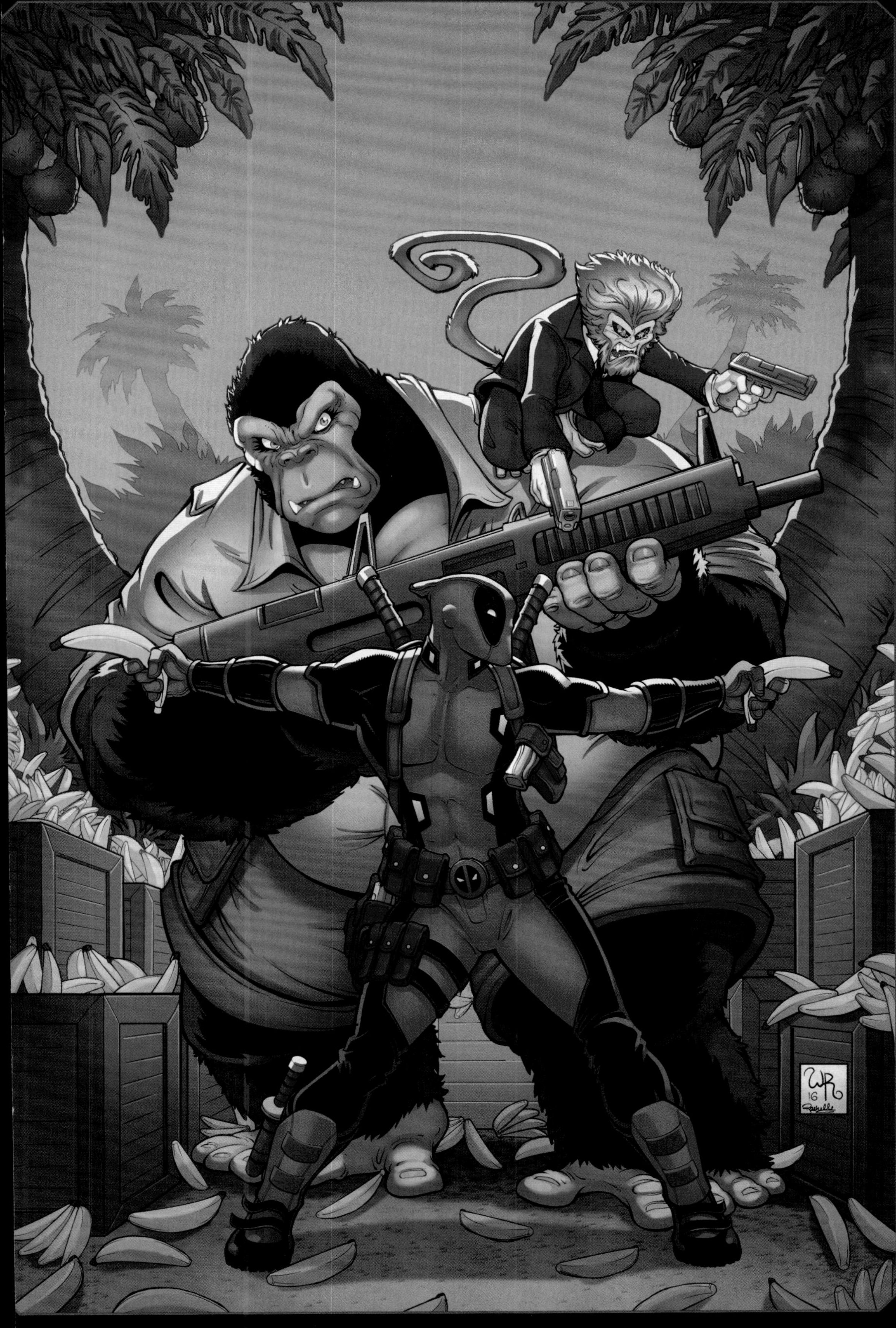
WR
16
Rachelle

WILL ROBSON & RACHELLE ROSENBERG

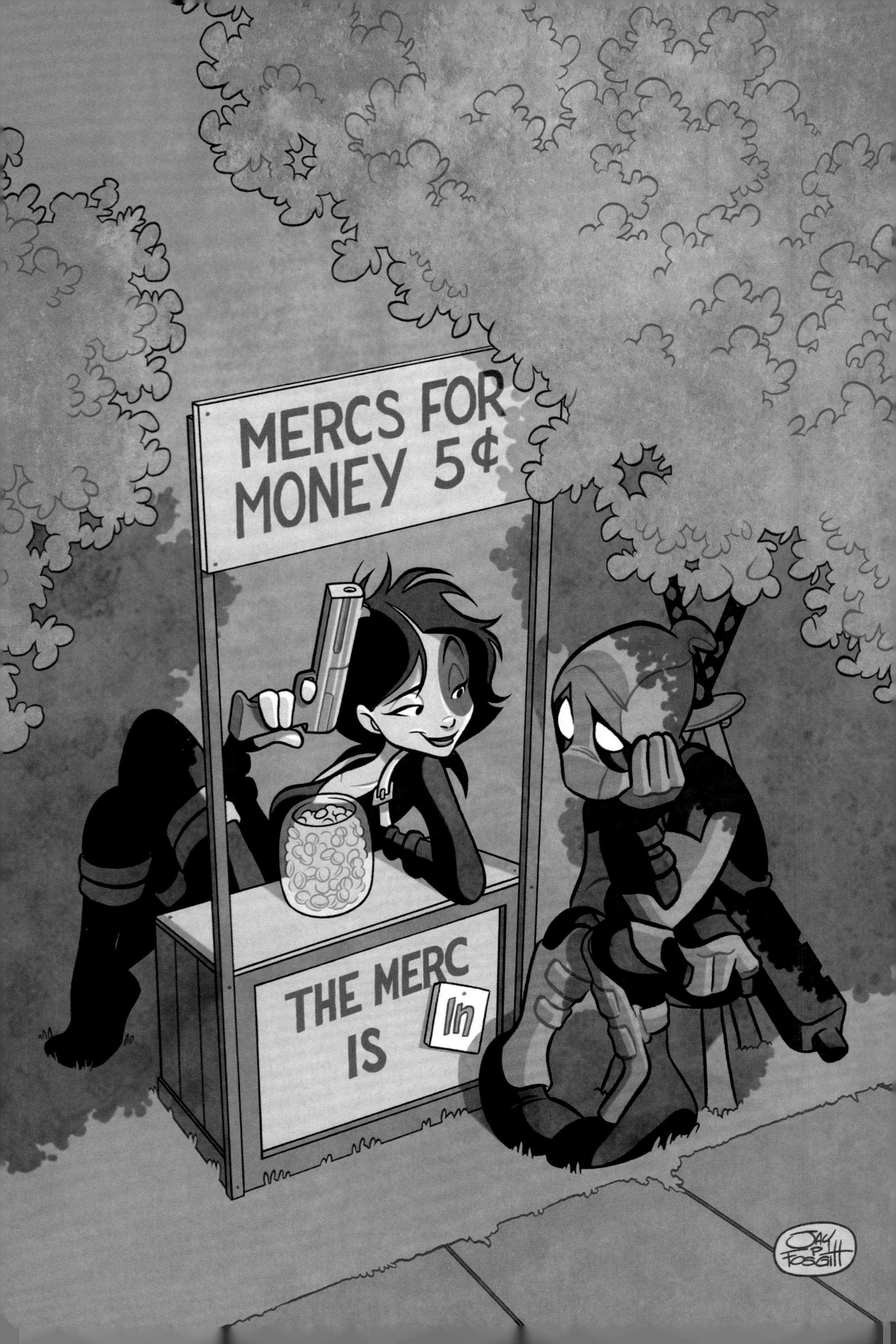
MERCS FOR MONEY 5¢
THE MERC IS In
JAY P. FOSGITT

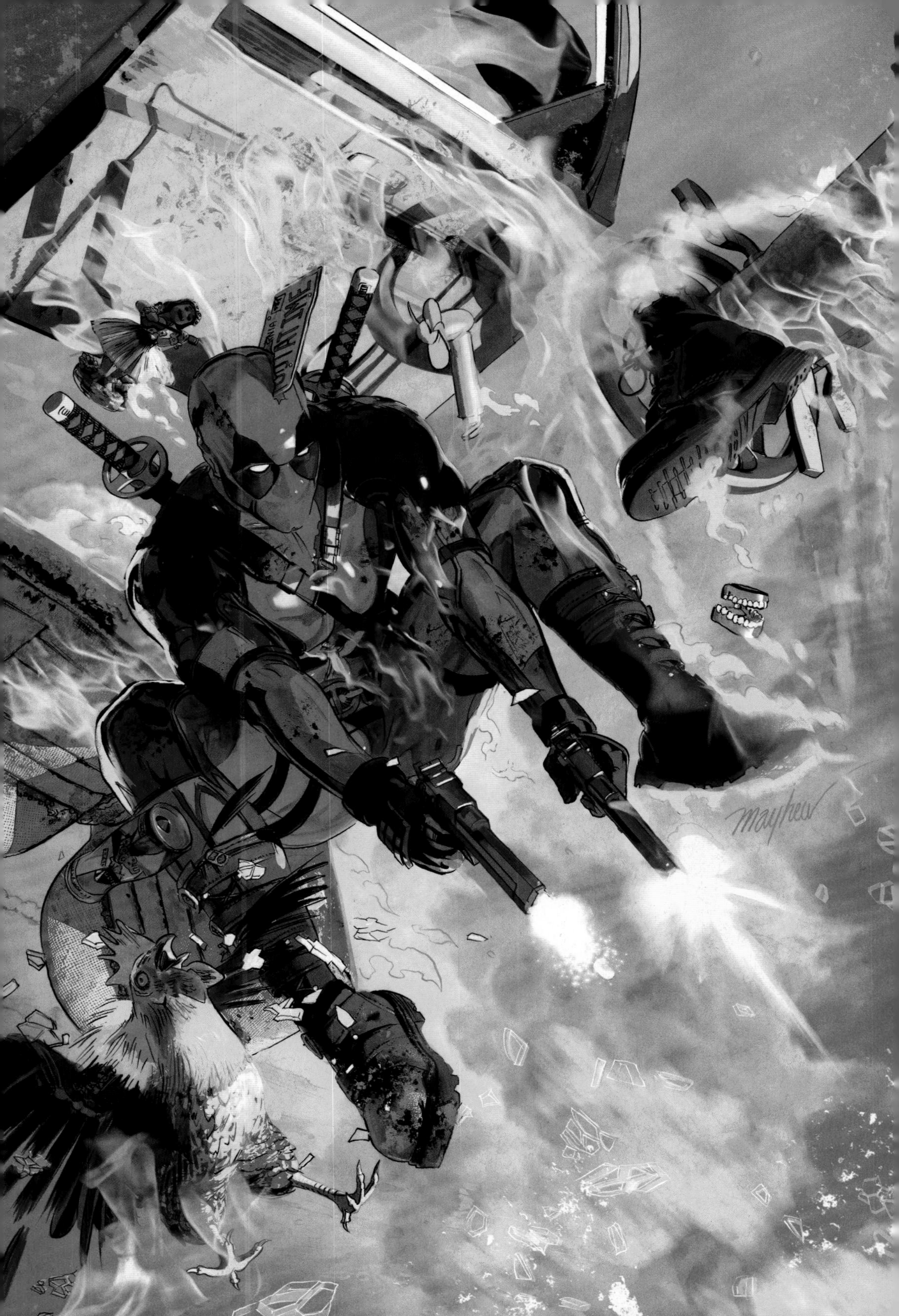
OUTATIME
mayhew

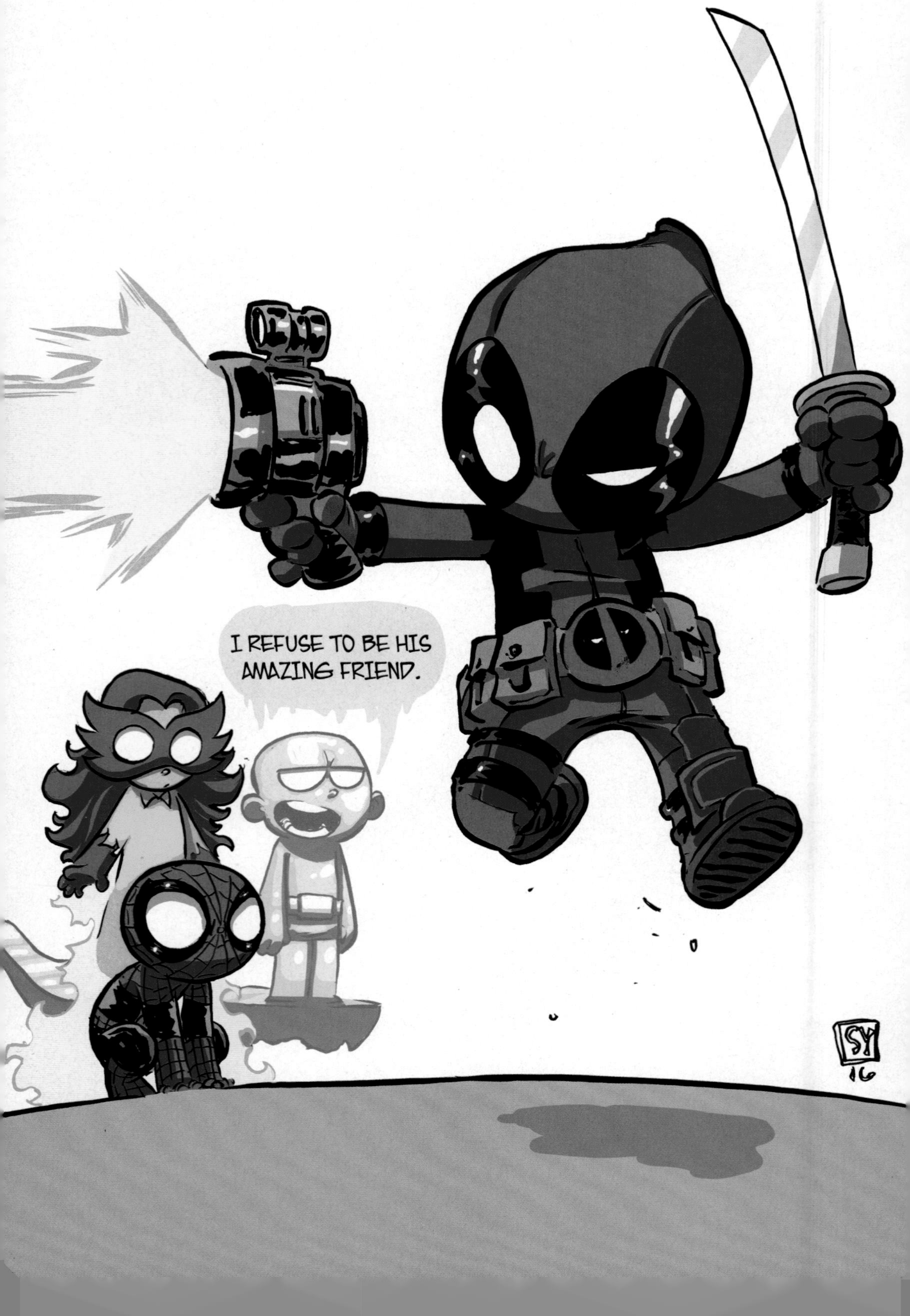
I REFUSE TO BE HIS AMAZING FRIEND.
SY 16

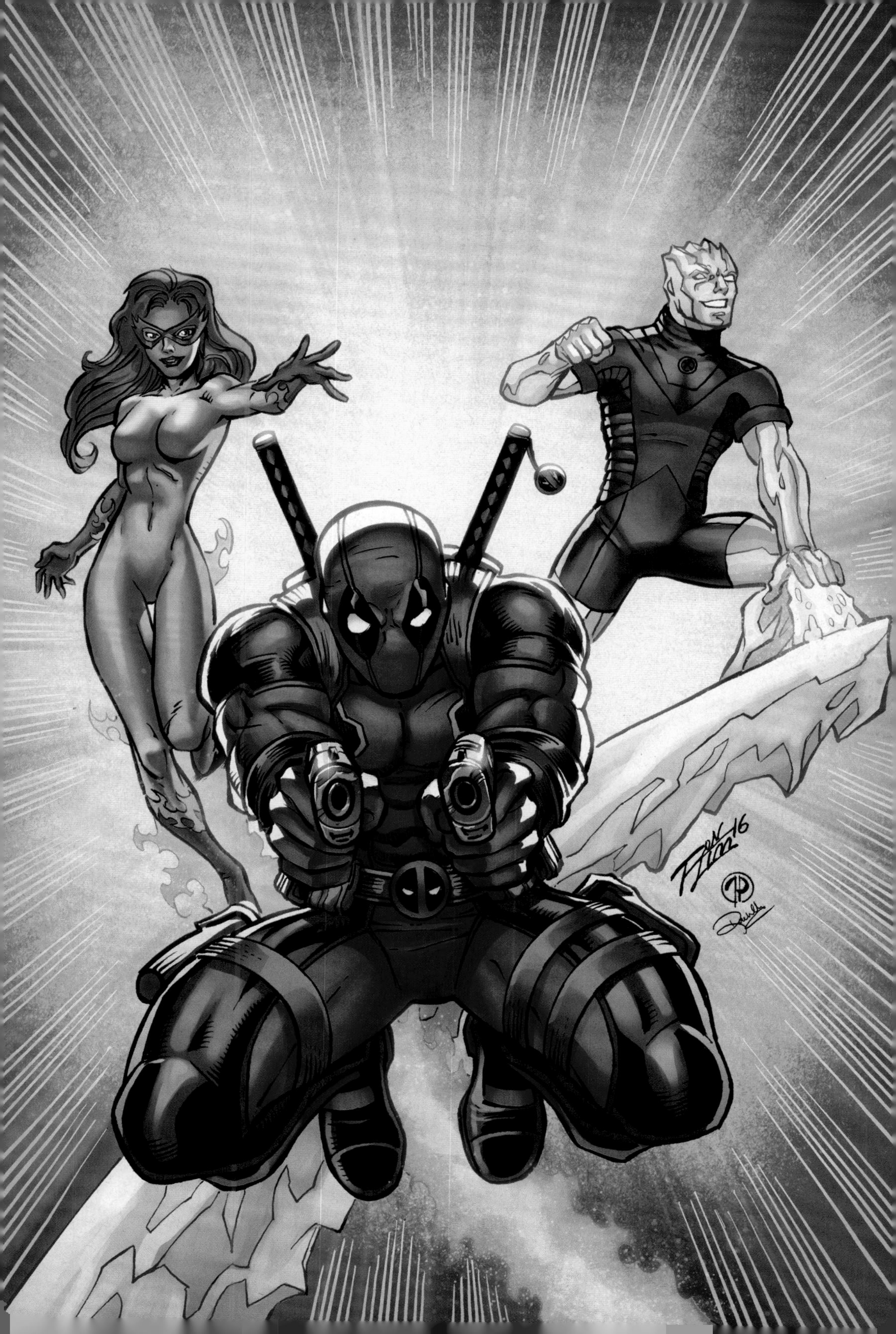

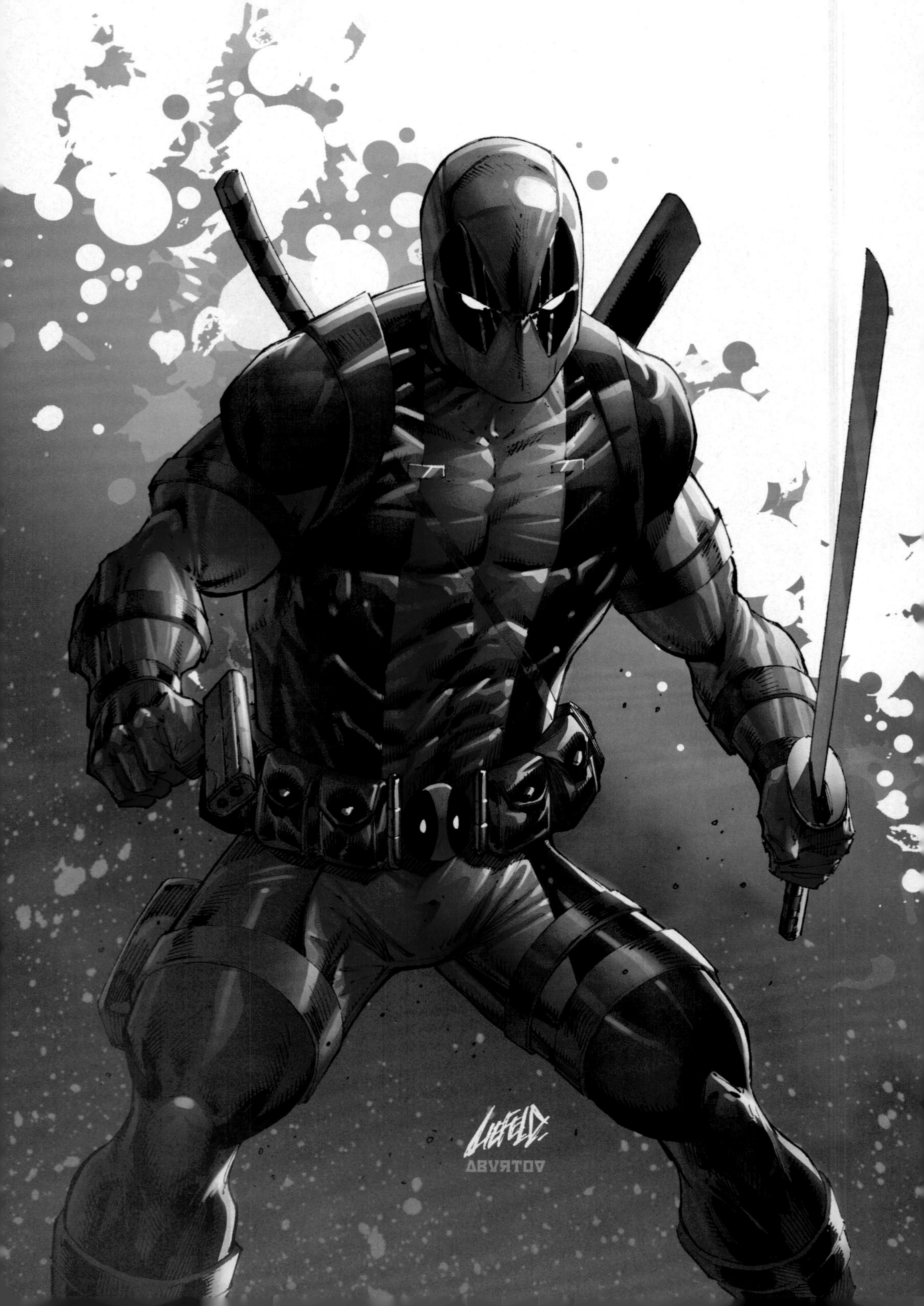
LIEFELD
ABURTOV

NÜ FLESH
page layouts by
ADAM WARREN

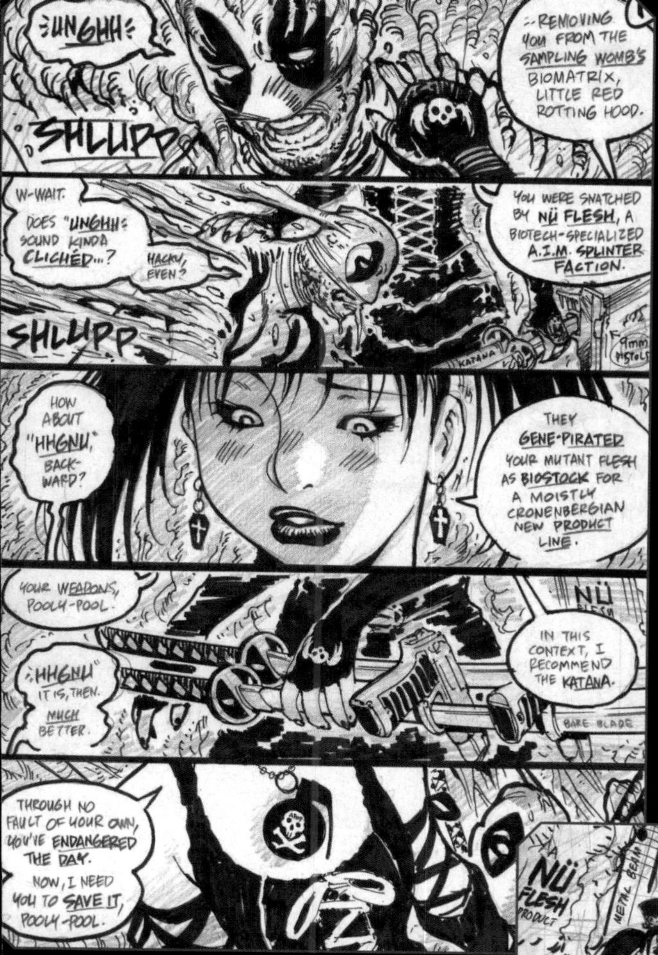

UNGHH
...REMOVING YOU FROM THE SAMPLING WOMB'S BIOMATRIX, LITTLE RED ROTTING HOOD.
SHLUPP
W-WAIT. DOES "UNGHH" SOUND KINDA CLICHÉD...?
HACKY, EVEN?
YOU WERE SNATCHED BY NÜ FLESH, A BIOTECH-SPECIALIZED A.I.M. SPLINTER FACTION.
SHLUPP
KATANA
9MM PISTOL
HOW ABOUT "HHGNU," BACKWARD?
THEY GENE-PIRATED YOUR MUTANT FLESH AS BIOSTOCK FOR A MOISTLY CRONENBERGIAN NEW PRODUCT LINE.
YOUR WEAPONS, POOLY-POOL.
NÜ FLESH
"HHGNU" IT IS, THEN. MUCH BETTER.
IN THIS CONTEXT, I RECOMMEND THE KATANA.
BARE BLADE
THROUGH NO FAULT OF YOUR OWN, YOU'VE ENDANGERED THE DAY.
NOW, I NEED YOU TO SAVE IT, POOLY-POOL.

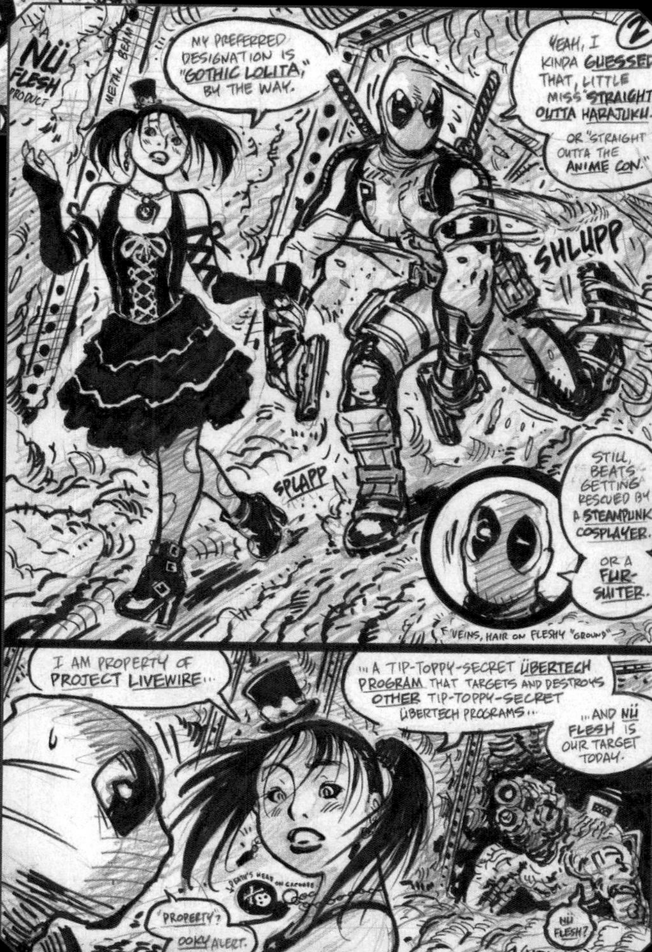

NÜ FLESH PRODUCT
METAL BEAM
MY PREFERRED DESIGNATION IS "GOTHIC LOLITA," BY THE WAY.
YEAH, I KINDA GUESSED THAT, LITTLE MISS "STRAIGHT OUTTA HARAJUKU."
OR "STRAIGHT OUTTA THE ANIME CON."
SHLUPP
SPLAPP
STILL BEATS GETTING RESCUED BY A STEAMPUNK COSPLAYER.
OR A FUR-SUITER.
VEINS, HAIR ON FLESHY "GROUND"
I AM PROPERTY OF PROJECT LIVEWIRE...
...A TIP-TOPPY-SECRET ÜBERTECH PROGRAM THAT TARGETS AND DESTROYS OTHER TIP-TOPPY-SECRET ÜBERTECH PROGRAMS...
...AND NÜ FLESH IS OUR TARGET TODAY.
DEATH'S HEAD ON CAMEO
"PROPERTY"? OOKY ALERT.
NÜ FLESH?

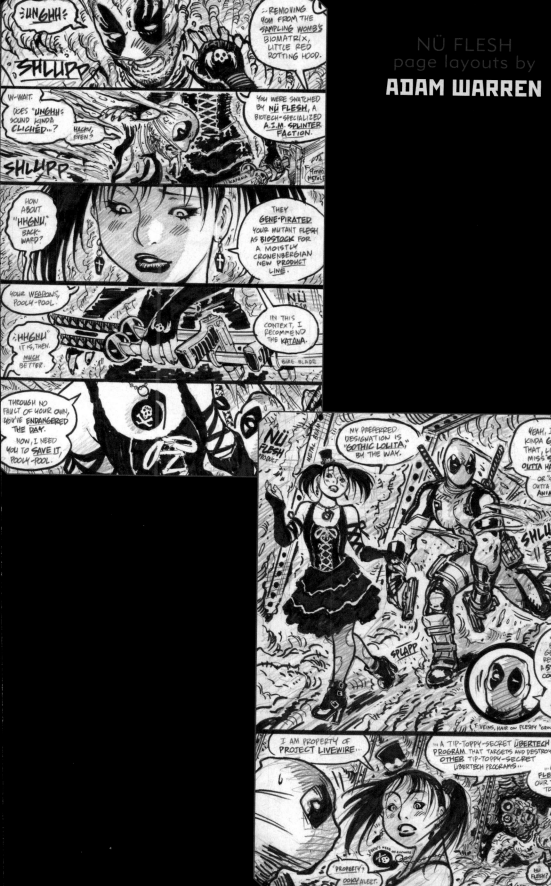

NÜ FLESH
page layouts by

ADAM WARREN

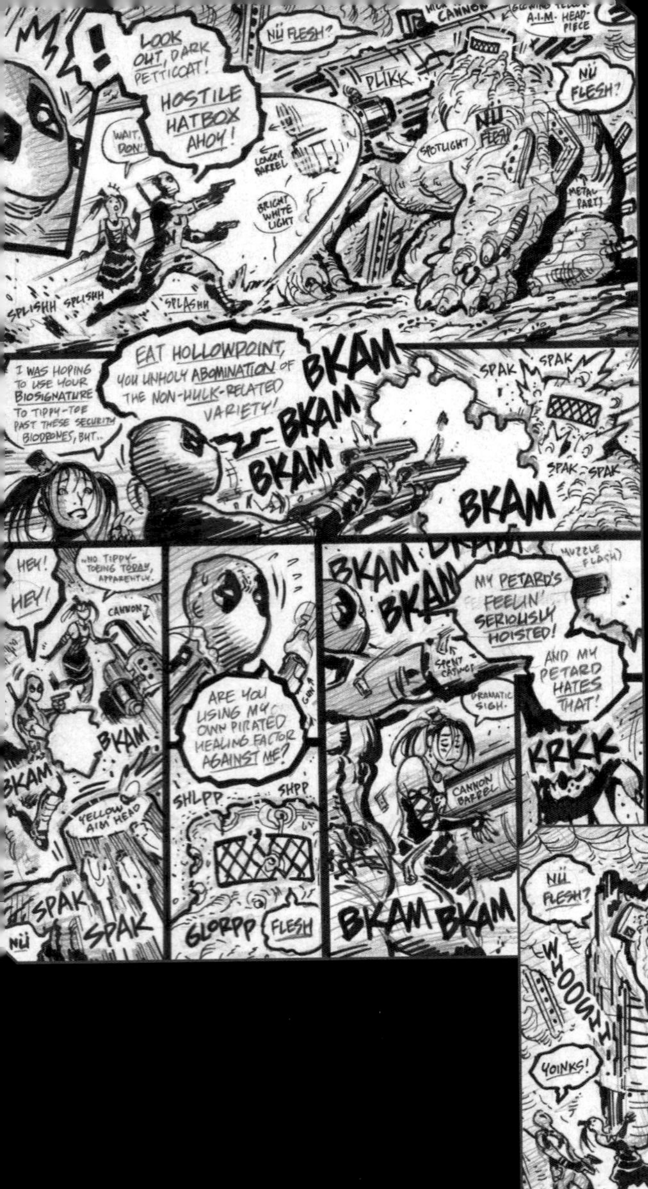
LOOK OUT, DARK PETTICOAT!
HOSTILE HATBOX AHOY!
WAIT, DON'
NÜ FLESH?
A.I.M. HEAD-PIECE
PLIKK
NÜ FLESH?
NÜ FLESH
SPOTLIGHT
LONGER BARREL
BRIGHT WHITE LIGHT
METAL PARTS
SPLISHH SPLISHH
SPLASHH
I WAS HOPING TO USE YOUR BIOSIGNATURE TO TIPPY-TOE PAST THESE SECURITY BIODROMES, BUT...
EAT HOLLOWPOINT, YOU UNHOLY ABOMINATION OF THE NON-HULK-RELATED VARIETY!
BKAM
BKAM
BKAM
BKAM
SPAK SPAK
SPAK SPAK
BKAM
HEY!
HEY!
...NO TIPPY-TOEING TODAY, APPARENTLY.
CANNON
BKAM
BKAM
YELLOW AIM HEAD
SPAK
SPAK
NÜ
ARE YOU USING MY OWN PIRATED HEALING FACTOR AGAINST ME?
SHLPP
SHPP
GLORPP
FLESH
BKAM
BKAM
MUZZLE FLASH
MY PETARD'S FEELIN' SERIOUSLY HOISTED!
AND MY PETARD HATES THAT!
SPENT CASINGS
DRAMATIC SIGH.
KRKK
CANNON BARREL
BKAM BKAM

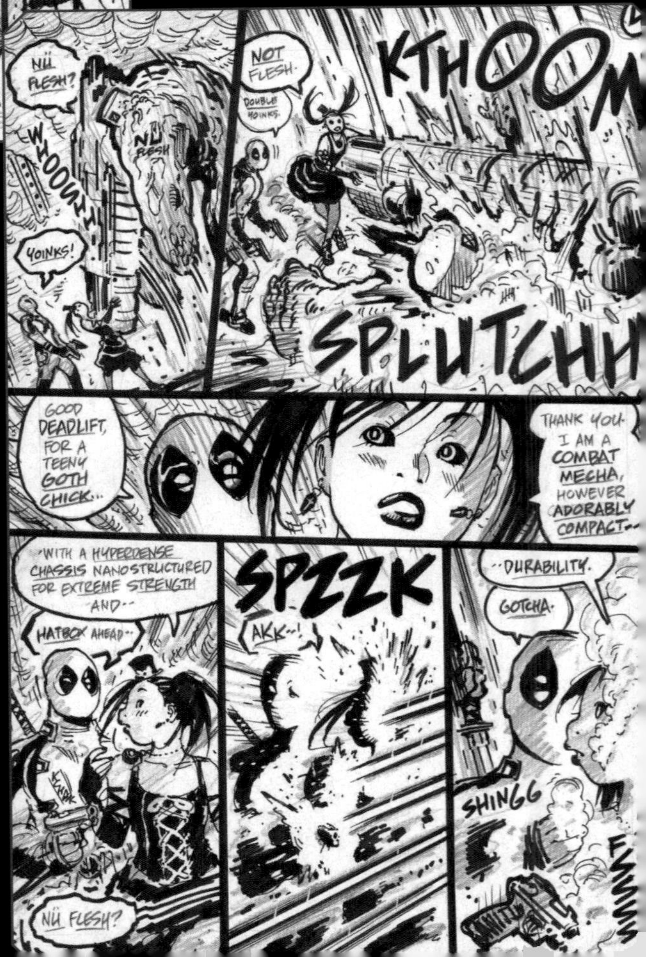
NÜ FLESH?
NOT FLESH.
DOUBLE YOINKS.
KTHOOM
WHOOSHH
NÜ FLESH
YOINKS!
SPLUTCHH
GOOD DEADLIFT, FOR A TEENY GOTH CHICK...
THANK YOU. I AM A COMBAT MECHA, HOWEVER ADORABLY COMPACT—
"WITH A HYPERDENSE CHASSIS NANOSTRUCTURED FOR EXTREME STRENGTH AND—
HATBOX AHEAD—
SPZZK
AKK—!
...DURABILITY.
GOTCHA.
SHINGG
NÜ FLESH?

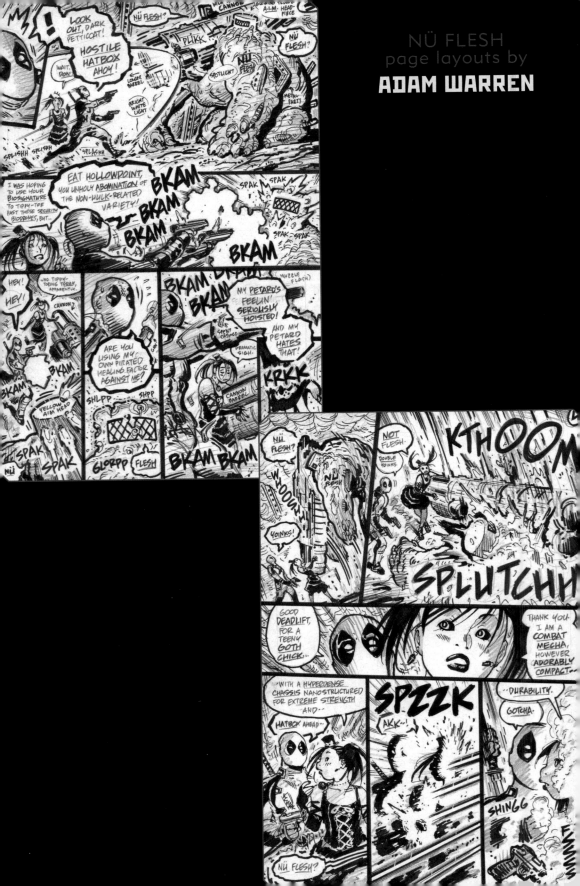

NÜ FLESH
page layouts by
ADAM WARREN

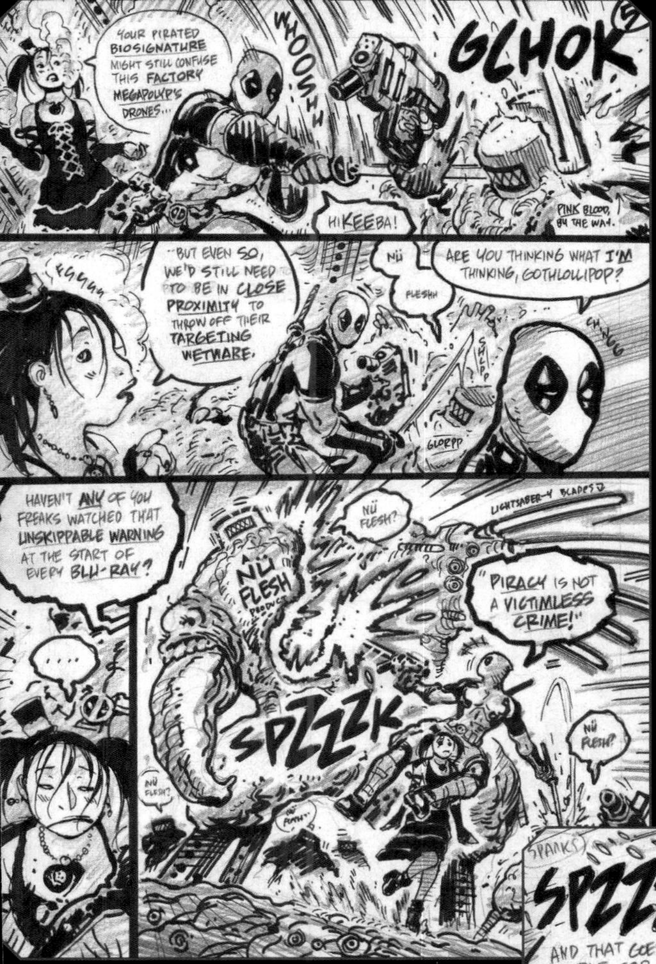
5
YOUR PIRATED BIOSIGNATURE MIGHT STILL CONFUSE THIS FACTORY MEGAPOLYP'S DRONES...
WHOOSHH
GLCHOK
HIKEEBA!
PINK BLOOD, BY THE WAY.
...BUT EVEN SO, WE'D STILL NEED TO BE IN CLOSE PROXIMITY TO THROW OFF THEIR TARGETING WETWARE.
NÜ FLESHH
ARE YOU THINKING WHAT I'M THINKING, GOTHLOLLIPOP?
GLORPP
HAVEN'T ANY OF YOU FREAKS WATCHED THAT UNSKIPPABLE WARNING AT THE START OF EVERY BLU-RAY?
NÜ FLESH?
LIGHTSABER-Y BLADES?
NÜ FLESH
"PIRACY IS NOT A VICTIMLESS CRIME!"
....
SPZZZZK
NÜ FLESH?
NÜ FLESH?

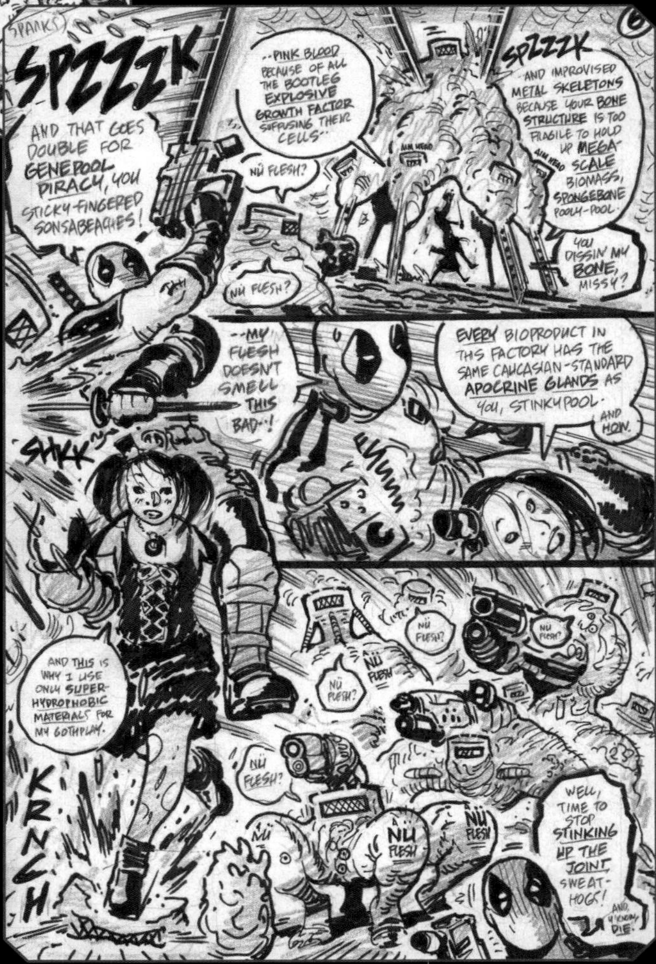
6
SPARKS
SPZZZZK
AND THAT GOES DOUBLE FOR GENEPOOL PIRACY, YOU STICKY-FINGERED SONSABEACHES!
...PINK BLOOD BECAUSE OF ALL THE BOOTLEG EXPLOSIVE GROWTH FACTOR SUFFUSING THEIR CELLS...
SPZZZK
...AND IMPROVISED METAL SKELETONS BECAUSE YOUR BONE STRUCTURE IS TOO FRAGILE TO HOLD UP MEGA-SCALE BIOMASS, SPONGEBONE POOLY-POOL.
NÜ FLESH?
YOU DISSIN' MY BONE, MISSY?
NÜ FLESH?
--MY FLESH DOESN'T SMELL THIS BAD--!
EVERY BIOPRODUCT IN THIS FACTORY HAS THE SAME CAUCASIAN-STANDARD APOCRINE GLANDS AS YOU, STINKYPOOL.
AND HOW.
SHKK
AND THIS IS WHY I USE ONLY SUPER-HYDROPHOBIC MATERIALS FOR MY GOTHPLAY.
NÜ FLESH?
NÜ FLESH?
NÜ FLESH?
KRNCH
WELL, TIME TO STOP STINKING UP THE JOINT, SWEAT-HOGS!
AND, Y'KNOW, DIE.

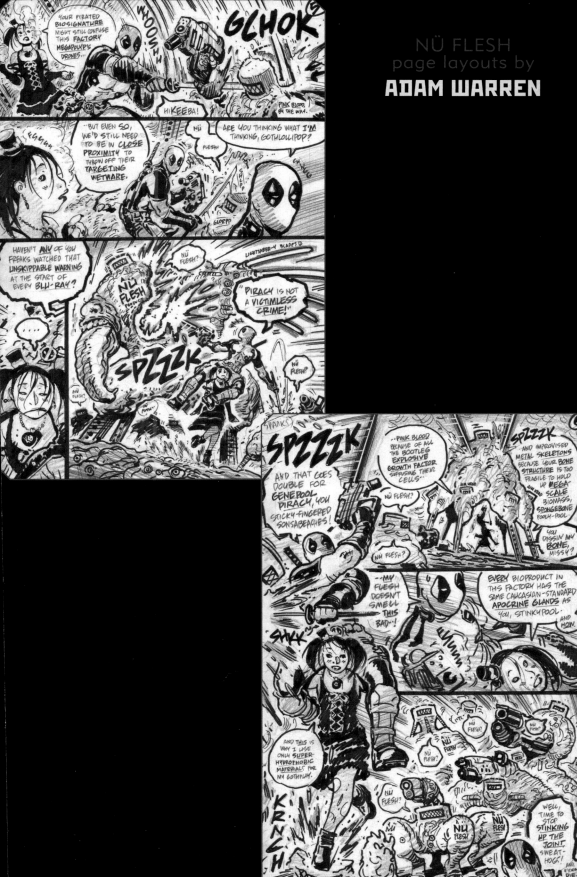

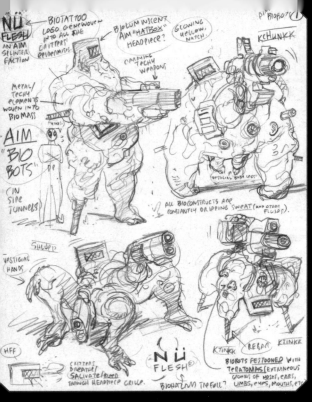

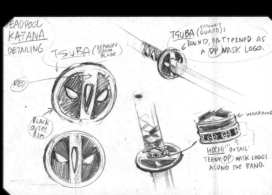

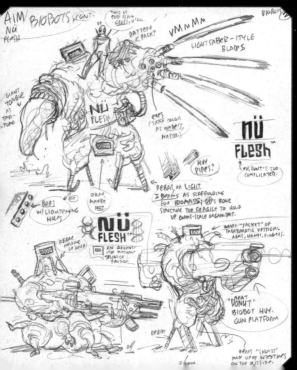

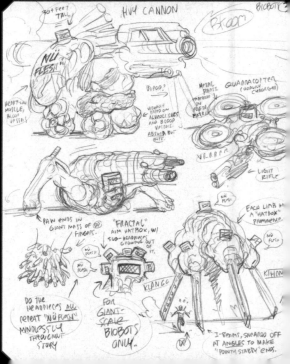